Jesus and the Cross

Princeton Theological Monograph Series

K. C. Hanson, Charles M. Collier, D. Christopher Spinks,
and Robin Parry, Series Editors

Recent volumes in the series:

Anette I. Hagan
*Eternal Blessedness for All? A Historical-Systematic Examination
of Schleiermacher's Understanding of Predestination*

Stephen M. Garrett
God's Beauty-in-Act: Participating in God's Suffering Glory

Sarah Morice-Brubaker
The Place of the Spirit: Toward a Trinitarian Theology of Location

Joas Adiprasetya
*An Imaginative Glimpse:
The Trinity and Multiple Religious Participations*

Anthony G. Siegrist
*Participating Witness: An Anabaptist Theology of Baptism
and the Sacramental Character of the Church*

Kin Yip Louie
*The Beauty of the Triune God:
The Theological Aesthetics of Jonathan Edwards*

Mark R. Lindsay
*Reading Auschwitz with Barth:
The Holocaust as Problem and Promise for Barthian Theology*

Brendan Thomas Sammon
*The God Who Is Beauty: Beauty as a Divine Name
in Thomas Aquinas and Dionysius the Areopagite*

Jesus and the Cross

Necessity, Meaning, and Atonement

PETER LAUGHLIN

With a Foreword by Neil Ormerod

PICKWICK *Publications* · Eugene, Oregon

JESUS AND THE CROSS
Necessity, Meaning, and Atonement

Princeton Theological Monograph Series 208

Pickwick Publications
An Imprint of Wipf and Stock Publishers
199 W. 8th Ave., Suite 3
Eugene, OR 97401

www.wipfandstock.com

ISBN 13: 978-1-62032-391-5

Cataloguing-in-Publication data:

Laughlin, Peter.

Jesus and the cross : necessity, meaning, and atonement / Peter Laughlin ; with a foreword by Neil Ormerod.

xvi + 256 pp. ; 23 cm. Includes bibliographical references and indexes.

Princeton Theological Monograph Series 208

ISBN 13: 978-1-62032-391-5

1. Jesus Christ—Crucifixion. 2. Atonement—Biblical teaching. 3. Jesus Christ—Historicity. I. Ormerod, Neil. II. Series. III. Title.

BT453 L194 2014

Manufactured in the U.S.A.

Portions of chapter 2 were previously published as "Divine Necessity and Created Contingence in Aquinas." *The Heythrop Journal* 50.4 (2009) 648–57. They are re-published here with permission.

To my wife, Sharyn,

for her abiding love,
enduring patience,
dedicated support,
and unwavering belief.

Content

Foreword

I CAN STILL REMEMBER AS A YOUNG THEOLOGY STUDENT COMING ACROSS the book *The Aims of Jesus* by biblical scholar, Ben Meyer. It was a heady time for theology students with the appearance of works by Hans Küng (*On Being a Christian*) and Edward Schillebeeckx (*Jesus: An Experiment in Christology*) both reflecting the impact of critical biblical scholarship on our understanding of Jesus. Within the excitement of these works, Meyer's book stood out as something different, serious, scholarly, patient and measured in its conclusions. But one thing that really struck me was the implication of the title—Jesus had intentions, aims, a purpose to his actions. Central to Meyer's work was the uncovering of those aims. It was no longer good enough to say Jesus went around doing good like some super boy scout; one had to ask what good Jesus was doing and why he did that type of good rather than another type. Only then would we understand the nature of his mission and its relationship to the coming Kingdom of God.

Sadly Meyer died too young, too young to see his work taken up with enthusiasm by a generation of Biblical scholars—Tom Wright, James Dunn, Scott McKnight and others—looking for alternatives to approaches based on methodological skepticism. What Meyer had found in the critical realism of the polymathic Bernard Lonergan, this generation of scholars found in Meyer, an approach based on data, hypothesis formation, and an accumulation of evidence for their position.

This present work by Peter Laughlin extends the conversation with both the biblical text read through the lens of critical realism, and with the broader insights of Lonergan. Patiently and methodically Laughlin seeks an answer to two basic questions: how can we understand Jesus' death as redemptive? And what relationship, if any, exists between our understanding of Jesus death as redemptive and the meaning Jesus himself gives to his death? As Laughlin points out, the history of Christian theology is littered with answers to the first question, but what is surprising is how little attention has been given to the second. While all Christians agree that Jesus' death and resurrection have saving significance, we are hardly so clear as to how or why this is the case. That it might have something to do with the meaning Jesus himself gave to his death is rarely if ever pursued.

Reasons for this vary, from agnosticism that we can uncover such a meaning or purpose, to horror at the notion that his death could be given any meaning, let alone a divine redemptive meaning. There are many hurdles to overcome and Laughlin carefully addresses each in turn. The first is to unpick the knotted skein of questions in relation to necessity and contingency, of God's relationship to the created order and God's permissive will in relation to the problem of evil. These are profound and difficult questions, but using Lonergan's work, *Grace and Freedom* as his guide Laughlin turns to the theological resources of Thomas Aquinas to find a path through the maze, to both remove God from responsibility for evil, while maintaining the divine prerogative to create meaning, *ex nihlio,* from the nothingness of evil. Such a creative act does not condone or justify evil, but is God's creative response to the brute fact of evil in human history.

This is an important step because it frees Laughlin from the commonly expressed concern that Christian theologies of the death of Jesus somehow turn God into a divine child-abuser, needing the death of Jesus to appease his anger at human sinfulness. As Laughlin clearly argues, God is not responsible for human sin, and the death of Jesus was the consequence of human sin. Therefore God is not responsible for, or wills in any way the death of Jesus. But given the death of Jesus at the hands of sinful men, the question is, how does God (and Jesus) respond? Quoting Ben Meyer, Laughlin notes, "Jesus did not aim to be repudiated and killed, he aimed to charge with meaning his being repudiated and killed."

The next issue is the question of the relationship between history and theological meaning. Should there be any connection at all between the faith proclaimed by the Church (theological meaning) and the historical events constituted by meaning and value of Jesus' life and death? As Laughlin puts it more bluntly, "why should the theologian care about what Jesus of Nazareth thought of his impending death?" Indeed it is not difficult to demonstrate how little theological thought has sought to incorporate Jesus' own self-understanding into its account of the atonement. For example, would Jesus have recognized himself within the feudal framework of Anselm's *Cur Deus Homo?* Again Lonergan's discussion of meaning and history are decisive in working through the issues here. Lonergan's notions of carriers and functions of meaning and of authenticity suggest the theological importance of Jesus' own meanings. Through a consideration of incarnate, linguistic and symbolic carriers of meaning Laughlin pieces together the evidence needed to answer the question of the meaning Jesus gave to his impending death. Here it is not Aquinas, but contemporary biblical scholarship that he must examine, interrogate and critique, with those scholars who have most taken up Ben Meyer's call for a critical realist approach to exegesis coming to the fore.

With a particular focus on symbolic carriers of meaning Laughlin focusses his attention of the cleansing of the Temple and the institution narrative of the Last Supper. In this reading he allows Jesus to be genuinely creative, not just repeating symbols from the past or locating all creativity within the early Church, but has Jesus bringing familiar Jewish symbols together to create a new meaning, constituting a new reality which the disciples (and ourselves) are invited to enter. As he says, "Jesus created the symbolism of the Last Supper to reveal that God's eschatological work (occurring in and through him), would redeem his followers for life within a new covenant community and to guarantee them a place at the eschatological banquet to come."

As Laughlin notes of this, "to some this conclusion will be too orthodox to possibly be true, to others it does not go far enough." Rereading this some years after Peter originally wrote his doctorate under my supervision, it reminded me of his intellectual courage and determination to go where the evidence led him, regardless of prevailing orthodoxies but with a faithful commitment both to the truth and to his Christian faith. As he argued in his chapter on faith and history, faith should never be an impediment to the quest for truth; in fact if our faith is authentic we can and must welcome the demands of historical investigation, while also recognizing the limits of what can be affirmed historically. This book is a testament to this dual commitment, tackling the most difficult questions with a serene confidence that intelligent investigation and attention to the evidence can lead to a cautious conclusion which is congruent with the best of our Christian faith tradition.

Neil Ormerod
Professor of Theology, Australian Catholic University.

Preface

THEOLOGY AND HISTORICAL JESUS STUDIES COULD BE COMPARED TO estranged cousins who through some strange turn of events happen to arrive at the same family party unbeknownst that the other was going to be there. Having seen each other across the room, much effort is then expended on both sides ensuring that a sufficient number of other guests remain between them so as to prevent a direct confrontation. For their part, theologians tend to decry the various quests for the historical Jesus as misplaced adventures into history that result in nothing but irrelevancies for faith. On the other hand, historical Jesus scholars are quite critical of the theologian's practice of playing ostrich—willfully hiding their head in the sand, hoping that the flurry of historical activity around them will go away without disturbing their carefully laid and systematized nest.

This is nowhere more evident than in the understanding of what happened when Jesus hung on the cross. Theologians have tended to systematize the cross event into an overarching salvific narrative which has no need for, or any sense of, the historic particulars. Whereas the majority of historical Jesus scholarship understands the cross to have no real meaning at all, it is simply what happens when one goes up against the established might of Rome. For the former, the perilous task of peeling back the layers of history to try and discover the "real Jesus" yields nothing of the truth and can be safely ignored. For the latter, theological interpretations of Jesus' death are merely later accretions of the faith community which are stitched together by devoted followers in the hope of making sense of what happened to their dearly beloved, and recently departed, leader.

But the problem for both cousins is that the Jesus who is confessed as Christ is both a historical figure of history *and* the founder of the Christian faith. One can therefore not talk about Jesus in isolation from the other as if only one perspective had any claim to credibility. The Jesus who walked and talked during the first century of the Common Era is the Jesus that inspired and evoked the faith of Christian belief. And thus the Jesus of history is important to our understanding of the Christ of faith. Indeed, this is a tired old split that needs to be finally laid to rest and both cousins need to realise that they've been talking about the same person after all.

This work is an attempt to bring the cousins to the same table to discuss the death of Christ in order that we might learn from one another and so that the Christian faith might be the richer for it. To be sure, the task is difficult—the cousins were estranged for a reason. But just because it is difficult does not make it any less worthwhile a task. In fact, we must try because if Jesus is really both God and Man as the Council of Chalcedon affirmed then the connection between the cousins has already been made in the person of Christ. History, of course, is not theology and theology is not history. But the theological confession that the eternal Word was made flesh, inevitably invites historical analysis. Bringing such analysis to bear on the intention that Jesus had for his death must in turn, impact the theologian's soteriological conceptions.

And herein lies the crucial contention of this book. Contemporary articulations of how and why Jesus' death functions to "save" humanity are going in considerably different directions to the Church's traditional teachings. Of course, different articulations are to be expected as each new community appropriates the salvation found in the cross event for themselves, but there must still be coherence with the Christian tradition if such re-articulations are to be considered faithful. This work argues that such coherence is found to the extent that new models and motifs are able to demonstrate their connection with the meaning with which Jesus imbued his death. Whether this work is ultimately successful in such a task will be left to the reader to decide. But if it contributes to the conversation and encourages others to add their voice then its goal would have already been achieved.

A work such as this is never the product of one mind and acknowledgement and thanks need to be expressed to the following. To Professor Neil Ormerod and Professor Raymond Canning of the Australian Catholic University who oversaw my doctoral program. In particular, Professor Ormerod was tireless in his reading and re-reading of the original dissertation and his penetrating insights and keen appreciation of the issues involved have helped to sharpen my own understanding beyond measure. I also thank Rev. Ming Leung former director of the Alliance College of Australia for allowing me to consume many of his hours in discussion and for granting me permanent office space at the College whilst I was completing the dissertation. I would also like to express my thanks to another former director, Rev. Russell Warnken, who perhaps more than any other fostered a love for all things theological. Finally, it would be impossible to express sufficient thanks to my wife Sharyn, her constant words of affirmation and unflagging encouragement have kept me going when the mountain looked too big to climb. It is to her that this book is dedicated.

Canberra
December, 2013.

Abbreviations

CD   *Church Dogmatics*. Karl Barth. Translated by Geoffrey W. Bromiley. IV vols. Edinburgh: T. & T. Clark, 1955–1969

CWBL   *Complete Works of Bernard Lonergan*

JP   *Søren Kierkegaard's Journals and Papers*, I-VII. Translated by Howard V. Hong and Edna H. Hong, assisted by Gregor Malantschuk. Bloomington: Indiana University Press, 1967-1978

Metaphys.   *Sententia libri Metaphysicae*. Thomas Aquinas. Edited by M.-R. Cathala, revised by R. M. Spiazzi. Turin: Marietti, 1950

Phys.   *In Aristotelis libros Physicorum*. Thomas Aquinas. Edited by P. M. Maggiolo. Turin: Marietti, 1954

PL   *Patrologia Latina*

SCG   *Summa Contra Gentiles*. Thomas Aquinas. 5 vols. Notre Dame: University of Notre Dame Press, 1975

Sent.   *Scriptum Super Sententiis*. Thomas Aquinas. Amersham: Avebury, 1980

ST   *Summa Theologiae*. Thomas Aquinas. 61 vols. Cambridge: Cambridge University Press, 2006

WA   *Weimarer Ausgabe*

1

Introduction: Cross Intentions

At the beginning of Christianity there are two crosses:
One is a real cross, the other a symbol.[1]

—Jürgen Moltmann

IN HER INTRODUCTION TO *CROSS EXAMINATIONS*, MARIT TRELSTAD REmarks that the meaning of the cross is dependent upon the context in which it is found.[2] One can hardly dispute her point: a burning cross on the lawn of an African American home in the mid twentieth-century does not have the same meaning as a cross mounted at the focal point of a contemporary African American church. Nor does the symbol of the cross have the same meaning when worn as a fashion accessory today as it once did in its crude representations on the shields of Constantine's army. Like any symbol the cross is open to the changes of context in which it is found, its meaning dependent upon the collective intentions of those appropriating it.

But the cross is not just any symbol, it is the symbol *par excellence* of the Christian faith and so there is an understandable reaction against any suggestion that its meaning is dependent upon variable contexts. Surely the salvific meaning of the cross is fixed in the event itself—forever locked down in Christ's outstretched arms and pierced feet. And indeed, ever since the early Church reflected upon what happened on the cross, Christians have proclaimed a consistent message: "Christ died for our sins" (1 Cor 15:3). But the question of how Christ's death functions to "save" us from our sins remains. What is it, in other words, that makes the atonement "work"? And it is here that Christian reflection has not been univocal,

---

1. Moltmann, "The Cross as Military Symbol for Sacrifice," 259.
2. Trelstad, *Cross Examinations*, 3–4.

its many voices offering up a range of images and metaphors all of which attempt in some way to capture a facet of the truth that is confessed. And it is here, too, that Moltmann's point in the epigraph is valid, for while there is a "real" cross locked away in human history, the "symbol" of the cross has grown large through Christian reflection, becoming much more than a simple retelling of the facts themselves.

This point is readily discernible even from within the pages of the New Testament. What we find expressed therein is not a reduction of the power of the cross to a single understanding but a number of metaphors and images that collectively weave a tapestry of meaning: Jesus' death is, amongst others, the death of the Paschal lamb (1 Cor 5:7), the inauguration of a new covenant (Heb 8:8; 9:15), the paid ransom price (Mark 10:45), a sin offering (Rom 8:3) and an example to follow (1 Pet 2:21). The fact that these multiple reflections exist is perhaps why the Nicene Creed simply stated without any elaboration that Christ died "for us and for our salvation."[3] It seems the early church quickly recognized that the meaning of the cross readily transcended any one interpretation. Of course, since the creed does not specify how salvation is actually effected by the cross, theories of atonement are left to describe for themselves how it is that the cross functions *pro nobis* to their communities. And so diverse motifs emerged as differing cultures and contexts appropriated the cross event anew.

An obvious example is the emergence of the Satisfaction motif during the Middle Ages. It was the developing feudal context of that era that led Anselm of Canterbury to take offence at the then traditional motif, which had systematized the cross' victory into an explanation of how God had tricked Satan into giving up his hold on fallen humanity.[4] Horrified at the thought that God should have to respect Satan in any way, Anselm contended that what was really at issue was the fact that honor was owed to God by a rebellious humanity who had failed to uphold their responsibilities in the lord-vassal relationship.[5] The death of the incarnate Son was the only means by which that responsibility could be met, thereby restoring the honor lost to God and righting what was wronged.

---

3. It might also be said that one of the reasons for this lack of precise definition in the creeds was due to the fact that none of the post-apostolic presentations on the atonement were deemed heretical enough to evoke an official or "orthodox" church response. See Brümmer, *Atonement, Christology and the Trinity*, 66.

4. Anselm, *Why God Became Man?*, I.6.

5. Ibid., I.7, II.6, II.15.

Anselm's conception was not only logically and contextually coherent it also made a lot of popular sense. The First Crusade was being preached and there was a strong drive to rid the infidel from the Holy Land in order to restore God's honor.[6] Therefore to portray salvation in the same terms had immense popular appeal and gained easy and immediate traction. However, there is also no doubt that this interpretation would have made little sense *prior* to the rise of feudalism, and indeed, much of the motif's power was lost with feudalism's decline. But what is often glossed over in what Anselm achieved is that the satisfaction motif was a clear departure from the traditional (ransom) understanding of how the cross saves. He did not consider it necessary to hold on to the previous articulation at all costs but rather saw the need for a new framework of understanding that connected with his own context. What is interesting, is that far from decrying Anselm's work as an abandonment of received truth, the Christian community welcomed his reflections as a valid and appropriate way of conveying the mechanism of salvation. Naturally, not everyone agreed and Anselm's work prompted additional reflections, the most notable being Peter Abelard's moral influence theory. But what such fluidity demonstrates is that cultural context has an important and indeed fundamental role in the development and appropriation of the cross' saving significance. It is therefore not unorthodox in and of itself to postulate alternative meanings for the cross event that differ from previous reflections.

And for this reason alone it would be rather presumptuous to declare Christian reflection on the atonement closed or to consider the soteriological narrative definitively told. On the contrary, it must be strongly asserted that it is not possible to simply repeat the words of the Bible, Fathers, or the Reformers and expect to gain a hearing within our own contemporary context. Their terms and expressions are valuable, but this does not relieve us of the responsibility to articulate the saving message of the Gospel in contemporary language and within the constituted meaning of our own culture. Indeed, this is the very thing that the biblical writers, Fathers, and Reformers did themselves and it is what made their contribution so contextually meaningful.[7]

6. For the idea of crusading during this period see Riley-Smith, *The First Crusade*, 31–57.

7. This does not mean that their language is of no use today, for it provides a discernible and valuable starting point for our own reflection. But the need for ongoing reflection is not diminished by an appeal either to tradition or the biblical witness. Gunton, *Yesterday and Today*, 3–5.

Simply put, changing cultures and contexts demand new articulations, or at least re-articulations of salvific motifs, in order that the saving significance of the cross can continue to be meaningfully appropriated. Of course, this means that an essential characteristic of individual reflections which needs to be acknowledged is that they are inherently *temporal*.[8] "Images of Christ and conceptions of salvation bear the mark of the prevailing cultural consciousness and are only temporarily relevant," writes Herman-Emiel Mertens. "They are not always and everywhere equally useful."[9] Yet because of the universal significance of the cross in Christian redemption, Mertens' point often gets overlooked. The overwhelming theological temptation is to elevate (our favorite) motifs above cultural considerations and declare them to be equivalently universal. This is arguably what Bernard of Clairvaux did in energetically defending the Anselmian motif against Abelard's moral influence theory.[10] And if so, then Saint Bernard is not alone. More than once in Christian history has today's contextual theology comfortably drifted into tomorrow's entrenched dogma. What makes sense to us now is naively assumed to make sense to everyone and to do so for all time. As Douglas Hall recognizes, the problem with some atonement theologies,

> is that they are sometimes so perceptive and brilliant that they last beyond their appropriate time—and, at the same time, they are perpetuated longer than they should be because too few Christians have the courage to enter into the new, emerging darkness and prefer to rely on the old light of entrenched soteriologies.[11]

Without a doubt, the old light is both familiar and comforting, but as time goes on it does struggle to illuminate the far corners of the present. But this is not to say that it is time for the old light to be disconnected, it is merely an acknowledgement that there is a need for other lights to shine as well. Indeed, this is the experiential reality of the cross. Its power is always evidenced anew in the lives of individuals as the death of Jesus of Nazareth overcomes the horror of their fallen contingent existence. And just as that existence is not static but always changing from culture to culture and from generation to generation, so too there is a dynamism in salvific experience that cannot be limited to the static expressions of its activity.

8. Green and Baker, *Recovering the Scandal of the Cross*, 214.

9. Mertens, *Not the Cross*, 63–64.

10. Bernard, of Clairvaux, *Contra quaedam*, c.8, in PL 182.1069.

11. Hall, *The Cross in Our Context*, 130.

While some will no doubt counter this last statement with concerns of relativism, it is a position that is evidenced by the continuous recreation of human life when brought face-to-face with the crucified and risen Christ. We must never forget that it is *people* who are saved—not theological expressions. Unsurprisingly then, I find much value in the recent scholarly criticism that is concerned to reawaken the wider Christian community to the particularities of their own *Sitz im Leben*. Christ's death remains *pro nobis*, but the challenges facing our own communities must be considered in understanding how it is that the death of Christ functions "for us," in the here and now. This is certainly not to deny that there is a universal problem for humanity that requires a divine solution, but it is to say that such a solution is inherently personal and is received as such. Positively, this conclusion means there is a great deal of space for Christians to find within the death of Christ a saving meaning that speaks directly to their individual and generational circumstances. Negatively, it inevitably means an endless stream of difference, nuance, continuity and even potential antithesis, as various accounts of what Christ was doing on the cross are appropriated by differing communities.[12] So while Christian theology can point to its historical unity in proclaiming the cross' soteriological purpose, its explanation as to precisely how the death of Christ is the means of salvation must be acknowledged as a point of ongoing discussion.

Do Limits Exist?

The obvious question to ask is whether there are any limits to interpreting the saving significance of the symbol of the cross. What is it that makes an interpretation faithful to the Christian tradition over against another that might not be? How do we judge between them? What makes us contend for one over another? As I have argued, community context must play a part in a motif's viability, but this simply recognizes the *differences* that arise in various contexts and the allowances needed for them. How can the theologian be sure that the results of their contextual investigations remain, despite their diversity, faithful to the Christian tradition?

Joel Green and Mark Baker briefly address this question towards the end of their *Recovering the Scandal of the Cross*.[13] They conclude that there is, in fact, no way to guarantee short-term fidelity to authentic Christianity whilst the frontiers of Christian mission remain just that, frontiers.

12. Ray, *Deceiving the Devil*, 1.
13. Green and Baker, *Recovering the Scandal*, 217–21.

Previous perspectives are both important and suggestive but are not determinative for the believer who is trying to communicate the good news to a community which needs to hear it as "good news" for them.[14] However, they do express confidence for the longer term, a confidence they base in three particular faith statements. Firstly, they uphold that human ways of speaking about God, particularly God's activity in salvation, cannot fully circumscribe that divine activity and therefore there is no "one" way to talk about God's saving work and multiple motifs are to be expected. Secondly, is a commitment to the Scriptures as the basis for Christian faith and contextual presentations of the atonement will need to demonstrate adequate reflection on, and faithfulness to, the appropriate texts; and thirdly, is the belief that the Holy Spirit continually works through the community of God's people in creative and cautionary ways. These three points are certainly valid reflections and they are recognizable as an attempt to provide freedom for diversity in atonement theory whilst maintaining a foundation within the biblical witness. In this I find little with which to disagree, but in terms of the question posed these points do little to provide an answer. They more or less take a "wait and see" approach, in that there is a providential belief that "it will all be right in the end" but for now there is nothing, aside from perhaps fidelity to the biblical witness (whatever that might actually mean in practice), which could be considered theologically proactive. But is this all that can be said?

What I wish to contend is that a faithful atonement motif will demonstrate a degree of continuity *with the meaning that Jesus of Nazareth constituted for his death*, an emphasis, it must be said, which is not particularly evident in some of the more recent articulations. It is no doubt a poor parallel, but modern atonement discussions could be said to treat the Jesus of history as something of a novelty act. He is brought out with a flourish to defend in some way the theologian's perspective, and then just as quickly returned to the top-hat so as to not disturb the remainder of the show. Three representative examples to help describe what I mean by this will be given shortly, but it seems to me that if we are to take the doctrine of the incarnation seriously then we must also treat the historical intention of Jesus of Nazareth with the same respect. Yet this point is not as axiomatic as one might expect. There has been, and continues to be, significant debate as to whether the meaning Jesus created for his death is actually important, or even *relevant* to the Christian faith. The debate is by no means trivial either, for in practice (whatever our actual intentions

14. Ibid., 218.

may be), Jesus' self-understanding plays very little part in Christian inter-pretations of the cross. What we find throughout the Christian tradition is systemizations of a universal soteriology rather than direct historical questions as to what Jesus thought his death would accomplish. David Brondos puts the differential well:

> Ultimately, Jesus dies not because his words and actions were viewed as offensive or dangerous to the Jewish and Roman authorities, but because his death is regarded as necessary for some theological reason: only through the cross could forgive-ness be won and sin, death and evil overcome in us and our world. Instead of looking to history to determine the causes of his death, we look outside or above history to some type of "metastory": the stories of salvation which we tell have to do, not so much with a first-century Galilean Jew in conflict with the religious authorities of his day, but with God's holy nature and the satisfaction of its just demands, the enslavement of all humankind to Satan, sin, death and evil and our subsequent liberation, or the creation of a "new humanity" embracing all who follow Christ's teachings and example or participate in his death and resurrection.[15]

The criticism of traditional models here is clear, but it seems to me that contemporary motifs also continue this trend, in part because of the modern skepticism concerning the reliability of historical knowledge, but also because of the theological interest to capture the universal salvific meaning of the cross for the contemporary context. This is not to say that theologians believe the cross was meaningless for Jesus of Nazareth, just that there is little theological interest in what that meaning might have actually been.[16] It is this focus on the universal soteriological narrative that allows Marit Trelstad to comfortably assert along with Moltmann that for the theologian there are in fact two crosses. There is the historical cross upon which Jesus was crucified and there is the cross of theological interpretation.[17] The two are joined in history, but as far as their meaning or interpretation is concerned they may as well be different entities.

Of course, the primary theological benefit of maintaining a distinc-tion between faith and history is the freedom for the theologian to face the question of "why did Jesus die"? unencumbered by the exigencies of

---

15. Brondos, "Why Was Jesus Crucified?," 485.

16. A point that comes to full fruition in Brock and Parker, *Proverbs of Ashes*.

17. Trelstad, *Cross Examinations*, 3.

the actual historical event. This is a point that Trelstad embraces since it clearly enables the theologian's vantage point to shape the particular symbolic meaning of the cross he or she wishes to appropriate. It is, therefore, not history that is important but its theological interpretation—and truth be told it is not at all clear that this is a bad thing. In many ways the distinction between faith and history functions to "protect" the theological task from the contingencies of history and even worse, the predilections of historians.

But one could also rightly ask whether or not this distinction inevitably divorces our understanding of the cross from the aims and intentions of Jesus himself? The answer must, of course, be given in the affirmative, but from the kerygmatic perspective does it really matter? After all, do we need to restrict ourselves to what Jesus thought he was doing in the first century, especially since it is possible that Jesus himself did not fully appreciate the meaning of his own death?[18] What impact would it have on Christian faith if it could be proven that Jesus of Nazareth actually had *no* conception that his death would have universal saving significance? For Bultmann, who was prepared to accept that Jesus' death could have been historically meaningless, the answer is absolutely nothing.[19] What is important to the faith community is not the underlying history of Jesus' death, but the contemporary preaching of its meaning and the subsequent existential encounter that occurs between the believer and the crucified Christ. On this he was quite clear:

> The salvation-occurrence is nowhere present except in the proclaiming, accosting, demanding, and promising word of preaching. A merely 'reminiscent' historical account referring to what happened in the past cannot make the salvation-occurrence visible. It means that the salvation-occurrence continues to take place in the proclamation of the word.[20]

From this perspective it appears that history has nothing to say to such an existential encounter and should be left in the past where it belongs and not unceremoniously dragged into the present.

Moreover, there is considerable danger in allowing history to dictate to theology because one is immediately forced to make a decision in regard to which history one should be referencing. The proliferation of the various "Lives of Jesus" in the nineteenth century, for example, made

18. O'Collins, *Interpreting Jesus*, 79.

19. Bultmann, "The Primitive Christian Kerygma," 22–24.

20. Bultmann, *Theology of the New Testament*, I.302.

trying to determine the particular "Jesus" one should put faith in incredibly difficult. Indeed, Lessing had already concluded that the exigencies of history are incapable of providing a basis for religious truth. It was simply far safer to stay on this side of the ditch and reflect on the ahistorical truths of orthodoxy than submit those truths to the uncertain waters of historical analysis.[21] A skeptical eye focused on the results of the "Third Quest" for the historical Jesus would easily relish Lessing's point. But can Christianity be successfully divorced from history? Many do not believe so. Even Bultmann's students struggled to maintain his historical pessimism and in a famous lecture by Ernst Käsemann the question was raised as to the impact such a position has on theological legitimacy.[22] Of particular concern was the potential damage that could occur to the doctrine of the incarnation, for without a firm footing in history it would inevitably become a lacuna, a nice idea about a justifying and saving God, but an idea that could just as easily have been the invention of the apostle Paul. But if God really did became flesh as the New Testament proclaims then we cannot abstract the eternal meaning of the cross from its historical actuality.

This is not to say that we therefore need a Christology from below over against a Christology from above.[23] To maintain such a distinction would inevitably lead to theological difficulties since *both* are required to be held in tension if a Chalcedonian Christology is to be upheld. The very fact that the human and divine, the eternal and the temporal, are present in one place and in one time means that, methodologically, there is always a double movement. The content of Christological language is required to be from above and, at the same time, from below.[24] In arguing then, for the importance of the intention of Jesus of Nazareth to a theology of atonement, I am not suggesting that a theological perspective must be minimized nor that the historical particulars are necessarily of greater

21. Hence his much quoted dictum: "accidental truths of history can never become the proof of necessary truths of reason" (Chadwick, *Lessing's Theological Writings*, 53).

22. Käsemann, "Das Problem Des Historischen Jesus."

23. Indeed, as far as Pannenberg is concerned, to assert the value of the incarnation from the outset effectively rules out the approach as a Christology from below. Pannenberg, *Jesus—God and Man*, 33.

24. Any Christology that is excessively from above runs the risk of abstracting Jesus from history, just as an excessive emphasis on a Christology from below will abstract Jesus from eternity. Theology has continually demonstrated that there are elements of truth in both methods which is why they must be held in dialectic. Gunton, *Yesterday and Today*, 13.

significance. What I seek to do is to draw both theology and history together, upholding the importance of one without denying the value of the other.

I well recognize that such an endeavor has significant pitfalls and is often criticized as fanciful, if not actually impossible. It will, therefore, need to be extensively defended and we will do so primarily in chapter three. But for now the point to be made is that Jesus' intention for his death—that is, the meaning he created for it—should be investigated in the first instance for what it might contribute to a theology of the atonement. This is not to say that our atonement motifs must be limited to what we know of Jesus' self-intention, but it *is* to say that our motifs should not be articulated in abstract. Faith in the preached Christ cannot be allowed to float free from the Jesus of history. Without such an anchor, Christology itself pays the ultimate price.

Jesus' Intention in Recent Atonement Motifs

So how do contemporary atonement motifs deal with the Jesus of history? As one might expect, contemporary *Christ*-ian discussions on the atonement often do claim to be faithful in some way to the intention of Jesus, yet it is also immediately clear that what is claimed as Jesus' intention differs markedly from one presentation to the next. It is also apparent that the historical particulars of Jesus' mission, and of even his Judaic context, are most often pushed to one side in order to facilitate the fortuitous discovery that Jesus actually had an intention similar to the author's own presentation. What I have yet to discover is a theological work that attempts to seriously integrate the results of historical Jesus research into its own atonement discussion. This lack is, in fact, one of the main motivations for this present study as there is an urgent need to lay the necessary groundwork for a valid theological appropriation of history. For now, however, the immediate task is to provide some examples as to how the intention of Jesus is presently being appropriated in atonement discussions. It should go without saying that the three works chosen below are by no means the only examples that can be given but they are representative of the approaches being taken today.

We begin with Alan Mann's *Atonement for a "Sinless" Society*, which focuses on how redemption can be received by postmoderns through the locating of salvation in the possibility of the wholeness of self. The second example is from Mark Heim's *Saved from Sacrifice*, which appropriates a

Girardian anthropology to explain how Jesus' death functions to create the potential for a peaceful human society. And finally, John Milbank's *Being Reconciled* interprets Jesus' death as the divine offer of the capacity of intra-human forgiveness. While each of the soteriologies on offer will be briefly described, the focus here is not on evaluating the merits of their particular perspectives *per se*, but on how they variously appropriate the constituted meaning of Jesus of Nazareth.

Alan Mann: Atonement for a "Sinless" Society

A great example of an attempt to contextualize the atonement into contemporary terms can be found in Alan Mann's *Atonement for a "Sinless" Society*.[25] Contending that the current Western world no longer lives with the sense of sin and guilt that was characteristic of previous generations, Mann asks how Jesus' death might adequately respond to the primary problems of alienation and shame that now plague the postmodern, post-industrialized self. For while the intense emphasis on "self" in the postmodern era might have "freed" people from guilt (in that nothing "I" do is any longer wrong for *me*), it forces people into an alternative state of shame since it highlights their inability to realize their ideal-selves. Therefore what the postmodern craves, contends Mann, is "ontological coherence"—the meeting of the ideal and real selves—a meeting that will release the postmodern from the crippling effects of self-deficiency. Yet paradoxically, the way to ontological coherence is through mutual and unpolluted relationships, the very thing a postmodern cannot do because of their self-emphasis.

This, says Mann, is why the story of Jesus' death is so significant for the postmodern. It is a narrative of ontological coherence because Jesus who publicly announces his ideal self at the Last Supper (my body broken for you) demonstrates that his real self is one and the same by willingly hanging from the cross.

> Therefore, as Jesus stretches his arms out along the crossbeam, he is, at one and the same time, symbolically holding together his own story and 'exposing' his real-self without fear of incoherence or the malady of chronic shame that haunts the postmodern self; for he is, at this moment, "at-one."[26]

---

25. Mann, *Atonement for a "Sinless" Society.*

26. Ibid., 136–37.

Being "at-one," is the fulfilment of human authenticity because it is the moment at which our real-self (the actuality of our life) becomes our ideal-self (the person we aspire to be).[27] In so doing Jesus opens himself up to the "Other" and guarantees the presence of mutual and unpolluted relationships. It is, says Mann, this "Other-focused" living that brings about the *at-one-ment* so craved for by the post-industrialized self. However, owing to ontological incoherence, the postmodern is unable to follow Jesus into this "Other-focused" living on their own. The boundary must somehow be removed and it is removed, argues Mann, through the story of Jesus' death; it is only this narrative that has the potential to be the necessary counter-story to ontological incoherence.[28] Mann's presentation is significantly more nuanced than that just described, but at its heart is the contention that Jesus' death represents the fulfilment of ontological coherence and is therefore the divine way forward for human authenticity.[29]

But how is the reality of Jesus' ontological coherence to be appropriated by the postmodern? Mann comments that there is no *one* way; how the death of Jesus reconciles the isolated, alienated self to the "Other" can only be a personal interpretation since no two encounters with the storied-Jesus are ever the same. Yet he does offer a possible narrative, one that takes place through participation in the Eucharist, for it is this identifying rite that "allows the atoning work of Jesus to manifest itself in the lives of those who encounter it."[30] Through the Eucharistic liturgy, postmodern people are brought to an awareness that there is an absence of the "Other"—both human and divine—in right relationship with them. Hence it is the Eucharist that enables postmodern people to discover not just each "Other," but the transcendent "Other" to whom they can be reconciled; an "Other" who can recreate them without the chronic shame that so imprisons them.

It is not my purpose here to discuss the strengths and weaknesses of Mann's presentation but to ask how he appropriates the intention of Jesus of Nazareth in telling his atonement story. On one hand his thesis actually requires him to narrate Jesus' intent, because as he himself acknowledges, "without the intent of Jesus the cross itself becomes nothing more than a

27. Ibid., 38.

28. Ibid., 137.

29. Ibid., 134. On this, he quotes Douglas Hall approvingly: the cross reveals the "compassionate determination of God to bring humankind to the realization of its potentiality for authenticity" (Hall, *The Cross in Our Context*, 91).

30. Mann, *Atonement for a "Sinless" Society*, 10.

hollow act."[31] If Jesus' death is truly to be an example of ontological coherence then it cannot be an accidental event. It must be intentional and, indeed, he quotes Ben Meyer's insightful words from *The Aims of Jesus*: "Jesus did not aim to be repudiated and killed, he aimed to charge with meaning his being repudiated and killed."[32] On the other hand, however (and rather perplexingly given his quotation of Meyer), Mann contends that the historical Jesus has nothing to contribute to his narrative of atonement.[33] In fact, the historical Jesus is an "unnecessary distraction, for it is of no concern to the postmodern on their search for salvation."[34] There is then an interesting dialectic. Jesus' intent is necessary if his death is truly to be an example of ontological coherence, yet the historical Jesus has no possible bearing on such an intent. No doubt part of the reasoning behind this rejection of the historical Jesus lies in the postmodern incredulity towards historical truth, a point we will ourselves have to address in the third chapter. But primarily the rejection stems from a desire not to be limited to a narrative of "facts," which having occurred in a time and place long obscured by history, could not possibly offer a narrative that is able to be appropriated by the postmodern as their own. "[W]e seek" Mann writes, "a narrative possibility that is bearable and conceivable, and one that can be owned by the individual as meaningful and sufficient."[35] For the postmodern, the historical Jesus apparently provides no such possibility.

So what intent does Mann contend that Jesus narrates? Given our discussion thus far, it is of no surprise to find that Jesus' intention is strikingly revealed in the Last Supper. The meal is important not only because in Jesus' ministry meals were moments of reconciliation (Matt 9:10–13; Luke 14:1–4; 19:1–9) but because here at the final meal Jesus narrates his purpose for coming. The breaking of bread and the offering of wine symbolically narrate Jesus' intention to die and this reveals to the postmodern Jesus' ideal self. His intent to die will ultimately prove his ontological coherence because on the cross his real-self is displayed without shame. This coherence opens the door to the "Other" even to the "Other" that betrays and abandons him. Mann notes that Jesus maintained an openness to the "Other" right to the very end. His intent can therefore be seen in the giving

31. Ibid., 113.

32. Ibid., 107, quoting Meyer, *The Aims of Jesus*, 218.

33. Mann understands the "historical Jesus" to be the Jesus reconstructed by historical research. We will have more to say about this in the third chapter.

34. Mann, *Atonement for a "Sinless" Society*, 107.

35. Ibid., 108.

up of his life so that "living within mutual, undistorted, unpolluted self-relating and 'Other-relating' may become a real possibility."[36]

The question I have for Mann's thesis is whether the rejection of the historical intention of Jesus of Nazareth functions to remove Jesus from the meaning of the cross. The intention that Mann finds in the Last Supper narrative is patently not that of Jesus of Nazareth, as indeed, Mann acknowledges. It is, instead the meaning of a post-Easter reflection created to respond directly to the cultural situation Mann is addressing. The meaning that Mann therefore finds is not the meaning inherent in the historical event, nor is it the meaning of the incarnate Son, but a meaning shaped along the lines of a perceived soteriological need. Perhaps this is the cost of coherent contextualization, but need it be? Is the narrative of the Jesus of history so out-of-touch with the humanity of today? Mann acknowledges that his presentation will cause consternation among many Christians for its perceived unorthodoxy, but the problem I have is not in the novelty of its presentation but in its ahistorical precondition. To assert that the import of the narrative that confronts the postmodern is not the storied intention of one man two thousand years ago but the divine story of ontological coherence that finds its ultimate expression in that one man is to separate the divine meaning of the cross from the intention of Jesus himself. But as I intend to argue, the two cannot be separated; the divine meaning created for the cross event is the very meaning Jesus of Nazareth constituted for it.

S. Mark Heim: Saved from Sacrifice

This recent offering from Mark Heim is one of the better presentations of Christian atonement from the perspective of Girardian anthropology.[37] Previous efforts by both Raymund Schwager and Anthony Bartlett have demonstrated just how valuable the Girardian insight is to a re-reading of the Gospels,[38] and Heim writes similarly, drawing particular attention to the importance of the passion narratives themselves. In his engaging style he argues that Jesus' death is the decisive revelation of the scapegoat mechanism in history and having revealed the mechanism, the Gospels declare its power forever broken. Thus, the key feature of the book is the contention that the significance of the cross is found in the way it reveals

36. Ibid., 114.

37. Heim, *Saved from Sacrifice*.

38. Schwager, *Jesus in the Drama of Salvation*; Bartlett, *Cross Purposes*.

the dynamic of scapegoating violence that encompasses both individuals and communities.[39]

And what is this "dynamic of scapegoating violence"? Girard posits that it is the mechanism by which peace and order is restored to a community that has suffered from internal conflict. As a community's cohesion begins to crumble due to hidden (and what Girard terms *mimetic*) rivalry it seeks a way to restore order from the threatening chaos and it does so by searching out a scapegoat, an individual (or group) who can be blamed for the current crisis.[40] The chosen victim needs to be marginal to the society as a whole and lack the ability to retaliate or seek vengeance, while also being sufficiently vulnerable to being seized, accused, and killed.[41] Once the chosen victim has been identified the society carries out the murder, and because it is really believed that the scapegoat caused the crisis, peace returns to the community following their removal.[42] Over time, the society begins to see the chance victim as the one who brought salvation from the crisis and saved the community from possible destruction. Thus, the scapegoat is transformed into a hero and in some cases even deified, as it appears that they alone brought peace and reconciliation.

Girard argues that this mechanism is quite possibly the constitutive element of hominization,[43] but Heim (who remains cautious about such global statements) suggests that one does not have to accept the totality of Girard's argument to recognize that "his insights are a reality actually functioning in human religion and societies" both past and present.[44] Thus, the point Heim wishes to make is not that Girard has found the cause of all culture and religion but that the scapegoating mechanism actually works, even though one might consider it horrendous that it does.

So, from this perspective, what is the soteriological function of Jesus' death? Heim contends that the narrative of Jesus' death is, in fact, two stories laid on top of one another. The first is a description of Jesus' execution as an example of the sacrificial mechanism in action. The second is the story of God's redemptive action "in, with and under" the story of the

39. Heim, *Saved from Sacrifice*, 10.

40. On mimetic rivalry see Girard, *To Double Business Bound*, 140. Girard, *Things Hidden*, 18.

41. Hunsinger, "The Politics of the Nonviolent God," 63.

42. "The purpose of the sacrifice is to restore harmony to the community, to reinforce the social fabric" (Girard, *Violence and the Sacred*, 9).

43. Girard's understanding of the hominization process is well summarized by Alison, *The Joy of Being Wrong*, 15–20.

44. Heim, *Saved from Sacrifice*, 11.

first.[45] It is readily evident that as a candidate for sacrifice Jesus makes a classic case. He is of humble birth, an outsider from Galilee whose healings and exorcisms have shown him to be aligned (in the minds of some) with demonic powers. His popularity and disdain for the recognized rulers and authorities has made him dangerous and he is charged with the worst possible offences both before God (blasphemy) and Roman rule (sedition). At his trial everyone abandons him and he is put to death with collective unanimity and peace is miraculously restored to the nation.[46] This latter point is recognized by both the Gospels of John (11:45–53) and Luke (23:12), an acknowledgment that indicates the appropriateness of understanding Jesus' death as an example of scapegoating violence. In fact, from this perspective, Heim comments that what is actually redeemed through Jesus' death *is* the status quo. In other words, the Gospels do present a theory about the value of redemptive violence, but it is a value believed in and propagated by the persecutors. "Atonement is precisely the good they have in mind," Heim writes, and it is this drive for sacrificial atonement that actually kills Jesus.[47]

But for the community to believe its own scapegoating lie it must be totally blind to what it is doing to the victim. For if the innocence of the victim was to be exposed, then the death of the victim would be revealed as a murder (and hence be unjustified) and its efficacy as a saving event would be completely undermined.[48] Indeed, Heim argues that this is exactly what the passion narratives declare and this revelation is what God is unveiling through the cross. The narrative certainly includes the sacrificial mechanism, it is still there in all its horrific detail but the difference now is that *we see it*, the very fact of which undermines the effectiveness of the mechanism. Heim explains:

> The sacrificial necessity that claims Jesus is a sinful mechanism for victimization, whose rationale maintains it is necessary that one innocent person die for the good of the people. The free, loving 'necessity' that leads God to be willing to stand in the place of the scapegoat is that this is the way to unmask the sacrificial mechanism, to break its cycles of mythic reproduction,

45. Ibid., 17.

46. For the threat of conflict and return of peace from a historical perspective, see Fredriksen, *Jesus of Nazareth*.

47. Heim, *Saved from Sacrifice*, 125.

48. "Sacrifice would not be effective if we explicitly knew what we were doing; its benefits depend on our conviction that we are doing something else" (ibid., 121).

and to found human community on a nonsacrificial principle: solidarity with the victim, not unanimity against the victim.[49]

Heim acknowledges that this understanding could be interpreted in terms of a Gnostic revelation, making salvation a matter of mere knowledge rather than the more traditional forensic act common in other motifs.[50] But he stresses that the revelation requires a transcendent act of grace to perceive and is not something that can be arrived at from a "Pelagian" operation.[51] Nevertheless, there is a strong horizontal dynamic in this soteriology; a redeemed community is one that is not based on the scapegoat mechanism.

But does Heim believe that this was Jesus of Nazareth's intention? To endure the evil of sacrificial violence in order to unmask it and thus release his followers into a non-sacrificial community? He believes it likely, suggesting there are indicators in the Gospels that Jesus was aware of the scapegoating mechanism and that he acted in such a way that it would be revealed. He begins his analysis with Matthew 23:27–39, the so-called Pharisaic woes in which Jesus casts himself in a long line of prophetic succession. Far from stressing his uniqueness, Jesus emphasizes the fact that he is being treated just as all the prophets have been treated. Indeed, he goes further than this and identifies himself with all the righteous blood that has been shed on the earth, from Abel to Zechariah, the last of the recorded murders in the Hebrew Scriptures. Heim finds in this identification a deliberate connection with all the scapegoating victims of history; Jesus chooses to align himself with them.

There are two other possible references to the scapegoat mechanism in the "Pharisaic woes." The first is Jesus' use of the phrase "whitewashed tombs," which for Heim must go beyond a general condemnation of hypocrisy to the mythical practice of sacrifice as Girard describes it. The reason for this is that the tombs are described as beautiful on the outside (just like the mythical cover stories and the social benefits that result from the sacrificial death) yet full of bones and filth within (corresponding to the bodies of the victims, along with the unacknowledged lies and the arbitrary violence—the uncleanness—of their persecution). The second reference is understood from Jesus' emphasis on deception. The Pharisees

49. Ibid., 114.

50. Ibid., 13. See the interesting discussion in Alison, *The Joy of Being Wrong*, 83–85.

51. Heim, *Saved from Sacrifice*, 197. Anthony Bartlett explains this point particularly well. Bartlett, *Cross Purposes*, 148–49.

claim that they would not have taken part in the shedding of innocent blood had they lived in the days of their forefathers. But Jesus responds by criticizing them for their own re-creation of the very same scapegoating dynamic that was evidenced in the prior murders. Heim notes that since Jesus' comments were directed at the pious and virtuous Pharisees, it cannot be a lack of morality or ethics that is primarily in view. "Jesus is not talking about something that bad people do and good people don't. It is the mechanism by which the community of people, good and bad, maintains itself."[52]

That Jesus understood this to be the case is found, suggests Heim, in the Synoptic quotation of Psalm 118:22–23. This Psalm draws attention to the fact that it is the rejected stone that becomes the cornerstone, an apt analogy of the rejected victim becoming the structural foundation of corporate harmony. It is, therefore, not a matter of a few "bad apples" that take matters into their own hands but society itself that requires the rejected stone to build upon. So what is the "Lord's doing" that is "marvelous in our eyes"? It is the fact that the mechanism is now unveiled and so undone.[53] This is why, when Jesus quotes Psalm 22 from the cross, it is not so much a cry of dereliction as an acknowledgement that the righteous victim, indeed, all righteous victims will be vindicated by God. The cry of forsakenness functions to reveal the scapegoat mechanism at precisely the moment when the mechanism's deception is normally at its height.[54] Hence, Jesus can pray for the nation's forgiveness for they act in ignorance, not aware of the controlling mechanism that Jesus reveals through his death.

Heim is more than ready to acknowledge that his argument is not all that can, or indeed, should be said about Jesus' understanding and we should not mistake him for presenting some kind of satisfactory whole.[55] However, he is convinced that Jesus' willingness to face death needs to be explained in terms of that death's revelatory quality. If we do not, then we obscure the unveiling of the sacrificial mechanism at best, and continue to perpetuate the myth of sacred violence at worst. On the contrary, says Heim,

> God takes advantage of the occasion of death in general to directly address a universal feature of human sin. God is willing to die for us, to bear our sin in this way, because we desperately

52. Heim, *Saved from Sacrifice*, 121.

53. Ibid., 123.

54. Ibid., 121.

55. Ibid., ix.

need deliverance from the particular sin this death exemplifies. Death and resurrection are located where they can make an irreversible impact on this horizontal evil in human life. God breaks the grip of scapegoating by stepping into the place of a victim, becoming a victim who cannot be hidden or mythologized. God acts not to affirm the suffering of the innocent one as the price of peace, but to reverse it.[56]

It must be acknowledged that all the necessary pieces of the soteriological puzzle are present in Heim's argument, but nonetheless, the question still needs to be asked as to whether he has correctly characterized the meaning that Jesus created for his death. The focus on Jesus' message and ministry in the Gospels is not obviously a revelation of the scapegoat mechanism *per se* but the coming of the kingdom of God. This is what Jesus proclaimed when he began his ministry and the consensus of historical Jesus scholarship is to locate Jesus' intentions for his ministry within the light of how he understood that event. It might, of course, be possible to argue that the revelation of the scapegoat mechanism is included in the wider scope of the "coming of the kingdom," but Heim certainly makes no effort to do so.[57] Even if he had, it is true to say that no historical Jesus scholar has yet picked up the Girardian insight and tried to square it with what is known from historical research. Perhaps such an endeavor is still to come, but at present there is little doubt that Girardian anthropology gets the rough end of the historical stick.[58]

John Milbank: Being Reconciled

Our third and final example is considerably different from the previous two because Milbank's work *Being Reconciled* is not strictly an atonement discussion.[59] His thesis is far broader, focusing as it does on the category of divine "gift," which he expresses positively through creation, grace, the incarnation and finally ecclesiology.[60] Of course, atonement too is a gift

---

56. Ibid., 194.

57. In fact, in Heim's work the kingdom of God is not referenced with any significance at all.

58. For example I was unable to locate any reference to Girardian anthropology in Dunn's comprehensive *Jesus Remembered*, and only a brief dismissive footnote in his earlier analysis of Pauline theology. Dunn, *Jesus Remembered*; Dunn, *The Theology of Paul the Apostle*, 213 n. 22.

59. Milbank, *Being Reconciled*.

60. On the type of "gifts" see particularly Rowland, "Divine Gifts."

and Milbank turns to it midway through the book in an attempt to explain how humanity's desperately needed gift, that of *forgiveness*, can be appropriated and effected. However, like all gifts it can also be refused and Milbank describes this refusal particularly in terms of evil and violence, the discussion of which takes place in the first two chapters.

Without getting drawn into his detailed argument we can note that Milbank is especially critical of any attempt to give evil its own ontological right, affirming instead the Augustinian conception of evil as a privation, which he contends is the only way to adequately make sense of evil's inexplicability. But surd as it may be, evil can nonetheless be overcome and this is done, says Milbank, through the act of forgiveness. Yet he also argues strongly that humanity is incapable of forgiving unless it first receives the divine gift of forgiveness, offered in and through the death and resurrection of Jesus Christ.[61] This, then, is what is defined as atonement: the divine enabling of human forgiveness. While an interesting take on redemption, Milbank's work is of primary relevance to us because he spends a whole chapter defending the *historicity* of the Gospel passion narratives. And as history, there must be a coherence between event and meaning, a coherence he attempts to locate in the depths of Jesus' abandonment.[62] But as before, Milbank's historical Jesus also takes the shape of his own soteriological presentation and there is little here that one could connect to historical Jesus scholarship. But before we engage in that discussion, a brief explanation of Milbank's thesis is required.

Since humanity is incapable of forgiveness without a prior transcendent act, Milbank turns to the incarnation to locate that transcendent act within the human sphere. Appropriating a high Christology, the argument is made that Jesus, the God-man, fulfils the role of the unique sovereign victim and by virtue of the divine *Logos*, is able to plumb the full depths and implications of suffering. "In this way a single suffering became also a sovereign suffering, capable of representing all suffering and of forgiving on behalf of all victims."[63] Moreover, the unique sovereign victim is able to forgive at the instantaneous moment of hurt because, unlike other human beings, Christ is able to experience suffering in an "accepting, actively receptive fashion."[64] Hence, for Christ to suffer is at one and the same time

61. Milbank defines five *aporias* of human forgiveness, discussion of which would take us too far afield. Milbank, *Being Reconciled*, 50–60.

62. In this it is similar to the Girardian approach but Milbank's analysis has its distinctive features.

63. Milbank, *Being Reconciled*, 61.

64. Ibid.

for Christ to forgive. An outcome that can only be described as a divine gift. Importantly, such a gift only becomes forgiveness when in "Christ it is *not* God forgiving us but humanity forgiving humanity."[65] Divine redemption is, therefore, found in the human reception of the gift of the capacity for forgiveness. And to emphasize the transcendent nature of this gift, Milbank comments that it must first be given by the Trinity to Christ's humanity before it can be subsequently offered to us. And humanity can only appropriate intra-human forgiveness by virtue of the Christ passing that capability to us through the "hypostatic presence" of the Holy Spirit.[66] It is, then, only the ecclesial community that has the capability to extend human forgiveness, for it is only by the power of the Holy Spirit that we can receive and subsequently offer such a gift.

The implications of Milbank's position certainly warrant considerable discussion, but our specific question is how does Milbank appropriate the intention of Jesus? From the brief analysis above it would seem that he does not. The high Christology invoked operates without historical interest and there is very little to suggest that the intention of Jesus of Nazareth could possibly have any value. Yet Milbank immediately follows this chapter on the Incarnation with a thorough defense of the historicity of the passion narratives in which he does address the intention of Jesus even if not directly. That he does so becomes very clear in his description of the coherence between historical event and imbued meaning, a coherence which is said to be all the more important because the incarnation guarantees that such created meaning will be universally effective.[67] And what was that meaning? As might be expected from the discussion above, Milbank contends that Jesus through his death intended to enter into solidarity with each and every human being as the sovereign victim. But he also notes that in the Gospel narrative Jesus did not just suffer as a victim but as a complete outcast, totally rejected by all of humanity. This emphasis on Jesus' victimhood is similar to that of Heim. Milbank, however, does not

65. Ibid., 61–62. For Milbank, God can never be a victim since it is impossible for God to suffer loss and hence there is no need for God to forgive. Singular support for this position is drawn from the mystical writings of Julian of Norwich who famously argued that God does not need to forgive, since God is never offended.

66. Ibid., 62.

67. "There are no events outside the assignment of meanings, and there are no construable meanings not ultimately including some reference to an active rearrangement of things in time" (ibid., 94).

take a Girardian approach here, but turns instead to the insight of Giorgio Agamben and his account of the *homo sacer* in Roman jurisprudence.[68]

> [According to Pompeius Festus,] after the succession of the plebs in Rome, it was granted to the plebeians to have the right to pursue to the death (singly or collectively it is implied) someone whom they have as a body condemned. Such an individual was declared *homo sacer*, and his irregular death was not exactly homicide, nor punishment, nor sacrifice. . . . Such a person was *sacer*, simply in the sense of cast out, utterly abandoned.[69]

Milbank contends that the passion narratives give an account of Jesus' death in precisely these terms: successively abandoned by Jewish sovereignty, Roman sovereignty and by the mob, Jesus goes to his death as an outcast, as a *homo sacer*. The implication of this position is enormous, for as the death of a *homo sacer* Jesus' crucifixion cannot be understood exactly as a murder, an execution or even a sacrifice—for these all imply that Jesus' humanity was still recognized. Instead, Jesus' death is the death of an outcast who Milbank contends had already been reduced in the consciousness of the mob to a level "beneath humanity," to that of "half-animality."[70] But it is here, outside the city, where the God-man offers the ultimate gift of forgiveness. Dying in solidarity with every victim, Jesus forgives on behalf of every victim and makes the way possible for human beings to truly forgive each other.

This understanding of the death of Jesus as *homo sacer* has several implications for Milbank's conception of the historical Jesus. First of all, in dying a sub-human death Jesus could not have died the death of a martyr, as a witness to some kind of universal cause. For if Jesus (the man) did actively imbue his death with some kind of meaning then he would not have died a sub-human death. On the contrary, as he was led away to be crucified it must have seemed that he went to his death at "the whim of a drunken mob," which ostensibly makes it a senseless and meaningless event.[71] To suggest otherwise (i.e., to give Jesus' death historical meaning) is to give dignity to Jesus' death, and to give him dignity misses the point of his death as a *homo sacer*. Milbank does not spell the point out, but it is

68. For his earlier critique of Girard, see Milbank, *Theology and Social Theory*, 392–98.

69. Milbank, *Being Reconciled*, 90.

70. Ibid., 97.

71. Ibid., 96.

implied that if Jesus' death had historical meaning then it could not have been in solidarity with every victim.

The second point has to do with Jesus' mission. Milbank contends that what is understood and rejected by the mob is Jesus' claim to be God; nothing more, nothing less.[72] This means that the resentment towards Jesus expressed by both the high priests (Mark 15:10) and by the people (Matt 27:18) could only have originated out of envy, an envy not of Jesus' popularity or remarkable authority but of his claim to be God in the flesh. This, says Milbank, is the real reason why the people "screamed out their resentment to Pilate."[73] For even if the people misinterpreted Jesus' actions in the Temple as a threat of destruction (since, according to Milbank, Jesus was "clearly" protecting the temple's integrity and was not out to destroy it), their self-deceit as protectors of the Temple remained nothing but a shabby cover for their envy of Jesus' "awesome elevation."[74]

Finally, Milbank notes that even if the Gospels did contend that Jesus died for the truth, it was not possible for that "truth" to be publically displayed at the time. As a *homo sacer*, Jesus' death had no meaning for anyone—including the disciples—and only became meaningful once the resurrection enabled such reflection. Hence, while Jesus' death was never without divine meaning, such meaning was not visible at the moment of his death. It is the resurrection that makes the meaning visible, for it is then that the capacity to forgive is offered to those who cowered in fear behind the locked doors of that upper room.

When, in our fourth chapter, we come to asking contemporary historical Jesus scholarship what it is that Jesus may have actually intended for his death, it will become very obvious that the intention of Milbank's Jesus as described here differs markedly from those accounts. For one thing, it is very clear that Jesus did have a cause—the inauguration of the kingdom of God—and hence, a meaningful martyr's death cannot be summarily ruled out. In addition, Jesus' actions at the Last Supper (something that Milbank does not address) have significant influence on the way his earlier actions in the Temple should be understood, and an envious rejection of Jesus is not all that apparent.

However, of more theological concern is the argument that Jesus goes willingly to his death merely to die in solidarity with every victim. Does this understanding really acknowledge the power of the incarnation?

72. Ibid., 95–96.
73. Ibid., 96.
74. Ibid.

Or does it function to drive a wedge between the life of Jesus and his death, making the former merely the prelude to the latter? Despite Milbank's theological insistence on the importance of the incarnation, his presentation can be criticized at this point. An unnecessary dichotomy is introduced between Jesus' life and death, a dichotomy that reinforces the existence of two disparate crosses in contemporary atonement research. So once again we find in Milbank that, as in Mann and Heim, Jesus' intention (or lack thereof) is described in terms that support the theological motif in question.

These examples could readily be multiplied but enough has been said to make the point. The intention that Jesus of Nazareth had for his death, *as far as can be determined from historical research*, is not well addressed in contemporary atonement discussion. Either Jesus' intention is considered completely irrelevant, or it is portrayed as reflecting the atonement motif in question and thus changes dramatically from one discussion to the next. In reality, both approaches have similar results: whatever it was that Jesus intended his death to achieve has very little bearing on the discussion at hand. But I ask again, should this be the case? It is my contention that the recent work on the historical Jesus does have a significant contribution to make to an understanding of the cross, and this contribution should be incorporated as far as possible into our presentations of the atonement.

In other words, I do not believe that it is sufficient to make the death of Jesus a datum of reflection in and of itself. Jesus' death is most securely a feature of his life, and must therefore be construed in its historical dynamic. Roger Haight puts it well:

> [His death] was due to his message, his preaching it, and his actions. His crucifixion was determined by the measure in which he confronted people or challenged their interests. Jesus' death flowed from the radicality and seriousness of his message; from his perspective, it was a function of his fidelity to his mission or cause, the cause of God, a mission of salvation to the people around him. Jesus gave his life for the kingdom of God, and all the evidence points to the fact that he gave it freely.[75]

Jesus' death is therefore connected to his life and must be understood within that context. Of course, today we are used to approaching Jesus' death dogmatically and in terms of abstract symbolic categories, but this should never blind us to the actual historicity of the cross. If Jesus' life had meaning (and I have yet to read anyone who suggests that Jesus lived a

75. Haight, *Jesus*, 85–86.

meaningless life), then it is also appropriate to ask what meaning he may have constituted for his death. And the answer, however tentative, should have some bearing on how theologians present the saving message of the Gospel to the community with which they are engaged.

But it will be immediately obvious to anyone familiar with the current state of atonement reflection that this position presents us with a significant challenge; for to uphold the Christian doctrine of Jesus of Nazareth as the Incarnate One and to also insist that Jesus constituted meaning for his death is to argue that divine meaning can be created for contingent events (even evil ones). This contention opens up a twenty-first century Pandora's Box because it insists that salvific meaning can be derived from violence and suffering, a present *aporia* if there ever was one. This is not a trivial concern and is a major motivation for the development of some of the more recent atonement discussions. It is, therefore, more than appropriate for us to spend some time addressing this question.

A Potential Hurdle: The "Myth" of Redemptive Suffering

To argue for the importance of Jesus' own intention for the cross in the development of atonement motifs immediately confronts us with a considerable challenge. The fundamental problem is this: If we claim that Jesus intended his suffering and death to have divinely constituted meaning then do we not also give divine value to suffering and death and thereby create divine validation for the perpetuation and/or enduring of other forms of human suffering? This at least is the fear, but it is a fear that is not merely derived from abstract theological concerns but from the lived experience of those who have been abused and oppressed. Liberation and Feminist theologians particularly draw attention to the fact that a theology of redemptive suffering does nothing to free people from their own experience of suffering and can actually have the opposite effect, encouraging them to remain within their oppressive and abusive situations. This is perceived, quite rightly, as abhorrent and has given rise to a fresh movement in both academic and popular theology that avoids any suggestion that God finds value in suffering and death. In itself, this raises questions of theodicy (to which we will have to return in the next chapter), but it does help explain just why the traditional models of atonement are held to thrust theology into this modern *aporia*. As J. Denny Weaver convincingly demonstrates, each traditional motif (including the Abelardian) relies upon the violence of the cross to effect salvation, and this reliance is said to do nothing but perpetuate the "myth" of redemptive suffering.[76] If, then, we are to contend that Jesus did create salvific meaning out of the sinful event of his own suffering and death then we must also adequately contend with this challenge.

An Overview of the Problem

In her inimitable style, Delores Williams castigates traditional atonement theology for its blood-lust, remarking at the women's re-imagining conference of 1993, "I don't think we need a theory of the atonement at all... I don't think we need folks hanging on crosses and blood dripping and weird stuff."[77] Her comments sparked significant controversy at the time and in the years following her perspective has often been repeated. To be sure, contemporary discussion on the atonement is still convinced that humanity is in need of salvation, but as Williams hoped, the idea that God could only forgive if somebody suffered has more or less become anathematized in recent Western scholarship. After all, is not the God of the Gospels a God of peace, love and forgiveness? A God who is revealed by Jesus of Nazareth to be the God who unashamedly welcomes home the prodigal without thought of vengeance, or the demand of satisfaction? How, then, if this picture is to be believed, can God be associated with the horrendous death of God's own Son, even if such suffering is for so grand a purpose as human redemption?

For many the obvious answer is that God cannot be so associated. Attitudes which are roundly condemned as morally reprehensible in human beings cannot, in any sense, be promoted as justifiable for God.[78] In any event, it is assumed to be axiomatic that violence is incontrovertibly opposed to the goodness of God.[79] Violence destroys, divides, sup-

---

76. Weaver, "Violence in Christian Theology." See also Weaver, *The Nonviolent Atonement*.

77. Quoted by Cyre, "Fallout Escalates," 71. In a more recent article Williams has continued this line of thought: "There is nothing of God in the blood of the cross" (Williams, "Black Women's Surrogacy Experience," 32).

78. Indeed, Brock and Parker remark somewhat provocatively that if Jesus' "executioners" did what was historically necessary for salvation, then state terrorism is a good thing and one must conclude that torture and murder are the will of God! Brock and Parker, *Proverbs of Ashes*, 49.

79. This is nothing new. As early as the second century we find Marcion striving to inoculate the God of the New Testament from any kind of violence by attributing

presses, abuses and nullifies. It is the direct opposite of *at-one-ment* and is, therefore, surely incapable of bringing about reconciliation. Thus, any attempt to shroud the violence of the cross with an aura of divine ordination must be summarily rejected. To not do so is to insist that violence is God's way of transforming people and communities into greater spiritual well-being.[80] It is to insist that violence is an appropriate mechanism for spiritual transformation. It is to insist that acts of evil are sometimes to be celebrated rather than condemned.

But perhaps the most significant criticism directed against any attempt to make the violence of the cross meaningful is the belief that such meaning (a) not only justifies violence but encourages *further* acts of violence to be done in its name; and (b) promotes the ongoing passive acceptance of personal suffering. It is, of course, to Christianity's shame that it has a history of sanctioning acts of violence and it can readily be demonstrated that the doctrine of the atonement has done little to prevent such acts.[81] Anselm's supporting visit to the front lines of the First Crusade whilst in the midst of writing his *Cur Deus Homo?* is cited as an obvious example, but both Augustine and Luther, neither a stranger to the atonement debate, were ultimately prepared to lend their theological weight to violent acts of repression.[82] Understandably, contemporary theologians find this to be a scandal. The cross was never meant to be a standard of war; it is an agent of reconciliation, a marker of divine love, a moment of unquestionable compassion. Inherently violent in itself of course, but by no means should the violence imparted upon that one individual be interpreted to provide justification for inflicting violence upon another.

The second criticism is particularly emphasized by both Feminist and Liberation theologians who readily cite instances in which the oppressed

---

all divine violence, including the violence surrounding the death of Jesus, to the Old Testament Demiurge.

80. Brock and Parker, *Proverbs of Ashes*, 44.

81. See for example, Gorringe, *God's Just Vengeance*.

82. I am not suggesting here that Anselm wrote *Cur Deus Homo?* as a theological buttress for Pope Urban II's call to arms. In fact, there is some evidence that Anselm was actually unsympathetic to the Crusade's cause, primarily because he felt that it was a distraction from the true calling to spiritual growth (Southern, *Portrait*, 169). However, it must be said that the publication of *Cur Deus Homo?* had no detrimental effect on the Crusade's perceived theological legitimacy. Further discussion on the link between atonement theology and violence can be found in Bartlett, *Cross Purposes*. Merback, "Reverberations of Guilt and Violence," 37–50. For a bemusing description of atonement theories as "nothing less than terrorism" see Peterman, "Redemption (Theology Of)," 11:985.

and abused were encouraged to go back to their situations of suffering precisely because of the meaning said to be inherent in the death of Jesus Christ. But far from being liberating, such situations merely function to perpetuate the oppression of the individual/community, encouraging them to passively acquiesce in their own suffering in the vain hope that something "good" might come from it. Brock and Parker want to know what good comes from a battered wife being sent back to her abusive husband by the parish priest only to be violently killed in one last terrifying outburst?[83] If such tragedies are the price of a theology of redemptive suffering, then it is a price that few are now willing to pay. Darby Kathleen Ray draws the conclusion rather effectively:

> To make meaning out of suffering and death . . . merely perpetuates them, and any religion or belief that does such a thing is demonic. God is a God of life, not death; God is life-giving, not death-dealing.[84]

The clear assumption here is that divine meaning is equivalent to divine justification and thus if the cross is to have divine meaning then its violence must also be justified. I will spend a fair portion of the next chapter challenging this assumption but it is certainly apparent that Ray believes this to be the case. Her emphasis on what God can and cannot do is arguably designed to "protect" God from the claim that the cross represents an example of divinely justified violence. In a way this effort is reminiscent of the earlier work of Dorothee Soelle, who famously argued in *Suffering* that God could in no way be involved in the death of Jesus of Nazareth, for to do so would inevitably portray God as sadistic.[85] Any attempt to maintain that salvation was somehow dependent on God causing the death of Jesus (whether directly or indirectly), would stand in danger of this portrayal. This is essentially her complaint against Moltmann's *Crucified God*, a work that she contends presents the quintessential argument for theological sadism. Left unchallenged such a view, she says, would have the potential to encourage Christians to ultimately—though probably unconsciously—love, honor and worship "the executioner."[86]

83. Brock and Parker, *Proverbs of Ashes*, 15–20.

84. Ray, *Deceiving the Devil*, 84.

85. Soelle, *Suffering*, 26.

86. Ibid., 28.

A Potential Way Forward

The conclusion to draw from this discussion is that the contemporary Western atonement debate is very concerned to do two things. The first is that God should be heralded as a God of love who does not engage in acts of violence, and should not in any way be said to derive value from such acts. And second, an appropriate atonement theology will not provide divine validation to any act of evil, for to do so inevitably perpetuates further acts of evil (whether performed or endured) in the name of God.

These twin points are enlightening because to my mind they reveal a more fundamental concern with the nature of God, and God's activity in creation, than with atonement theology *per se*. Of course, it is rightly argued that the lived experience of the oppressed and abused demands a theological understanding of God—and particularly of God's actions in salvation—that is unquestionably liberating, and incapable of any articulation in which oppression could somehow continue to be justified.[87] But it is more assumed than argued that this desire also requires the theologian to completely abandon any attempt to find meaning in the suffering and death of Jesus of Nazareth. I acknowledge that this is a possible conclusion, but I contend that this would be the case if, and only if, it could also be demonstrated that the creation of divine meaning out of an evil event *requires by necessity the event itself to be divinely caused*. But is such a conclusion really tenable? Is God the necessary cause of evil events? And if one wants to contend that the answer is no, does that thereby prevent an understanding in which God is able to create meaning out of the event without justifying and validating the event itself?

That divine meaning does equate to divine validation seems to be the prevailing assumption in contemporary research, but it effectively denies the possibility of either (a) divine meaning without divine causation, or at least (b) that an evil contingent event can have divine meaning created out of it. And herein lies the failure, I believe, of much of the current discussion on the atonement. In its justifiable eagerness to decry acts of violence and oppression, the debate also redefines God's relationship to creation (that is, the necessary to the contingent). Again, the motive for doing so may be healthy, but the results of this argument have major consequences that go beyond that of negating the possibility of divine violence to include every facet of the creator/creature relationship. For this reason alone an

87. This point is made very clear in Brown and Parker, "For God So Loved the World?," 1–30.

investigation into the relationship between divine action and the cross of Jesus is warranted, but a reason enhanced because what is at stake is the very possibility of salvific meaning itself.

In conclusion then, if we wish to uphold that there is divine meaning in the suffering and death of Jesus of Nazareth, the fundamental task is not to defend atonement motifs against the charge that they perpetuate suffering, but to argue that God can create meaning out of the cross event without requiring that event to be divinely caused. If such an argument can be presented then the contention that the historical intention of Jesus of Nazareth should have a role in faith's understanding of salvation can proceed without fear that it will be understood to justify acts of oppression and abuse.

The Road Ahead

The discussion thus far has emphasized the importance of historical meaning for our understanding of a theological event. But the task here, as I have already indicated, is not to try and prove the value of Christian salvation from an analysis of history. Salvation is, at the end of the day, a matter of personal faith and lived experience. One can point to its reality in the lives of millions of people around the world but one can never prove matters of faith from an investigation into a particular event that occurred at a particular place and time in history. However, it is also true that the doctrine of Christian salvation unashamedly finds its fulcrum in the historical events of Jesus' death and resurrection, and I believe that Christian theology cannot afford to lose the historical actuality of the cross underneath its symbolic power. In this, I agree with Milbank: along with the resurrection, it is the doctrine of the incarnation that imbues the historical life of Jesus of Nazareth with theological significance. To somehow draw a line at the resurrection and treat what lies beneath it as insignificant matters of historical interest, is to introduce a dichotomy between the historical value of Jesus' preaching and teaching and the theological significance of his death. On the contrary, the value to theology of Jesus' life is far from limited to the sheer fact of his death and resurrection and it is, therefore, appropriate to ask what Jesus may have intended his death to achieve.

However, in saying this I am not suggesting that we can simply move from historical reconstruction to theological significance by way, for example, of assigning metaphysical implications to particular events.[88] How

88. On the problematic nature of this see Haight, *Jesus*, 86 n. 105.

the intention of Jesus is to be successfully appropriated is something that we will need to work towards and is fundamentally dependent upon how we view the relationship between faith and history. But in itself this task raises some very important methodological issues, so a brief explanation as to how we will approach the question is also in order.

The next chapter presents an argument for understanding divine action in a way that does not negate the possibility of divine meaning being created out of contingent acts. To do this I will draw primarily upon the theology of Thomas Aquinas as mediated through Bernard Lonergan, since it is my contention that the classical doctrine of God provides a sufficient solution to the perceived problem of redemptive suffering. I am well aware that not all would agree, and some of the related criticisms of the classical doctrine will need to be addressed as we proceed. However, the primary purpose here is to provide adequate and coherent evidence for the possibility of there being divine meaning in a contingent event, a meaning that can be said to have universal significance without inevitably requiring that event to be transposed into the necessary.

Having demonstrated the coherence of this conclusion it becomes possible to comprehend the intention of Jesus of Nazareth as having divine significance. This is a Christological assertion to be sure, but as has already been made clear, this work is not an attempt to derive Jesus' divine status through historical means but to ask of history what it might contribute to a theology of the cross. Hence, I am not concerned to avoid a theological perspective when it comes to approaching the historical Jesus.

Once more this contention requires some defense, and the third chapter provides that discussion as it examines not just historiography but also the relationship between faith and history. Drawing primarily upon Bernard Lonergan's notion of critical realism as its methodological foundation, the chapter argues that not only can a historical event be reliably known, but that such knowledge can be adequately appropriated and incorporated into a theological understanding of that event. The reasons for turning to Lonergan here is threefold. Firstly, having widely drawn upon Lonergan in the previous chapter, it is more than coherent to continue to draw upon his insights as they relate to the faith-history dialectic. Secondly, Lonergan's description of critical realism is foundational to Ben Meyer's presentation of Jesus of Nazareth and through Meyer's work has had significant (and acknowledged) influence on N. T. Wright, James Dunn and Scot McKnight.[89] Hence, there is an inherent consistency in our

89. Meyer, *The Aims of Jesus*; Dunn, *Jesus Remembered*; Wright, *Jesus and the Victory of God*; McKnight, *Jesus and His Death*.

discussion on Jesus' intention since we draw heavily on these particular authors. Finally, Lonergan's further conception of constitutive meaning provides a link between Dunn's idea of *impact* and the transformation of meaning that results. Facing a challenge to their existing world mediated by meaning, the disciples were forced to respond to the meaning constituted by Jesus of Nazareth, a response that is indicative of the meaning itself. From this perspective, the Gospels remain historically valuable despite their acknowledged theological agenda for the very reason that they are a reflection of the engendered impact.

However, for meaning to have an impact it must also be carried and it is the carriers of meaning that provide the necessary framework for historical investigation. Drawing again on Lonergan's understanding, three carriers of meaning (the incarnate, linguistic and symbolic) are identified as being of particular value and these carriers become the structural premise for the following analysis into the intentions of Jesus of Nazareth.

So what meaning, then, did Jesus of Nazareth create for his death? This is the fundamental question of the fourth chapter and it is approached, as was said, through an investigation into the incarnate, linguistic and symbolic carriers of meaning. From the outset, however, it must be recognized that a thorough investigation into the historical Jesus, even from the limited perspective of what he may have intended for his own death, remains impossible within the confines of the present project. We will therefore limit the investigation to those scholars who have embraced a critical realist model of historiography and indeed, given the discussion above this should come as no surprise. Furthermore, one of the benefits of a critical realist perspective is that it allows for the carriers of meaning to be meaningfully investigated. While only a selection of the relevant data can be questioned, enough can be gleaned to draw, albeit tentatively, a conclusion about what Jesus intended his own death to achieve.

Again, it must be emphasized that the import of this study is not to develop a new presentation of the historical Jesus, nor is it to direct theology to the "only" meaning inherent in the cross. The point here is to investigate the meaning that Jesus constituted for his death and to bring that judgment to bear on contemporary understandings of the atonement.

The final chapter is a discussion on how this might be done in practice. Drawing upon the distinction between judgment and understanding, the chapter argues that the salvific judgment that Jesus constituted for his death is able to be understood in differing, and contextually sensitive ways, without negating the intention of Jesus himself. This does not mean, however, that all contemporary models of atonement are equally valuable nor, indeed, equally faithful to the intention of Jesus. In particular those models which fail to accept that divine meaning can be created for suffering and death cannot be considered faithful to Jesus' intention, and must for that reason be considered unfaithful to the Christian tradition itself. But it is argued, that models of atonement that go beyond the understanding that Jesus articulated are not necessarily wrong, as long as they remain faithful to the constituted salvific intent.

Context-sensitive articulations of salvation are necessary if Christian theology is to continue to impact the world for Christ. It is, however, the present contention that a contextual presentation does not require the minimization or abandonment of the historical intention of Jesus of Nazareth. On the contrary, the salvific meaning that God creates for the evil event of Jesus' death is revealed in the constituted meaning with which Jesus imbues that death. It is, therefore, appropriate to investigate what Jesus may have intended his death to achieve and having done so, to investigate how that intention might be successfully appropriated for contemporary articulations of that saving grace. However, the first step is to examine the relationship between divine action and the cross of Jesus of Nazareth. To this we now turn.

2

Divine Action and the Contingent Cross

That God could create beings free over against himself is the cross which philosophy could not bear but upon which it has remained hanging.[1]

—Søren Kierkegaard

IN PHILOSOPHY, SOME THINGS ARE UNDERSTOOD TO BE BECAUSE THEY could not be otherwise; whereas other things could have been otherwise but just so happen to be. These vague intuitions are of course codified into more technical terms: it is *necessary* that some things are so, merely *contingent* that other things are so. A key metaphysical question for philosophers then, is to ask what things are necessary and what things are contingent.[2] From a theological perspective this question is often framed in terms of the distinction between God and the created realm. In classical theism at least, only God is strictly necessary and everything else is contingent because the latter depends in some way on God for its very existence. This conclusion is readily reached from *a posteriori* reflections on the nature of contingents themselves. The very fact that some things might not be suggests that there is something greater than contingents and that "something" is somehow able to explain their very existence. Hence, Leibniz famously suggested a principle of sufficient reason; there must be sufficient reason why something that might not exist actually does exist, since to exist *causa sui* is simply impossible in something that might not be.[3]

In Christianity, as in the other two great monotheistic religions, that sufficient reason is God who freely brings contingents into existence

1. Kierkegaard, JP, 1:1237 (1838).
2. Swinburne, *The Christian God*, 96.
3. Leibniz, "The Monadology," 272; Leibniz, "Principles of Nature and Grace," 262.

according to the divine good pleasure. Creation is therefore a free initiative on the part of God who brings a dependent universe into being (*ex nihilo*) because it simply pleases God to do so. Thus, creation cannot be necessary in the same sense that God is necessary with the result that it cannot be thought of as concomitant with God.[4] Such an understanding functions to reinforce creation's dependence on the creator and allows for the related emphasis on cause and effect to be made. Yet affirmations of ongoing dependency immediately raise the question of how God operates in creation and to what extent that operation directs or influences creaturely action.

Such a discussion is required because a theological examination into the death of Jesus of Nazareth must face the question of the divine operating in the created world: How is God involved in the events pertaining to the death of Jesus? The New Testament answered this question by paradoxically balancing both the divine and human perspectives: The crucifixion of Jesus is carried out at the hands of wicked men yet under the direct purpose and foreknowledge of God (Acts 2:23; 4:28). But how the two perspectives actually relate is no-where disclosed, the biblical writers were presumably content to leave such details to the *mysterium paschale*.

Nevertheless, the question refuses to go away. What do we mean when we say that a necessary God is somehow involved in the cross event? Does the salvific importance of the cross require us to postulate that the event was a logical necessity as well? In other words, did God necessarily cause the crucifixion of Jesus of Nazareth in order to be able to forgive a rebellious humanity? If so, there would be little to recommend a theology of creaturely free will. But even more telling is the potential justification that this view grants to human acts of violence. For if the death of Jesus was logically necessary—in that it was impossible for it not to happen— then the evil and violence of the event itself would be divinely sanctioned, and we would be forced to concede that God participates in innocent suffering and death. On the other hand if we were to contend that Jesus' death was *not* necessary, then the cross could be understood to be a contingent event that occurs as a result of the free actions of human beings. Hence, Jesus would not die because God providentially willed him to, but because God's people ultimately and freely rejected Jesus and his message.

Yet such a view is not without its own difficulties either, especially since an emphasis on the freedom and autonomy of the created realm has the potential to sideline God's providential activity completely. Indeed,

---

4. See Burrell, *Freedom and Creation*, 7–9.

desperate attempts to prevent an understanding of the cross in which God has the hammer and nails in hand, tend to result in the denial that there was any divine involvement at all. A denial that readily gets extended to also negate the potential for divine meaning. I would contend, however, that such a denial is not required. Genuine contingency is not precluded when divine meaning is created out of an event, nor is contingency denied in God's ongoing and sustaining activity in creation. Thus, there is potential to simultaneously affirm both the cross' contingency and its capacity to contain divine meaning.[5]

The task, then, of the present chapter is to affirm Christianity's right to proclaim the importance of the cross for human salvation in the midst of the event's contingency, in the fact that it might not have been. The approach taken is firmly classical as I find differing theistic viewpoints provide little in the way of genuine alternatives, although the challenges they bring to the classical position do help sharpen its focus. Some of these challenges will need to be addressed as we proceed, but the primary purpose here is to present enough evidence to suggest a coherent argument for the basis of a traditional, though at once fresh examination of the cross' salvific power.

This being the case I take up the task with Thomas Aquinas as he is undoubtedly one of the most, if not the most systematic and careful exponent of the classical position. Of course, Aquinas' corpus is a little like the Amazon forest, vast and rarely appreciated unless one takes along an appropriate guide. For this reason we will rely heavily on Bernard Lonergan who is becoming more frequently recognized as one of the twentieth centuries foremost authorities on Aquinas. His first published foray into the mind of the great Parisian thinker, *Grace and Freedom: Operative Grace in the Thought of Thomas Aquinas* will be our primary guide.[6] However, before examining Aquinas' understanding of the necessity/contingency dialectic, we begin with some much needed theological groundwork into the nature of a necessary God.

---

5. I recognize that from a modernist perspective this assertion will be contentious because there is an expectation that divine involvement requires a logical necessity. If a necessary God so dictates that a certain event occurring within the created realm has divine meaning, then surely that event cannot fail to be or else it seems that God's purposes will be frustrated. However, this perspective also assumes that God is unable to create meaning out of a contingent event without also transposing that event into the necessary. This chapter will challenge that assumption.

6. Lonergan, *Grace and Freedom*.

A Necessary God

The classical conception of God as necessary being can readily be traced back to a Hellenistic philosophy grounded in the relationship between cause and effect. The fundamental question to ask in this respect is why there is something rather than nothing.[7] Even prior to Plato, philosophers struggled with the reality of a world that was continually in a state of becoming. Parmenides in particular found little comfort in a world that was caught somewhere between being and non-being, concluding its movement was illusory and consequently unknowable.[8] Plato, who appreciated much of Parmenides' thought nevertheless dismissed the latter's epistemological skepticism and postulated in response his own hierarchical division of reality.[9] The world of the senses does exist and can to some extent be known, but it exists as only a shadow or reflection of the eternal world of forms. The latter is uncaused, unchanging and eternal; the former is ever in a state of motion, always becoming but never actually be-ing.[10]

Comfortably falling on either side of Plato's "divided line" then is the distinction between the necessary and the contingent. The necessary is that which does not change, it lies beyond and indeed behind the world, being comprehended through the intelligibility of reason. The contingent, on the other hand, is that which we apprehend through our senses and is a reality that remains forever transitory. In this world there exists a cycle of generation and corruption that precludes any necessity of being, for what is necessary is by definition that which is uncaused and eternal. So where then do these contingencies come from? Clearly they cannot come from themselves because that which at one time did not exist cannot bring itself from non-existence into existence on its own.[11] Undoubtedly the necessary world of forms is somehow involved since contingencies are more or less reflections of that higher realm. Yet Plato acknowledges that the world of forms does not have the power to generate contingent copies of itself. This is why he has Timaeus concede the existence of a creator demiurge

---

7. Leibniz, "Principles of Nature and Grace," 262.

8. Since it involved a movement from "what is" into "what is not," change is unintelligible and therefore for Parmenides unknowable (it is impossible to know "what is not"). The movement we sense can only be an illusion. Parmenides, *Fragments*, fragments 7 and 8.

9. For Plato's critique of Parmenides see Plato, "Sophist," 237e.

10. Plato, "Timaeus," 27d.

11. "That everything that becomes or is created must of necessity be created by some cause, for without a cause nothing can be created" (ibid., 28a).

who utilizes the pre-existent and necessary world of forms to create the realm of becoming *qua* becoming.[12]

When we turn to Aristotle we find his treatment is similar though, of course, he begins not from the standpoint of the Platonic idea of being but rather with the empirical reality of becoming. The focus is thus on motion, on generation and corruption since that which is undergoing change does so because it is so acted upon to make that change.[13] Therefore, Aristotle recognizes that the source of contingent motion cannot be found in the moving thing itself because potentialities cannot be actualized (i.e., begin to move) without some external cause which imparts the force of that motion.[14] This "external cause" must at some prior iteration be unmoved or there would be an infinite regress of movers, a conclusion Aristotle rejects.[15] Hence, there must be some logically first "unmoved mover" in order to explain the existence of all other motion. In addition, this unmoved mover must be both eternal and necessary since non-eternal and contingent movers cannot explain all motion.[16] Therefore, in both Plato and Aristotle there is an explanatory movement from effect to cause that predicates a transcendent, necessary being which by its necessity explains the existence of this-worldly contingents.

There is no suggestion that Plato's demiurge and Aristotle's unmoved mover can be directly equated with the Christian God. Christianity is adamant that while God is indeed transcendent over the world, God is also immanent in the world—a belief that is notably absent from the other concepts. But nevertheless, the impact of both philosophers on later Christian theism is well documented and is evident not least in the classical cosmological arguments for God's existence. Here the movement from effect to cause, moved to unmoved and contingent to necessary forms a central element in classical theism's *a posteriori* arguments and is seen in both Platonic (Augustine) and Aristotelian (Aquinas) forms.

Significantly, one of the characteristics of the *a posteriori* argument is the effort to describe what God *is* (albeit in a limited sense) on the basis

12. Ibid., 28b–29c.

13. "Now, all those who treat of nature claim that there is such a thing as change, because they are concerned with how the world was created and they focus exclusively on coming to be and ceasing to be, for which the existence of change is a necessary prerequisite" (Aristotle, *Physics*, 8.1).

14. "[W]hat can be changed must be changed *by something* and it must be something that has the ability to cause change" (ibid., 3.1, emphasis original).

15. Ibid., 8.5.

16. Ibid., 8.6.

of what God is *not*. The classic use of the *via negativa* is found particularly in Aquinas' so-called "five ways", the third of which focuses exclusively on the move from the contingent to the necessary. Here in a manner reminiscent of Aristotle, Aquinas takes what God is manifestly not (caused, moved and contingent) and by way of contrast, argues for what God actually is (uncaused, unmoved and necessary). But this approach continues to be criticized by modern theistic perspectives because at its foundation is a concept of God that is essentially distinct from the created order. For if God is what nature is not then the question of how God can relate to nature becomes somewhat problematic.[17]

In classical theism's defense one could point to the long history of Christian appropriation of the *via negativa* not to mention a clear scriptural precedent.[18] Nevertheless, how the necessary and transcendent God of classical theism can hold an effective relationship with a contingent creation—without overruling the latter's contingency—is something that we will need to address. But before we get to that point there is the prior question of what we can learn about divine necessity from Aquinas' third way (*tertia via*).

Earlier in his *Summa Contra Gentiles*, Aquinas reflected on the nature of the contingent order and came to the conclusion that there must exist some necessary being that can explain the presence of contingents.[19] This argument is again presented in the first part of the *Summa Theologiae* in slightly modified form as the third of Aquinas' five cosmological arguments.[20] As we would expect in an *a posteriori* argument, Aquinas begins with the observation from sense experience that certain things are possibles (i.e., contingents). By this he means that they have the possibility of existing and not existing because we experience them being "generated and corrupted." But it is impossible for all things which exist to be of this kind since, Aquinas argues, that which has the possibility of not existing did at one time not exist. On this basis he is able to conclude that at some

17. Gunton, *Being and Becoming*, 2.

18. Most notably in Psalm 139. Philo, Dionysius, and Maimonides are among the most influential early exponents of the negative way. Gregory Rocca is right to point out that Aquinas does also speak positively about God but this is always tempered by our lack of intuition regarding God's essence or being. Rocca, "Aquinas on God-Talk," 649–50.

19. Aquinas, *Summa Contra Gentiles*, 1.c.15. Hereafter SCG.

20. Aquinas, *Summa Theologica*, I. q2. a3. Hereafter ST. The major addition is the third point of the argument in ST, that at some time no contingent entities would exist at all.

time nothing at all would exist[21] and, therefore, nothing would exist now[22] because what does not exist does not begin to exist except through something else that exists. Aquinas naturally notes that the present existence of the world means that something does in fact exist and thus he draws the conclusion that not all beings can be contingent beings; there must be some necessary being. Yet it is logically possible that the necessary being was itself caused by another necessary being, but as Aquinas had already shown with efficient causes (in his "second way"), one cannot regress to infinity in caused necessary beings. Hence, there must be an uncaused necessary being which causes the necessity of the others. This being Aquinas calls God.

The detail and contested elements of the "proof" need not detain us here because the issue of interest is not the argument's success (or lack thereof) of proving the existence of God but the deductive reasoning that moves from the contingent base of sense experience to transcendent necessity. In particular, the question of interest to us is what kind of necessity does Aquinas actually argue for here? He has sometimes been accused of intending logical necessity, in that the *tertia via* is said to demonstrate the logical impossibility for God not to exist.[23] If this were the case then Aquinas would also have to contend that the negation of the proposition,

21. Exactly what point in time Aquinas has in mind here is a matter of debate. The context appears to imply a past time in which nothing would exist, but it could be that he is arguing logically rather than temporally in which case he would be affirming that a universe of contingent beings cannot explain itself. However, I prefer a past time context because the movement from generation to corruption is a movement through time and generation must always be prior to corruption. So if nothing exists then nothing has yet to be generated and therefore nothing has ever corrupted. See, for example, Wippel, *The Metaphysical Thought of Thomas Aquinas*, 464.

22. There is a recognized problem with this point: If we accept that all things that exist have the power to not exist then it does not logically follow that at one time nothing at all existed. Why should not corruptible beings, for example, overlap with each other so that while they may come to be and pass away there is never any time in which nothing at all exists? In other words, "each thing at some time or other is not" is not equivalent to "at some time or other everything is not." Hence, Anthony Kenny actually prefers the earlier argument in SCG 1.c.15, which while similar in its overall process does not include this logical step. Kenny, *Aquinas on Being*, 136. For an alternative evaluation of the argument in ST see Wippel, *The Metaphysical Thought of Thomas Aquinas*, 466 n. 63.

23. See, for example, the discussion in Gunton, *Becoming and Being*, 4. An alternate response is given by Anthony Kenny who comments that in the *tertia via* Aquinas cannot mean logical necessity since his proof for the existence of God is not concluded when he has established that there exists a necessary being. Kenny, *The Five Ways*, 47–48.

"God exists" would entail a self-contradiction similar to what occurs if one was to negate the proposition "the sum of all angles in a triangle equals the sum of two right angles." But this is difficult to square with Aquinas' own critique of the ontological argument in which he contended that God's existence is not self-evident from a human perspective. Indeed, it is quite clear from Aquinas' writings that he held the proposition "God is not" to be just as valid as the proposition "God is," which means that he cannot be intending logical necessity here.[24] In fact, this point is readily demonstrated by recognizing that the mark of contingency in the *tertia via* is transiency, or temporal finitude. By contrast the mark of the necessary being is that it does not have a beginning or end in time—in other words, the necessary being is an eternal being. Hence, Aquinas defends God's necessity not on the basis of a logical reflection that presupposes a necessary being but because a necessary being is the only way to *adequately explain* the contingency of the temporal realm. The importance of this heuristic element cannot be overemphasized since the very reason for positing a necessary God as opposed to a contingent God is the requirement to explain the existence of contingents. Only an unchanging, eternal and necessary being can ultimately make sense of this.[25]

However, we should recognize that this does not mean that we can simply equate contingency with transience and necessity with eternal existence. Eternity is certainly one of the conceptual elements of a necessary being, but it is not by itself sufficient. It is quite possible to conceive of a being that exists eternally, not because it cannot be destroyed, but because even though it can be destroyed the power that could destroy it refrains from doing so. Such a being would only have temporal necessity even though it might exist eternally.[26] This is partly the reason for the last step in Aquinas' *tertia via*, there must be some first necessary being that underwrites all others. It is only this uncaused being in the causal chain that can be called God. That there is only one uncaused being is an axiom of Christian theism. Thus, to appropriate a term from Richard Swinburne, I would suggest that Aquinas intends divine necessity to be understood as *ontological necessity.*[27] That is, God is deemed to be necessary not because

24. ST I. q2. a1. See also Aquinas, *1 Sent.* d3. q1. a2.

25. Hence, Eberhard Jüngel: "God is necessary in order to understand the world as world" (Jüngel, *God as the Mystery of the World*, 30).

26. Hick, "God as Necessary Being," 732.

27. Swinburne, *The Christian God*, 118–22, 146–47. It should be noted that Aquinas often uses the term *absolute* necessity in his writings and we will encounter this at various times below. Where it does occur it should be understood in the sense of ontological necessity.

we cannot conceive a God who is not necessary, but because the very existence of contingents requires an ontologically necessary being that has no active or permissive cause.

The result of this methodology is to introduce an ontological hierarchy that qualitatively separates the cause from the effect. God, as ultimate cause—or creator—is distinguished from all effects not by an order of magnitude but by essence itself. Thus God stands out from the multiplicity of beings within the created order on account of the coincidence of essence with existence.[28] In other words God's essence is to exist, or expressed more formally, God's aseity is an integral notion of what it means to be an ontologically necessary being. In contrast to the universe and created contingents which exist *ab alio* and rely for their existence on some factor or factors beyond, only God exists *a se* in total independence as a sheer unconditioned, self-existent being.[29] For this reason it is incorrect to suggest that God is only necessary in relation to contingent entities.[30] So while it is true that Aquinas arrives at a necessary God on the basis of contingent existence, having reached this point it becomes clear that even if no contingencies existed, God would still be necessary. For God is without beginning or end, without origin, cause or ground of any kind whatsoever. "God *is*, as the ultimate, unconditioned, absolute, unlimited being."[31] All other classical predications of God hang upon this datum.

Deus operator in omni operante

A major implication of this theistic understanding is the ongoing role that God has, as the necessary first cause, in the operation of all things that are moved. In this Aquinas diverges fundamentally from Aristotle whose cosmic scheme had no place for divine design since what was important for Aristotle was simply the sufficient reason for the existence of motion and not the particular purpose such motion might have.[32] In contrast, Aquinas was convinced that God did have a purpose for the created realm and its continuing motion was due to the providence of God. God is thus not only the cause of all motion but also the divine intellect that guides

28. See McGrath, *Nature*, 168–69. Stump, *Aquinas*, 129–30.

29. Hick, "God as Necessary Being," 733.

30. As Pannenberg makes clear: Pannenberg, *Systematic Theology*, 1:83 n. 55.

31. Hick, "God as Necessary Being," 733.

32. On Aquinas' view, Aristotle's first mover could not cause anything except perpetual motion. See Lonergan, *Grace and Freedom*, 285–86.

and brings that motion to its appointed end. The alternative is to conclude that God aimlessly creates and arbitrarily operates in the creature without a designated *telos*—a conclusion Aquinas explicitly denies. That denial is found in the definition of providence itself:

> [God] creates every goodness in things, as we have already shown. It is not only in the substance of created things that goodness lies, but also in their being ordained to an end, above all to their final end, which, as we have seen, is the divine goodness. This good order existing in created things is itself part of God's creation. Since he is the cause of things through his mind, and, as we have already made clear, the idea of each and every effect must pre-exist in him, the divine mind must preconceive the whole pattern of things moving to their end. This exemplar of things ordained to their purpose is exactly what providence is.[33]

Providence is therefore defined as the operation of God's intellect in moving all things to their proper end. The "proper end" is here identified as divine goodness, a conclusion Aquinas had already reached in an earlier article.[34] What he means by this can be clarified through an extension of Aristotle's position in the *Nicomachean Ethics* in which we find the ultimate goal or end of being defined as "the good."[35] What is the good? It is *eudaimonia* says, Aristotle, often translated "happiness" but a happiness that is not transitory for it includes the implication of a life that is flourishing.[36] Aquinas in general agrees, but unlike Aristotle, Aquinas understands that the end is not just *eudaimonia*—which is devoid of divine life—but *beatitudo*, which includes as the ultimate good the knowledge of God. Thus, the final fulfilment and ultimate goal of the human being is found in his or her union with God, or as Aquinas expressed it, the divine goodness.[37]

33. ST I. q22. a1.

34. ST I. q21. a4. The context here is a discussion on the mercy and justice of God in perfecting humanity. Cf. IaIIae. q2. a5; IaIIae. q2. a7.

35. Aristotle, *Nicomachean Ethics*, 1.1.

36. Ibid., 1.4. Commentators recognize that "happiness" is a misleading translation of Aristotle's *eudaimonia* since "living well and doing well" for one's whole life is emphatically not the same as saying "I felt happy when I woke up today." One is either *eudaimon* or not, absolutely. Etymologically the word roughly means "having a good guardian angel," but Aristotle never made much of this. Bostock, *Aristotle's Ethics*, 11f.

37. "Complete happiness (*beatitudo*) requires the mind to come through to the essence itself of the first cause. And so it will have its fulfilment by union with God as its

Given the contingency of the creature and its dependence on the first cause for even its very existence, it is clear that the creature's ultimate end of divine goodness must also be dependent upon God for fulfilment. Therefore it could be said that it is God's ultimate aim to return human beings to God and to unite them to Godself.[38] This plan is what is known as providence, the actual carrying out of the plan is referred to as divine governance:

> For things are said to be ruled or governed by virtue of their being ordered to their end. Now, things are ordered to the ultimate end which God intends, that is, divine goodness, not only by the fact that they *perform their operations*, but also by the fact that they exist, since, to the extent that they exist, they bear the likeness of divine goodness which is the end for things . . . God, through his understanding and will, is the cause of being for all things. Therefore *he preserves all things in being* through his intellect and will.[39]

Here Aquinas indicates that divine governance is carried out through two means: operation and preservation. The latter is undergirded by two key beliefs: (1) creatures are made by God *ex nihilo*; and (2) creatures depend on God for their being. In other words, if anything is to exist at all then that existence is totally dependent upon God continuing to will that those things do in fact exist.[40] Or expressed in another way; if God wished to annihilate the created realm it would not need some divinely violent outburst to realize, the simple cessation from preserving action would warrant the same result.[41] This is the natural consequence of the two beliefs outlined and requires no further explanation.

---

object" (ST IaIIae. q3. a8). For a more detailed exposition of the final end of humanity in Aquinas' thinking see Hoye, *Actualitas Omnium Actuum*, 145–52.

38. Stump, *Aquinas*, 456.

39. SCG 3.65.2f. Emphasis mine. Cf. SCG 3.67.3.

40. ST I. q104. a1; SCG 3.65. In this sense preservation is continued creation. Aquinas was followed here by Occam and Descartes, the latter arguing that since the existence of the creature depends at every moment on God's creative activity we cannot infer from its existence at an earlier point its continued existence at the next. God's preserving work is therefore considered to be a continuation of creation with the only real difference being found in the fact that, in preservation, the creature has already been granted existence by God. Descartes, *Meditations*, III, 36. Strictly speaking then, God cannot "intervene" in creation because God has never stopped acting within it. Burrell, *Freedom and Creation*, 70.

41. ST I. q104. a3. ad3.

More complicated is how divine governance should be understood in terms of the first term that Aquinas uses, that of the operation of the creature. At issue is the understanding that divine governance is more than just preservation and conservation, for preservation is not sufficient in and of itself to cause motion in the creature. In the *Prima Secundae* we find that "no created thing can proceed to any act whatever except through the power of divine motion."[42] And again in *De potentia*:

> God is the cause of any *action* whatever insofar as he gives the power of acting, and insofar as he preserves it, and insofar as he applies it to action, and insofar as through his power every other power acts.[43]

That is, unless God actually operates in the operation of the creature, the creature itself cannot operate. The picture this usually elicits is one of "occasionalism" wherein God is the real actor and the creature merely the occasion for the action to occur. But this would assert a God who is parallel to the universe and one particular, or univocal notion of acting.[44] On Aquinas' view of creation neither can be true and we will examine the genuineness of secondary causes shortly. The other important implication is the effect such a position has on creaturely free will and again this is something we will return to in due time. But first, in regard to divine action in the creature, the technical terms of interest are *premotion* and *application* and it is worth briefly examining them here.

The Aristotelian concept of premotion, which Aquinas adopts without significant change, arises in response to the question as to how motion actually begins. Consider for example two objects in a state of rest. One of these objects is a mover, the other the moved yet the moved object is not yet moving because the state of rest is still actualized. Hence, there is some cause either on the side of the mover or that of the moved that is bringing about this state of rest.[45] Motion is clearly possible—there is a mover and a moved—but it is not yet actual. As Bernard Lonergan explains, "For actual

42. ST IaIIae. q109. a9.

43. Aquinas, *de potentia*, q3. a7. Translation in Lonergan, *Grace and Freedom*, 308 n. 157.

44. For details see Burrell, *Freedom and Creation*, 69.

45. "[A] state of rest is the privation of movement; but a privation is not had in what is susceptible of a habit or form except by reason of some cause; there was therefore some cause, either on the side of the motive force or on that of the movable, which was the reason for the state of rest; therefore, while that lasted, the state of rest always remained" (*In VIII Phys.*, lect. 2 §976. Quoted by and translated in Lonergan, *Grace and Freedom*, 278 n. 55).

motion it is further necessary that they [mover and moved] be in such a situation, mutual relation, or disposition, that the one can act on the other."[46] In other words, the state of rest must be overcome in order for the mover to be able to act on the moved. It is this overcoming, or bringing together of the mover and the moved that is the premotion. The example that Lonergan gives is that of an iceberg. The cold of the iceberg and the heat of the equator are not sufficient in themselves to cause the iceberg to melt. What is necessary is that the two be brought into proximity with each other so that the motion (the act of melting) can begin to occur. In like fashion the creature cannot begin to move (act) unless it is brought into propinquity with the mover. Of course as we have already seen in the *tertia via*, the very fact that a movable contingent creation exists requires that creation to be in relationship with the transcendent first cause. The point to be made here then is not in the denial of a God-independent created realm but rather in the emphasis that all action carried out within that created realm requires the enabling operation of God.

The second technical term, that of *application*, follows immediately from this conclusion and in the quotation from *De potentia* 3 above Aquinas confirms that God applies all things to action.[47] The idea of application is essentially captured by the statement that God moves all things to their appointed ends by his intellect.[48] Application must therefore include the concept of premotion and indeed Aquinas does use the verb *applicare* when he is clearly referring to the former operation.[49] However, application is more than just premotion because the operation of God in the creature is not just the operation of a mover on the moved, but the operation of an intellectual agent. Recall that Aristotle's unmoved mover operated without design or providence since all that was required was a final cause for the continuance of motion. As an intellectual agent, however, Aquinas' God acts as both final and efficient cause bringing about the motion of the creature to its appointed *telos*.

As an example consider the nature of fire. Even though it can do nothing but burn, it does not do so unless it is within proximity of something combustible, has oxygen to consume and is not prevented from burning by a bucket of water. Each of these conditions is required yet they have nothing to do with the nature of fire. In fact, each of these conditions

46. Ibid., 277.

47. See also SCG 3.67; SCG 3.70; ST I. q105. a5.

48. Lonergan, *Grace and Freedom*, 280.

49. Lonergan cites an example from *In IX Metaphys.*, lect. 4, §1818. Ibid., 281.

also has conditions that must be fulfilled, and those conditions in turn have conditions and so on *ad libitum*.[50] So for that particular fire to burn there must be a string of contingent causes that are so moved to converge at that particular place and at that particular point in time that only one who could envisage "all finite causes at all instants throughout all time" could possibly bring it about.[51] This is the application of the divine intellectual agent that so orders the world-order into an intelligible unity.[52] Indeed in Aquinas' view this is what God does and he notably relates this action to his understanding of providence. In *De substantiis separatis*: God is "the cause of something only as understanding, since His substance is His understanding . . . Therefore God moves all things to their proper ends through His intellect and this is providence."[53] Application could therefore be described as intended premotion and is here defined by Aquinas as the means of providence.[54]

This understanding of divine governance results in the acknowledgement that the creature cannot have an operation unless in that operation is the operation of God. This is Aquinas' fundamental conclusion arising from the existence of a necessary God. *Deus operator in omni operante*: God operates in everything that operates. The technical term for this is *concurrence*, a term that refers to created agents operating by virtue of the creator's power. While a valuable term when correctly understood it has the unfortunate connotation of coordinate cooperation, the kind of cooperation that would occur, for example, when two agents row a boat. Here the agents are independent of one another, their efforts combined in vectorial addition to produce the desired effect. However, such an image is expressly forbidden by the doctrine of creation since it denies the dependence of the creature on the creator.[55] Instead, Lonergan argues concurrence should be understood serially in that the agent's actions occur one after the other, the creature (secondary cause) being appropriately dependent on the creator (primary cause).[56]

As would be expected the actual mechanics of this serial cooperation has attracted, and continues to attract considerable debate. However, for

50. Hefling, "Christ and Evils, 874.
51. Lonergan, "On God and Secondary Causes," 58.
52. Lonergan, "The Natural Desire to See God," 88.
53. Aquinas, *Treatise on Separate Substances*, 14.77.
54. See Lonergan, *Grace and Freedom*, 287.
55. Burrell, *Freedom and Creation*, 128.
56. Lonergan, *Grace and Freedom*, 303–4.

the present purpose it suffices to make a single remark: The fact that God operates in all the creature's operations does not mean that the latter's operations are illusory. I have already pointed out that this is not occasionalism. God is the primary cause, but God's providence is mediated through the actions of creatures—actions that are real, though secondary causes of their own.[57] Therefore, primary and secondary designations are only an indication of the inherent ordering of the causes. They themselves do not differ on account of intensity or on the basis that the primary is more a cause than the secondary. This differentiation, if allowed, would assert a univocal genus, *cause*, which is not the case.[58] The terms "primary" and "secondary" simply indicate the dependence of one cause on the other. As Aquinas puts it, "a secondary cause does not act except through the power of the first cause."[59] Each is a genuine cause, yet what makes the secondary cause secondary, is its intrinsic dependence on the one which is primary. If this were not the case then it would be true to say that God produces nothing with genuine causal power. Aquinas clearly disagrees:

> But this is impossible, . . . because it would deprive creation of its pattern of cause and effect, which in turn would imply a lack of power in the creator, since an agent's power is the source of its giving an effect a causative capability.[60]

Again, if secondary causes were not real causes then it is somewhat superfluous as to why God would bring about effects through them:

> If the active powers that are observed in creatures accomplished nothing, there would be no point to their having received such powers. Indeed, if all creatures are utterly devoid of any activity of their own, then they themselves would seem to have a pointless existence. . . . God's acting in creatures, therefore, must be understood in such a way that they themselves still exercise their own operations.[61]

After all, if I could produce an effect without going through certain motions I may as well dispense with the motions and directly produce the

57. SCG 3.90.

58. Burrell, *Freedom and Creation*, 97. It is often said that the primary cause is more a cause than the secondary cause because of the importance of the cosmic hierarchy on this classical synthesis. The higher always governs the lower. But this is a statement of dependence rather than priority and should be understood as such.

59. Aquinas, *Truth*, q24. a14.

60. ST I. q105. a5.

61. Ibid.

effect. On the contrary, divine "providence procures its effects through the operations of secondary causes."[62] Thus, God's operation in creatures does not impinge on the genuineness of the creature's actions. Secondary causes remain real causes.

Instrumental Causality

In a response article to Elizabeth Johnson's "Does God Play Dice?" Joseph Bracken reveals that he is uncomfortable with classical theism's emphasis on the God-world relationship being predicated on the basis of cause and effect.[63] According to Bracken, this position is inherently insufficient to comprehend both God and creatures as subjective beings and thus it loses the necessary intersubjectivity to correctly characterize the creator-creature relationship.[64] This is particularly evidenced, suggests Bracken, by the necessary dependence of the secondary cause on the primary cause in producing the one effect. While he acknowledges that the divine nature must be present to the creature in order for the creature to act (in terms at least of the act of being), he disagrees strongly that "two ontologically independent subjects of the act of being each wholly produce one and the same finite effect."[65]

Lonergan acknowledges that this is the obvious difficulty with Aquinas' understanding of concursus; How can two causes do one "producing"?[66] In Bracken's judgment this could only be possible if the secondary cause is wholly instrumental to the primary cause. As we might expect from the foregoing discussion Aquinas actually agrees, yet Bracken finds that this position is unacceptable. Consider for example the case of a hammer in the hand of the carpenter. The carpenter chooses to use the hammer to drive the nail instead of his or her hands. The hammer is a real cause of the nail being driven into the wood because hammers really do hit nails. But the hammer itself does not have the ability to agree or disagree with the task and therefore it cannot contribute, nor indeed refuse to contribute, to the task. There is thus no intersubjectivity, no I-Thou to

---

62. ST I. q23. a5. Again, cooperation here should be understood serially: the primary act in serial with the secondary act.

63. Bracken, "Response," 720–30. Johnson, "Does God Play Dice?," 3–18.

64. Bracken, "Response," 721–22.

65. Ibid., 723.

66. Lonergan, *Grace and Freedom*, 307.

the relationship between the carpenter and the hammer, merely cause and effect, an effect the hammer is merely instrumental in achieving.

The complaint then is rather obvious: instrumental causality fails to appreciate the personal relationship between God and the creature but perhaps even worse, any instrumental cause is incapable of doing other than what the primary cause empowers because it is merely instrumental. The only viable solution suggests Bracken, is to assert the ontological independence of the secondary cause and hold that single effects must be produced by way of a shared venture between both primary and secondary causes. Either the venture is shared in equal measure or, as Bracken indicates is particularly the case in the God-creature relationship, the venture "is primarily done by the secondary cause (the creature), albeit under the direction and with the inspiration of the primary cause, God."[67] The point here is that rather than being instrumental, the human agent complements the divine agent and both contribute towards the one outcome.

The problem with Bracken's thesis is paradoxically the basis for his solution—the distinction he makes between the operation of the divine nature and divine person(s).[68] He may, of course, be right when he remarks that there is some "ambiguity in the Thomistic understanding of God as subsistent being," but that ambiguity does not require the distinction that Bracken seeks to exploit.[69] The conclusion he draws from the classical notion of God's simplicity, viz., a divine inability to relate to creatures, presumes that causal language must be impersonal. Indeed, Bracken is right to note that much of the discussion about divine intentionality in relation to the creature in classical terms *is* by way of "cause of being" rather than analogous discussions of persons and their activities. Partially this is because of the limitations of analogy, something of which Aquinas was more than well aware, but more so because of the stress that he particularly wished to give to the dependence of the creature's operation on God. As soon as this dependence is sidelined the creature inevitably gains its *theo*-independence to the extent that not even God can create the creature without the latter's incipient acceptance of that creative offer.[70]

67. Bracken, "Response," 724.

68. Ibid., passim. This distinction is expounded further in Bracken, *The Divine Matrix*, 29–37. Essentially Bracken's complaint is that Aquinas' terminology fails to recognize the distinction between the subjective reality of God as Supreme Being (as three interrelated subjects) and the underlying nature of God. For Bracken this distinction is necessary if God can be said to truly relate to creatures.

69. Bracken, "Response," 720.

70. "The human being is never simply an inert thing brought into existence by the

Bracken finds in this true intersubjectivity but it appears to make a mockery of *creatio ex nihilo*. This is one of the reasons for the repeated emphasis of God's ongoing operation in the creature throughout the forthcoming discussions on both freedom and creaturely responsibility. We cannot escape the fact that the creature does depend on God for its very existence and thus the God/creature relationship needs to be characterized on that basis. Furthermore, it is erroneous to conclude that impersonal language implies a denial that God acts as a "personal being," to use the phrase that Bracken employs. In fact, whenever it is said that God is the cause of being it must be inherently understood that God is the cause of that being *as* a personal (i.e., intelligent) being. This must be the case since the very assertion that whatever exists is given its existence by God (whose very being is to exist), is to point towards what is most intimate and individual about things.[71] And the fact that God brings about persons implies that God has, as an aspect of the divine nature, the formal character reflected in the personal existence of that creation, that is, personal existence itself.[72] Towards the end of *Insight*, Bernard Lonergan remarks:

> As man, so God is a rational self-consciousness, for man was made in the image and likeness of God. But what man is through unrestricted desire and limited attainment, God is in unrestricted act. But an unrestricted act of rational self-consciousness, however objectively and impersonally it has been conceived, clearly satisfies all that is meant by the subject, the person, the other with an intelligence and a reasonableness and a willing that is his own.[73]

There is thus no need, nor indeed is it even possible to mark the activity of the divine nature as impersonal. When God acts in the operation of the creature, whether by conservation or providence, it is always God as personal being who is doing the acting.

But what of Bracken's concern for the nature of instrumental causality? We have already given above various reasons why secondary causes should be understood as genuine causes and these need to be kept in mind

---

unilateral activity of a Creator God. It comes into existence partly through the gracious offer of a loving God and partly through its own incipient response to that offer of creaturely existence and activity" (ibid., 729).

71. Burrell, *Freedom and Creation*, 100.

72. Braine, *The Reality of Time*, 265–87, 293–96, quoted in Burrell, *Freedom and Creation*, 100.

73. Lonergan, *Insight*, 691.

here. But there are some additional comments that can be made about instrumental causation and these will somewhat paradoxically serve to reinforce Bracken's point—although for a very different purpose. To begin with, it is important to note that in his earlier writings, Aquinas commonly refers to the acts of creatures in terms of instrumental causation. In *De potentia*, for example, Aquinas correlates God and created agents as principal cause and instrumental cause respectively, even to the point of likening the *actio* of the created agent in terms of the artisan's instrument:

> Nor again could it be conferred on a natural power that it should move itself, or that it should maintain itself in being. And therefore as it is clear that it was not necessary to confer on the artisan's instrument that it should operate without the motion of art, so it could not be conferred on a natural thing that it should operate without divine operation.[74]

The argument in which this quotation fits is incredibly dense but the conclusion is familiar. In short, the operation of the creature is always dependent upon God as the operation of the artist's brush is dependent upon the artisan. The art that takes shape on the canvas occurs because it is the brush that applies the paint to the surface in the manner appropriate to the artist. The artist does not touch the paint nor does the artist touch the canvas. The entire effect is achieved through the application of the brush and thus like the hammer, the brush is a genuine cause of the art. Yet the brush itself can do nothing without the artist who applies the brush to the canvas and in a similar way, says Aquinas, the creature cannot operate without divine operation.

The analogy is of course simplistic. Human beings are not hammers nor paint brushes; we possess an intellect and will that relate to God in ways inanimate objects cannot. Yet this does not prevent the intelligent creature from being understood as an instrumental cause, for like the paint brush in the hands of the artisan, the creature cannot operate without the concurrent operation of God. In this sense Bracken was right to highlight the instrumental nature of the secondary cause and the inevitable dependence that ensues. It is in fact impossible in this scheme for the secondary cause to do what Bracken wants it to do—operate as an independent ontological entity. The secondary cause is always instrumental for it cannot move itself nor maintain itself in being nor does it have the power to produce effects on its own. But rather than reject this position, Aquinas accepts

---

74. Aquinas, *De Potentia*, q3. a7. ad7m, quoted and translated in Lonergan, *Grace and Freedom*, 292 n. 114.

it and acknowledges that the only way two causes can do one producing is if the lower agent always acts in virtue of the higher.[75] But again this is simply a reflection of the dependence inherent in creation itself. The only concession Aquinas makes is to change his terminology from principal/instrumental cause to first/secondary cause by the time of his major summa.[76] But it must be said that this is not a change in position but rather an attempt to help others avoid the conclusion that the creature does not have genuine causal activity. The creature may act as an instrumental cause, but that activity is for Aquinas both subjective and genuine.

To summarize then: as the necessary first cause of all that is, God not only preserves the created realm but also governs it in line with the divine providential plan. Divine governance requires that God be present in power to every acting thing, preserving it in being and applying it to action. God is thus operative in every creaturely cause and so the actions of creatures are in a sense the actions of God. If this was not the case then nothing would be able to operate at all.

This does not mean, however, that creaturely actions are only a chimera. God is the primary cause but creatures are genuine secondary causes of their own actions. Bracken is, of course, right to point out that such a position implicates God in the activity of the creatures. If God is present to everything the creature does through not only conservation but also empowerment then is not God somehow responsible for those actions? To take the same point but express it differently: even if the creature is a real cause of its own actions, does not the fact that it must be moved by a necessary God to those actions negatively impact the very possibility of contingency and human freedom? Does not the fact that everything is dependent upon God for its operation imply that all things that happen actually happen because God intends them to be? Is it not then the case that as the cause of all things nothing can occur without God and therefore all things happen by necessity—including the violent death of Jesus of Nazareth? Furthermore, how can we escape the conclusion that God is inexplicably responsible for this act? These are certainly important questions and any response must be carefully considered.

---

75. SCG 3.70. See also Lonergan, *Grace and Freedom*, 307.

76. ST I. q105. a5.

A Contingent World

If God is necessary, transcendent first cause and operates in the operation of the creature, the question arises as to how contingency—the possibility that something might be otherwise—is possible at all. Surely real contingency requires a contingent cause if it is to be truly contingent? How can a necessary God who acts in all things create a contingent creation? In his analysis of Charles Hartshorne's rejection of classical theism, Colin Gunton frames the issue in this way:

> But there can surely be no defence against the charge that a wholly necessary God and a free creation are logically incompatible. If God has to be free in order to create—or, for that matter, to reconcile, forgive, and redeem—then, however much the word *necessary* is qualified, it is impossible to reconcile this freedom with the demands of a thoroughgoing necessity.[77]

The conclusion seems inevitable: if God is wholly necessary then all acts that God undertakes must also be considered necessary and therefore creation, as an act of God, can in no sense be described as free or contingent. Furthermore, it follows that if creation is in fact necessary then all events that occur as part of creation must *a fortiori* be necessary as well. This includes all acts of creatures in which God is operating. Hence, there are no truly contingent acts because there is no possibility for those events to occur other than they do. If then we desire to affirm both God's freedom in creating and the contingency of the created order itself, then logically we must abandon the notion of a necessary God. Hartshorne himself places more emphasis on the problem in terms of knowledge rather than creation, but the point is still the same. Given the contingency of the world, does not the fact that some things may or may not have happened mean that God's knowledge of them is dependent (i.e., contingent) on them as well?[78] To claim to the contrary that God knows omnisciently all that is and will ever be requires that those contingent events be in fact necessary. Human freedom is thus a chimera and the classical God must be understood to be the necessary determiner of all that is.

Awareness of this difficulty did not need to await the post-scholastic period nor the arrival of a Newtonian mechanistic worldview. Aristotle had already pointed out the apparent inconsistency of affirming both created contingency and the necessity of divine knowledge and overcame the

77. Gunton, *Becoming and Being*, 18.
78. See, for example, Hartshorne, *Creative Synthesis*, 48.

problem by attributing all contingency to the pre-existent prime matter from which the world was formed.[79] Hence for Aristotle, the necessary unmoved mover was not the cause of the contingencies that were inherent in creation itself. Of course, Christian theism is adamant that God created the world *ex nihilo* and not from some pre-existent matter and therefore Aristotle's solution is *prima facie* untenable. So it seems we are either forced to go along with philosophers such as Spinoza and acknowledge complete determinism and the necessity of all things or we must reject the classical understanding of God as absolutely necessary.[80]

Moreover, it is not simply the possibility of creaturely freedom that drives this criticism but a fear that the transcendent, necessary God of classical theism is not capable of really relating to creation. I have already commented that Joseph Bracken believes that this is the inevitable result of a theism that emphasizes the God-world relationship in terms of cause and effect rather than in terms of intersubjectivity. It is argued that causes and effects are not necessarily agents endowed with subjectivity; they are simply agents in which the latter is dependent on the former. In such a case it appears that there is no element of personal relationship between God as cause and the creature as effect.[81] This too was the focus of Hartshorne's criticism. He was convinced that "to be" was "to be a subject" and therefore if God really *is*, then God is a subject and thus God must be vulnerable and open to the objects of divine knowledge.[82] It cannot then be just a matter of cause and effect. If God were not to be open and thus remain unaffected by creation, then, according to Hartshorne, God would fail to relate at all since to know is to be affected by the object one knows. In contrast, God must be understood to be in a real and reciprocal relationship with creation, a relationship in which God not only effects creation but that creation also affects God.[83] It is this relational need that requires in Process thought a dipolar view of God and the ultimate rejection of a God who is supremely the uncaused cause. Instead, God must be understood to have two poles; in some aspects God is uncaused (or admittedly God would not be God) but in order to know perfectly, God must also be in some aspects

---

79. See the discussion in Lonergan, *Grace and Freedom*, 77.

80. Spinoza, *Ethics*, 1.29. Process theists certainly take the latter option and postulate instead an alternate and dipolar picture of God in the hope of salvaging real contingencies.

81. Bracken, "Response," 722–23.

82. Hartshorne, *The Divine Relativity*, 60–75.

83. Ormerod, "Chance and Necessity," 267.

causally influenced.[84] Thus God is both uncaused and caused, the apparent contradiction being overcome by qualifying the two conditions as not in the same respect.

For the classical theist, however, this is an unacceptable conclusion for it results in God being dependent on creatures in order to be God. For Aquinas there is no property inherent in divinity that demands or results in creatures.[85] Creation does not occur as a result of God's nature but rather by God's intellect and will. Being related to creatures is, therefore, not a reality in God (*ipsum esse*), but God is nonetheless related to creatures because the creature is related to God.[86] However, the problem with this, remarks Bracken, is that it denies any potentiality in God and predicates the "relating" to the creature only. As *actus purus* God is incapable in the classical system of further actualization, of change that would result from real, two-way relating.[87] This is why in the Process scheme God must be understood to be dipolar, both uncaused yet caused or, in terms of our present discussion, both necessary and contingent. Gunton outlines clearly what is meant by this duality and it is worth quoting here in full.

> A corollary of God's being relative to the world is that he will know the world as contingent, and hence will have contingent elements or contents. (Naturally, as it is the knower who is affected by the objects of knowledge, the contents of God's knowledge at any given time will be contingent or dependent upon the state of the world at that time). Therefore, just as God *is* relative, so he is contingent, in his concrete reality; in fact, he is 'the supremely contingent being, in a certain sense the most contingent of all'. And so God, in respect of his contents as a supreme knowing mind, is contingent. . . . But, abstractly considered, God is not contingent but necessary, in fact the sole necessary being, for he *must* know infallibly all that is and was, and will know everything that will be, when it comes to take place. And so God's necessity consists in his contingency. He knows what he knows necessarily, and supreme contingency is seen to be necessary contingency.[88]

84. Gunton, *Becoming and Being*, 28.

85. ST I. q13. a7.

86. On this see the discussion in Burrell, *Aquinas*, 84–87. The necessity of creation is, of course, one of the major differences between Process and Classical theism.

87. Bracken, "Response," 725–27.

88. Gunton, *Becoming and Being*, 32.

We have then a God who is necessary in some respects but simultaneously contingent for true divine/creature relations to be possible.

Immediately it is apparent that a dipolar view of God has enormous consequences for classical theism. Predominant among these is that God can no longer be understood to be outside of time but is fully limited by temporal progression. God cannot know the future since true contingency requires it to be open and therefore God learns diachronically as events and choices are made.[89] As a consequence, God's eternality is not predicated because God stands outside of time but because God knows fully all that has happened up to this point in time.[90] So too God's receptivity to creation as a subject logically requires that God is affected by that relationship with the world. In other words, God cannot be immutable or impassible and still be in real relation to the world. Either God is unmoved, unloving and distant or God is a real "subject in relation" and God's being *is* becoming.[91] Hence the rejection of an ontologically necessary God who is the transcendent first cause of all that is requires a corresponding rejection of other classical predications of God: omniscience, impassibility and eternality to name just three.[92]

The criticism is not without its merits and its continued currency stems in large part from the desire to adequately meet the concerns of postmodern life. A God who is timeless, a-pathetic, immutable and beyond the vagaries of this experienced world seems no longer to resonate with our cultural core as it once did. Whereas impassibility and apathy once meant stability and comforting concreteness, now our culture demands a God who suffers with and alongside us.[93] In this vein Pinnock goes so far as to claim that the emphasis on human freedom and relativity in postmodernism actually *requires* that God be thought of "as self-limited" in relation to the world. God must be understood as a dynamic becoming entity rather than a static divinity who sits in "serene magisterial aloofness."[94]

---

89. Open Theists particularly emphasize this point. See, for example, Pinnock, "Between Classical and Process Theism," 314–17. More recently, Pinnock, "Open Theism," 240–42.

90. God is in this sense "supertemporal" (Hartshorne and Reese, *Philosophers Speak of God*, 146).

91. Gunton, *Becoming and Being*, 33.

92. Wolterstorff claims that the classical position is unravelled in this process to the point of undermining even God's aseity. Wolterstorff, "Does God Suffer?," 47, quoted in Pinnock, *Most Moved Mover*, 78.

93. Pinnock, *Most Moved Mover*, 88–92.

94. Pinnock, "Between Classical and Process Theism," 317.

Without denying the need for theologians to communicate in culturally relevant ways these comments are nonetheless more a caricature of the
classical position than a piercing critique. The religiously powerful passages in Aquinas' poetry and biblical commentaries, for example, would
be unintelligible if he really thought that God sat "aloof" from the world.
On the contrary, in Aquinas' mind, the classical God does relate to the
world and even though God remains absolutely necessary, it is possible for
creation to avoid being correspondingly determined. It is somewhat interesting to note that the solution provided by classical theists in this regard
is often overlooked or ignored in criticisms of their theistic position. Yet I
believe that its value will become evident as we try to unpack the relationship between the necessary God and the contingent cross of Christ.

Contingency and Conditional Necessity

Because the relationship between divine necessity and created contingency has a paradoxical appearance, the approach to any solution will
be correspondingly dialectical. On one side there is the question of the
possibility of contingency and on the other is the question of divine providence or how a necessary God relates to the world. As early as his commentary on the *Sentences*, Aquinas addresses the first side by confirming
that even though God is transcendent cause, real contingents do in fact
exist and that God's knowledge of them does not change their existence as
contingents.[95] Bernard McGinn comments that here Aquinas' response is
unhesitating and unequivocal. "Neither the fact that God is the necessary
cause of all things nor the fact that knowledge presupposes a determination in the thing known precludes the existence of contingent things or
God's knowledge of them."[96] Easy enough perhaps to state but given the
aforementioned criticism of this very point, on what basis is Aquinas able
to come to this conclusion?

The reason given here and outlined further in the *Summa Contra
Gentiles* is the classical predication of God's timelessness. Since God is
eternal, divine knowledge has the characteristic of eternality and therefore
God apprehends each successive temporal event in the eternal now. In
such a case all contingent events are fully known by God because God
sees them all at one and the same time. It must be pointed out though
that God's knowledge of these events, while immutable in the sense that it

95. Aquinas, *1 Sent.*, d38. q1. a5.
96. McGinn, "The Development of the Thought of Thomas Aquinas," 743.

cannot change over time, does not inevitably include the requirement to be immutable across all possible worlds.[97] What this means is that if things in the world had been different, then God's knowledge of them would have been different as well; hence in a different possible world, God would know something different from what God knows in this world. Thus there is no need in this view of God's knowledge to require that creatures do not have the ability to do other than they do in every possible world.[98] So Aquinas can coherently hold that creaturely contingency is a real possibility.

But even if we grant contingency across all possible worlds, does not God's knowledge of *this-worldly* contingent events in the eternal now render those events from a creaturely perspective logically necessary?[99] Not so, says Aquinas. The reason for this is that while God sees all things at once, the events themselves are only *conditionally necessary*, they are not logically necessary.[100] This distinction will appear again in relation to the second part of our dialectic but at this point conditional necessity refers merely to the proposition "if A, then A"—where the protasis does not posit a prior necessary cause, it simply affirms the reality of what appears in the apodosis.[101] In other words, and to use the example that Aquinas himself gives, it is necessary that Socrates be sitting because he is sitting (i.e., it is not possible for Socrates not to be sitting when he is in fact seated). However, it is not necessary that Socrates be sitting because at some prior time Socrates presumably made the choice to sit. Hence Socrates' sitting is only conditionally necessary because while it is necessary now that he be seated (because he is in fact sitting), it was not necessary for Socrates to be sitting now. For the sake of the argument suppose that Socrates at some later time (say t2) decides to go for a walk. In the eternal now God knows that Socrates is walking but again his walking is only conditionally necessary because although it is necessary that if Socrates is walking he is walking, it is not necessary that Socrates is in fact walking. Thus on this view, God can know with omniscience in the eternal present that a creature will have property A (sitting) but not property B (walking) at t1 and property B (walking) but not property A (sitting) at t2, *without precluding*

97. See Aquinas' discussion on immutability: ST I. q9. a1.

98. See Stump, *Aquinas*, 117.

99. A conclusion said to be unavoidable, Pinnock, "Open Theism," 242.

100. SCG 1.67.

101. See McGinn, "Divine Providence and Contingent Action," 744. Also Lonergan, *Grace and Freedom*, 104–5. The reader is reminded that the protasis is the antecedent of a conditional clause, the apodosis is the consequent clause.

the contingency of either event.[102] Therefore, just because God knows in the eternal present all that ever occurs does not mean that those events are prevented from being contingent.

It could be argued that this part of the solution fails on two accounts. Firstly it is dependent on an understanding of God's eternity that by no means has universal consensus and second, it presumes that the contingent events themselves were in fact contingent. In response to the first point we can say that as a classical solution to the problem of divine providence and created contingency it is appropriate to utilize classical predications of God's existence as a basis. Thomas is so insistent on God's timelessness that it would be inappropriate to disallow any recourse to it.[103] The intention here in any case is to demonstrate the coherence of Aquinas' solution from within a classical synthesis rather than defend that synthesis from every possible objection. The second point has more weight but it must be remembered that this is only one side of the dialectic and therefore takes for granted that real contingencies do exist. The question here is not whether God as necessary cause denies any possibility of contingents— that is the second part of the dialectic—but rather if there are contingents does God's knowledge of them deny their ability to be really contingent. Again, Aquinas' recourse to the eternality of God allows the negative answer to be given. So much then for the first part of the problem.

The second part of the dialectic faces the challenge that Gunton put forward as reason for the incoherence of the classical position: If God is the necessary cause of all that is, then it is logically incompatible to postulate the existence of real contingencies. As I have already noted above, Aquinas was not unaware of the problem and phrases the question in his own way in terms of divine providence. "If all things that are done here below, even contingent events, are subject to divine providence, then, seemingly, either providence cannot be certain, or else all things happen

102. Stump, *Aquinas*, 117.

103. Lonergan, *Grace and Freedom*, 103–4. As a further point of interest, modern science has effectively debunked the Newtonian model of absolute space and time. Now time, space and matter are all understood to be interconnected and explicated along Einstein's theory of General Relativity. Time is therefore unintelligible apart from space and matter which fits in nicely with the classical position that holds that all three are in fact created realities. The Process conception of God within time requires that God also be related to space and matter, a point that seems to have escaped most proponents of this view. See Ormerod, "Chance and Necessity," 276. For an excellent, though brief exploration of this point, see Pannenberg, "Eternity, Time and Space," 102–6.

by necessity."[104] On the surface the problem appears formidable, for either there is real contingency and God's purposes can be frustrated—something a classical theist strongly rejects—or God's providence is certain which seems to necessarily preclude the possibility of real contingents. But rather than collapse into a deterministic position in order to safeguard the certainty of divine providence, Aquinas endeavors to demonstrate that the antithesis is in reality a false one. This is achieved in two steps, the first being a denial of the fundamental assumption of the antithesis; the second is an assertion of God's will that allows for the cause of both necessary and contingent entities.

Beginning then with the rejection of the antithesis. There is an underlying assumption to the problem as presented that allows the antithesis to stand. This assumption is based on the notion that it is impossible for every contingent fact to have an explanation; or expressed more formally: For any contingent event C the fact which explains it cannot be a necessary fact, otherwise C would not be contingent. From this definition, contingency of effect requires at least one unexplained contingent fact in any possible proximate cause of the effect.[105] Aquinas has no real problem with this concept and in an early discussion on this issue acknowledged that contingency of effect does follow the proximate cause.[106] What is of concern is the subsequent assumption made that if God is the first and necessary cause then there can be no contingent proximate causes and *ipso facto* there are no contingencies. Aquinas calls this conclusion into question since just because God is necessary cause does not mean that all acts of God's will are in the same way necessary.[107] This line of reasoning is readily demonstrated with an appeal to creation.

We have already noted that God creates the world *ex nihilo* and is thus the cause of being for all creaturely existence. But it does not automatically follow from this argument that creaturely existence is ontologically necessary. If it did we would have to conclude that there is no possibility for God not to create but that God's will is necessitated by God's essence to create. However, Aquinas rejects this and holds that creation is not logically necessary since the proposition "God does not create" does not by itself entail a contradiction.[108] Indeed, creation is not required by

104. SCG 3.94.

105. Stump, *Aquinas*, 129.

106. Aquinas, *1 Sent.*, d38. q1. a5.

107. SCG 1.83. ST I. q19. a3.

108. See Stump, *Aquinas*, 123. Also, Lonergan, *Philosophy of God, and Theology*, 64–65.

some ineluctable logic or by the nature of deity so that God could not have willed not to create. The fact that something exists at all is wholly ascribed to the will of God as a gratuitous gift which arises freely from God's own goodness.[109] There is thus an asymmetrical relation between God and the world, characterized by perfect freedom on God's part and utter dependence on the world's part. It is this creative freedom that signifies creation's contingency for it must be independent of any necessity in God and yet at the same time totally dependent upon God's beneficent act of will.[110]

However, Aquinas does recognize that since God *has created* it is *conditionally necessary* for God to create. The reason for this is that if God chooses between two alternatives, neither of which are ontologically necessary, then logically the choice that God does not choose remains forever unavailable to God. Thus, having created it is no longer open for God not to create. Whatever God wills, then, in the act of willing cannot be changed but God's will remains free to choose what it is that God will in fact will.[111] The acts of God's will are thereby only conditionally necessary in this sense, they are not ontologically necessary for God. This allows Aquinas to come to the following conclusion in his *Summa Contra Gentiles*:

> The necessity of supposition [conditional necessity] in the cause, moreover, does not require an absolute necessity in the effect. But God wills something in the creature, not with absolute necessity, but only by a necessity of supposition [that which comes from a condition] . . . From the divine will, therefore, an absolute necessity in created things cannot be inferred. But only this excludes contingency.[112]

Aquinas then does not deny that God's providence requires that God be the transcendent cause that produces every effect. Indeed, as we have already seen, he insists that God is the cause of the creature's action since it is God who gives it the power to act. It is axiomatic then that divine providence extends to all creation but it does not automatically follow that all things are thereby determined. The reason is that conditional necessity in the cause can in no way produce absolute necessity in the effect. The fundamental premise that a necessary God cannot but produce necessary

---

109. ST I. q44. a4. ad1.

110. Torrance, *Divine and Contingent Order*, 33–34.

111. This point does not prevent all acts of God from being willed in a single simple act of will. See the argument in Stump, *Aquinas*, 125–26.

112. SCG 1.85.

effects is therefore ruled out on the basis that God does not will creation absolutely but conditionally.

The positive part of Aquinas' response readily follows. Since creation is conditionally necessary, it is open to God to freely will what God wills in creation in such a way that God not only wills the fact of their existence but also the mode of their existence, be that necessary or contingent. In the same article in which Aquinas details the importance of conditional necessity we read the following:

> God wills whatever is required for a thing that He wills, as has been said. But it befits certain things, according to the mode of their nature, that they be contingent and not necessary. There-fore, God wills that some things be contingent. Now, the efficacy of the divine will requires not only that something be that God wills to be, but also that it be as He wills it to be. . . . Therefore, the efficacy of the divine will does not remove contingency.[113]

On this understanding there can be no absence of contingency in the world created by God because part of what God wills with conditional necessity is that there be contingency in what God creates.[114] In other words God wills to create things with components that guarantee their contingency. What Aquinas concludes then is that effects can either be necessary or contingent according to the pleasure of God.

We see this again in the third part of his *Summa Theologiae* when he notes that God provides necessary and contingent causes as needed to produce either necessary or contingent effects.[115] God is therefore the *per se* cause of all that is, including contingents. As transcendent cause though, God effectively stands *outside and beyond the order* of created contingence and necessity.[116] As a result there is no incoherence between God as necessary cause and the reality of creaturely contingence in the classical schema. Lonergan, who refers to Aquinas' solution as the theo-rem of divine transcendence, summarizes it well: "because God is univer-sal cause, his providence must be certain; but because he is transcendent

---

113. Ibid.

114. See the further affirmation of this point in ST I. q19. a8. Cf. Lonergan: "What providence intends to be contingent will inevitably be contingent" (*Grace and Free-dom*, 108).

115. ST I. q19. a8. See also McGinn, "Divine Providence and Contingent Action," 751.

116. Aquinas, *Peri hermeneias*, Lect. 14. Lonergan, *Grace and Freedom*, 108.

cause, there can be no incompatibility between terrestrial contingence and the causal certitude of providence."[117]

The theorem has a number of suppositions and conclusions but they are all ones that fit comfortably into the milieu of the classical theist. A key point is that God stands outside of time and views all events in the created world at one and the same time in the eternal now. This understanding of God's relationship to the world allows Aquinas to come to the conclusion that the mode of contingents as contingents is not affected by God's knowledge of them. God knows infallibly, but knowledge does not prevent contingency. The more important conclusion is probably to be found in the assertion that God's *esse* as transcendent cause does not preclude the possibility of contingents. Because God creates out of conditional necessity and not absolute necessity, creation itself is utterly contingent and cannot *a priori* be considered predetermined. But God is, says Aquinas, nonetheless transcendent cause but this in itself does not prevent contingency because as transcendent cause God brings about events either contingently or necessarily according to God's good pleasure. Aquinas thus understands God to be beyond the created necessary/contingency dialectic. Hence the theorem of divine transcendence affirms the cogency of both divine providence and created contingency, and its success for Aquinas is demonstrated by his further application of the theorem to particular theological questions.[118]

Providence and Freedom

The classical predication of God as necessary being along with the affirmation of real contingency in creation brings us now to the point of addressing the question of creaturely free will. This is, in many respects, a molasses of a topic that could easily bring the overall argument to a standstill, caught up as it might be in the philosophical quagmire that tends to surround such issues. We will, however, attempt to avoid the mire given that our interest does not pertain to the modern debate, but is focused on the understanding of the operation of God in what at least appears to be the free and contingent operation of the creature.

The central question has to do with the possibility of creaturely free will within the reality of a God who operates as universal cause in every

117. Lonergan, *Grace and Freedom*, 79.

118. McGinn lists the following uses of the theorem from the Third Part of ST: q46. a2; q1. a2; q14. a2; q65. a4; q84. a5 ("Divine Providence and Contingent Action," 752).

secondary operation. For if the death of Jesus of Nazareth is to be ascribed to God's providential plan and that plan is, as is all of God's providential work willed efficaciously, then it seems no matter how one twists and turns the tapestry of the crucifixion the responsibility for the cross event inevitably falls to God. The one escape from this conclusion is the possibility of creaturely free will and this is the anchor upon which some of the contemporary motifs have made their moorings almost as if to ride out the storm of God's providential *actio*. The benefit to be sought after is clearly divine innocence. For if humanity is truly free to will their own actions then we could readily conclude that God cannot be held responsible for what they choose to do.[119] However, given our argument to date, the obvious theological danger is found in the temptation to elevate the free will ideal to such an extent that it effectively denies that God operates in the operations of the creature.[120] But as we have seen, there can be no isolation of God from the historical event of the crucifixion, for without God the crucifixion would never, nor could ever, occur. The question then is not whether free will triumphs over divine will—for that is a theological impossibility. The question is how should God's involvement in the contingent death of Jesus of Nazareth be understood? In other words, what is it that God actually wills in relation to the cross event? We will attempt to answer this question from within the framework of Aquinas' synthesis.

Free Will in Aquinas

It is natural in English to phrase the question of human freedom in terms of free will but there is no expression in Aquinas' Latin that corresponds exactly to this term. Aquinas certainly speaks of the will and he speaks of freedom but he does not speak of free will (*libera voluntas*) nor of the freedom of the will (*libertas voluntatis*). What he speaks of instead is free decision (*liberum arbitrium*) and from the commentary on the *Sentences* to the *Pars prima*, the fundamental thesis is that the free agent is the cause of its own determination.[121] In Aquinas' system it is the interplay between

119. This is essentially the free will defense to the problem of evil.

120. The requirement for indeterminism in the modern definitions of libertarian free will, for example, is symptomatic of such a position. Clarke, *Libertarian Accounts of Free Will*, xiii.

121. Kenny, *Aquinas on Mind*, 75. Lonergan, *Grace and Freedom*, 318. Eleonore Stump stresses that *liberum arbitrium* should not be confused for Aquinas' understanding of freedom of the will in general (*Aquinas*, 294–95). While it is the primary topic of discussion in *De malo* 6, elsewhere (ST I. q83. a3) Aquinas associates the term

the intellect and the will that gives rise to free decision. This immediately places Aquinas at odds with the Molinists as well as most contemporary discussions on free will which predicate human freedom only on the will and the will's ability to do other than it does.[122] Where Aquinas differs is not in recognizing the contingent nature of the will's act, for he too would agree that the will is free to do other than it does, but in rejecting its independence from other faculties. The will is not an isolated power in Aquinas' metaphysical system, for it operates in concert with the intellect. Thus the will's ability to choose between alternatives is never offered as the paradigm for human freedom but rather as its most obvious result.[123] What this means is that human freedom needs to be approached on a systems level rather than on an individual component level and therefore an understanding of the dynamic interplay between the will and intellect is an appropriate place to begin.

In simplest terms, the will is the power of wanting, but you cannot want what you do not know. The human act is thus a movement that proceeds from deliberate will; it is a knowing wanting, or put more constructively, it is a wanting governed by the intellect.[124] But what is it that the intellect knows that the will wants? The answer is the good of the end. What moves the will from potency to act is the very end that the intellect grasps as good. Why this is so is due, in Aquinas' view, to the understanding that the human agent is a creature created by a good God and therefore there is an inbuilt inclination or tendency in the human will towards the good.[125] This should not be viewed as an external constraint but rather

---

with only one of the acts of will needed to produce human action, namely the act of will which is *electio* (choice). It must be pointed out of course that the act of *electio* is required in the interplay between the intellect and the will in the differentiation of means by which the desired end is to be achieved. It is, as Stump argues, only one act but it is nonetheless a major one. As a result, and in the absence of more correct terminology, *liberum arbitrium* may continue to be used as a kind of shorthand reference for Aquinas' understanding.

122. For Molina, the will must be the sheer originator of free actions for them to be free. Burrell, *Freedom and Creation*, 127. On the non-Thomistic tradition of contemporary discussions on free will see Stump, *Aquinas*, 277 and esp. 533 n. 5.

123. Burrell, *Freedom and Creation*, 91–92.

124. McInerny, *Aquinas on Human Action*, 53.

125. "This is the good as common to all things. This is that to which the will by nature tends, like any power to its proper object. . . . Now since the will, like the mind [intellect], is a certain non-material force, there corresponds to it one common reality, namely being good. . . . This universal good embraces many particular goods, towards none of which is there a determinism within the will" (ST IaIIae. q10. a1). See also the similar discussion in ST I. q82. a4.

as an inherent condition of what it means to be human. In other words, the will is not coerced to desire the good but naturally orients itself to the good and subsequently acts in such a way as to accomplish the good.

This means that the orientation to the good is found not just vis-à-vis the end, but also vis-à-vis the means by which the end might be reached. As we find in the *Prima secundae*: "The character of being good, which is the interest of our power of will, is present, not only in the end, but also in the things that lead to it."[126] That is, the movement of the will is governed by the intellect's apprehension of the good in both the end desired and the particular means by which the end might be realized. So for example, in Nietzsche's famous "will to power," it is power which is understood as the good, and the will acts according to the "good" means identified by the intellect in order to achieve that end. The point to be made here is that it is not the will which determines the good to be sought. The will is limited in this regard to the power to act. Judgment as to what is good, whether or not that judgment be good absolutely considered, is the function of the intellect.[127]

We will have more to say about this particular point shortly but first a quick summary. Human action results from an interplay between intellect and will. The intellect presents to the will what it deems to be good in the circumstances and the will then wills to move to that good because it has a natural inclination to do so. The intellect thus moves the will not as efficient cause but as a final cause; it presents an end to which the will is motivated to move.[128] For this reason the will cannot be said to be autonomous or a self-starter, but acts in concert with the intellect, and the will's capacity to move is that of a moved mover rather than an unmoved mover.[129] If this logic is accepted, the means/end scheme at once realizes the need for a systems-oriented approach to the question of free will, since it is impossible for the will to act independently of the intellect.[130]

126. ST IaIIae. q8. a2.

127. Stump, *Aquinas*, 278–79. The will, of course, is not forced into action by the intellect and can resist the intellect's causation. The point here is that initial judgment is always the domain of the intellect.

128. ST I. q82. a4.

129. Burrell, *Freedom and Creation*, 88. For this reason it is somewhat anachronistic to try and locate Aquinas' account within the modern preoccupation with "libertarian" and "compatibilist" views of freedom, since these are more often than not based on the will as an unmoved mover. Such discussions must be based within Aquinas' own context.

130. The interrelated operations of both the intellect and will are considerably

It comes as no surprise then to discover in Aquinas four reasons why the will is said to be free, reasons that encompass both the will and the intellect.[131] For brevity's sake I will simply list them here and then provide a quotation from Aquinas which will allow us to demonstrate them in a given situation. The four reasons are:

1. Practical judgment is contingent

2. The means to the end is not necessary but an optional means

3. The apprehended good does not efficaciously move the will; and

4. The will may or may not move itself to its free act

And the quotation from Aquinas is found in his discussion on freewill in ST I. q83. a1:

> To clarify this, recall how some things act without judgment, so a stone falls to the ground; all things that lack knowledge are like this. Others act from judgment, but without freedom; thus brute animals. For a lamb perceives that a wolf is to be fled from by natural judgment which is not free; it does it by natural instinct not by deliberation, and this holds for any act of discernment by brute animals. But man acts through judging that something is to be shunned or sought after through his ability to know. Because this particular practical conclusion proceeds not from natural instinct but from reasoning from experience, he acts freely, being open to several possible courses. For in contingent matters reason can go either way, as is obvious in dialectical and rhetorical arguments. Now particular actions are contingent. And so in regard to particular acts reason's judgment is open to various possibilities, not fixed to one. It is because man is rational that such decisions must needs be free.[132]

Here Aquinas identifies three modes of action: the unconscious, the instinctive and the reasoned. In the first place the actions of the unconscious agent are only included by way of counter-example, for it is clear

---

more complicated than that just presented. For instance, in some cases the will also moves the intellect as in directing it to attend to some things and to neglect others. ST IaIIae. q17. a1; ST IaIIae. q17. a6. The intellect can also move the will in other ways, some of which we attend to below. Enough has been said, however, to allow us to proceed.

131. Lonergan notes that we cannot find in Aquinas these four reasons asserted in the same place. But nevertheless Lonergan argues that Aquinas does in fact assert all four and is not changing his mind nor correcting himself from one work to another. See the defense of this in Lonergan, *Grace and Freedom*, 320–21.

132. ST I. q83. a1.

that the very concept of free will does not apply when the agent is devoid of both intellect and will. Secondly, the instinctive action arises from judgment but it is an action that is unreasoned. The lamb does not weigh its options before fleeing, it simply responds to its natural impulses and attempts to outrun the wolf. Thirdly, and in contrast to the second point, reasoned action results from reflective judgment so that the human being is accountable for the decision taken. What this means is that while the human shepherd may also turn and flee from the wolf just as swiftly as did the lamb, the shepherd will also be accountable to the owner of the flock as to the action taken. The lamb will not be praised or blamed for fleeing, the shepherd on the other hand may very well be. Humans thus enjoy free decision on Aquinas' view because they are rational creatures.[133]

The key element of *liberum arbitrium* then is not in the will's ability to do otherwise but in the ability to make reasoned decisions, decisions that are contingent upon the circumstances faced. Taking the example of the shepherd and applying the four reasons that Aquinas gives for human freedom, we come to the following conclusions. In the situation the shepherd faced, the apprehended good which was presented by the intellect to the will was that of survival. There were other possible goods such as protecting the flock or even killing the wolf, but survival was judged by the intellect to be the good which should be presented to the will to be acted upon. Judgment is therefore contingent on any number of factors and thus the will is free. Secondly, the presented end, "survival" did not necessitate that the shepherd should flee; hiding from the wolf may have been an appropriate alternative. Therefore, the means to the end is not necessary to the end and so the will is free.[134] Thirdly, while it is true that the will is naturally oriented towards the good and thus is inclined to move towards the end presented to it by the intellect, that inclination is not efficacious. The apprehended good does not efficaciously move the will to the extent that the will is unable to resist it. Thus the shepherd, being motivated by the intellect to will to flee, could have willed to resist that means, which would have then forced the intellect to present another means to the good end.[135]

133. Which is why Aquinas comments that a person who, through madness, for example, has lost their intellectual faculties can no longer be considered to have free will. ST IaIIae. q10. a3.

134. The only time this would not be case is when there is only one available means to an end. The intellect would then have no choice but to present the one means to the desired end. But this does not negate free will for the judgment that selects that end as good is still free.

135. This results from what Aquinas terms as "counsel." The will is not forced to

This leads to the final and what Lonergan considers to be the essential reason, for it is not simply a matter of knowledge but a matter of act and so externally demonstrates the existence of free will.[136] The shepherd may or may not will to do anything the intellect has presented. It is certainly naturally inclined to do so, but the will is not forced by the intellect to do so. Thus, the shepherd is free to flee or free to not take any action at all. But it must be stressed that when the will does make a choice (*electio*), that choice follows from the intellect's apprehension of the good.

Freedom and the Necessity of the End

There is a problem with this understanding of liberty and it arises from the intellect's apprehension of the end good. As just outlined, human freedom requires the ability to make contingent judgment between ends and yet it is God, according to this schema, who determines the ultimate good of the end. Is the will not then moved of necessity to this end? The question essentially boils down to whether or not creatures can truly be free when their very existence is dependent upon the creator. There can be no doubt that in the means/end scheme articulated above, the will is a moved mover and the initial mover is not an independent intellect but is in fact the creator. Aquinas is very clear on this point:

> Man is the master of his acts, including those of willing and of not willing, because of the deliberative activity of reason, which can be turned to one side or the other. But that he should deliberate or not deliberate, supposing that we were master of this too, would have to come about by a preceding deliberation. And since this may not proceed to infinity, one would finally have to reach the point at which a man's free decision (*liberum arbitrium*) is moved by some external principle superior to the human mind, namely by God, as Aristotle himself demonstrated. Thus the mind even of a healthy man is not so much the master of its acts as not to need to be moved by God.[137]

In many ways this conclusion is a natural consequence of *Deus operator in omni operante* and again it is confirmed that it is God who gives the creature its power to act. To consolidate this point it is also apparent that the good to which God naturally aligns the will cannot be something that the

---

take action towards the end presented unless it chooses to do so.

136. Lonergan, *Grace and Freedom*, 320.

137. ST IaIIae. q109. a2. ad1.

created intellect can fully apprehend and present to the will on its own. By definition the ultimate good, which in terms of our earlier discussion we might frame as *beatitudo*, is a complete order of magnitude above *eudaimonia* and supremely beyond the faculty of the intellect to effectively comprehend. This means that it must be God who initially specifies the will to the good and Aquinas agrees: God, as the ultimate good, "alone fulfils the capacity of the will, and so he alone as object moves it sufficiently."[138] And in another place: "God moves man's will as the universal mover to the universal object of will, which is the Good. A man cannot will anything without this universal motion."[139] Humanity is therefore dependent on God for its very act.

But how then is the will not moved of necessity? Rather than try and argue against this conclusion Aquinas in fact agrees that the will is so moved.[140] However, the point to be grasped is that the sort of necessity in play here is not the sort that impinges on human freedom. In the first place, not all acts of the will are necessary acts. Certain goods do not move the will necessarily because they are neither the ultimate end nor necessary conditions for that end. In other words, our final happiness or *beatitudo* does not depend on them. So while the objects that our intellect grasps as good may indeed be good and contribute toward our state of happiness, they are not necessary to happiness. As Aquinas writes in *De malo*, "And so human beings, although they necessarily will happiness, do not necessarily will any of the things leading to happiness."[141] Secondly, he simply denies that the will is moved of necessity to will whatever it wills, because such a supposition undermines all attributions of praise and blame, amongst others. Again in *De malo*: "But this opinion is heretical. For it takes away the reason for merit and demerit in human acts, as it does not seem meritorious or demeritorious for persons to do necessarily what they could not avoid doing."[142] To be of any consequence, moral re-

---

138. ST I. q105. a4. See also: ST IaIIae. q94 . a2.

139. ST IaIIae. q9. a6. ad3.

140. "The ultimate end moves the will necessarily because it is the complete good" (ST IaIIae. q10. a2). And again in Aquinas, *De malo* 6: "[I]f we apprehend something as a suitable good in every conceivable particular, it will necessarily move the will."

141. Aquinas, *De malo*, 6. ad 9. Indeed, one can even will not to do those things at all. The will "is able [to] not actually will happiness, since the will can avoid thinking about happiness insofar as the will moves the intellect to its activity. And in this respect, neither does the will necessarily will happiness itself. Just so, persons would not necessarily become warm if they could at will repel heat" (*De malo* 6. ad 7).

142. Aquinas, *De malo*, 6.

sponsibility requires that the will not be moved by necessity. But Aquinas does not believe that the will is free some of the time and not free at other times. Even when the will does will of necessity it is still free and he comes to this conclusion because of the nature of necessity that is bearing upon the will and moreover, the nature of the creature in relation to the creator.

At the beginning of his disputation on the will in the *Prima pars*, Aquinas discusses the various types of necessity and he does so in terms of Aristotle's four causes; formal, material, efficient and final:

> There are many kinds of necessity. For the necessary is that which cannot not be. Now this can be from an intrinsic cause, whether material, as when we say that anything compounded of contraries must cease to be, or formal, when we say a triangle has to have three angles together equal to two right angles. Such is natural and absolute necessity. But necessity can also be due to an extrinsic cause, whether final or efficient. A final goal imposes necessity when it cannot be brought about, or cannot well be brought about, without something; thus food is described as necessary for life, a horse for a journey. This we term necessity given the end in view, and sometimes we call it utility. An agent cause imposes necessity when it applies force to the point where one cannot act otherwise. Necessity of this type is called coercion.[143]

Clearly two of these, formal and efficient are incompatible with any notion of human freedom. So self-evident is the incompatibility of formal causation with free will that Aquinas does not even grant it further comment. Geometrical theorems are not free to be true one day and untrue the next. Almost as obvious is the necessity that arises from an efficient cause, which Aquinas terms coercion. This occurs when some cause external to the agent produces in the agent a volition for some particular thing and with it we are well familiar. The agent does not act freely in either case and Aquinas dismisses them both as being the kind of necessity in play here.

In contrast the other two forms of necessity are, according to Aquinas, compatible with acts of free will and this is where the necessary willing of the ultimate good is to be located. The most obvious candidate for this is final causation for it is the necessity of the end that motivates the will to act. In this case the will is necessarily moved in two ways: firstly, when the end desired can only be attained in one way and secondly, when the end can be attained better or more conveniently by a certain means. Hence in the first case the will is necessarily moved to eat—not for pleasure or comfort,

143. ST I. q82. a1.

which may be good goals in themselves—but because the preservation of life depends upon it. Again, from the desire to sail the sea comes the necessary motivation of the will to seek a ship. But is free will negated by these necessary means? If one holds that free will requires total independence from any end, such as in indeterminate libertarianism, then the answer must be yes. Yet on Aquinas' view the will does not operate independently of the intellect and therefore cannot operate independently of an end. Free will is therefore not negated by a necessary means to a desired end.

Secondly, a thing is said to be necessary for a certain end when it is apprehended by the intellect as the best or most convenient way of attaining that end.[144] Aquinas gives the example of a horse being necessary for a journey. Clearly horses are not logically necessary for any journey but they are certainly a more pleasing way of travel than having to sweat it out on foot. This kind of necessity might therefore be termed aesthetic necessity, for the intellect is so moved by the beauty and right order of one particular means that the will could only ever be activated with respect to that means. Again this does not negate the possibility of free will for this necessary choice of means is not externally constrained but arises internally from the natural inclination to will the good.

Finally, the will is moved by natural necessity towards the good because as we have already seen, this is its created tendency. "Just as the intellect necessarily assents to the first principles of thought, so the will necessarily assents to the pursuit of our ultimate goal of happiness."[145] Aquinas readily acknowledges that this natural movement is indeed necessary but he is convinced that it does not imply that the human individual is not free and he comes to this conclusion on the grounds of the relationship between creature and creator.

> The very meaning of voluntary activity denotes an internal principle within the subject, this . . . does not have to be the utterly first principle, moving yet unmoved by all else. The proximate principle is internal, but the ultimately first moving principle is external, as indeed it is for natural movement, this being the cause setting nature in motion.[146]

144. In fact in the *Tertia pars* Aquinas identifies the incarnation as only being necessary in the same way that a horse is necessary for a journey—it is convenient to achieve a certain end. ST III. q1. a2.

145. ST I. q82. a1.

146. ST IaIIae. q9. a4. ad1.

What he is saying here is that free will does not have to be the cause of itself in order to be free. As a created creature, the "internal principle" that governs our activity is derived not independently from ourselves, but from the creator. Moreover, since God as the creator of all preserves the very existence of that creation, our internal operation can only be considered "internal" when understood in dependent relationship to the creator.[147] In other words, freedom is not dependent on independence. To be free means that one is not under the forced influence of another creature, it does not, and could not mean to be independent of God.[148] Freedom of the will is thus not antithetical to the operation of the creator within the creature, and indeed, it is only because of God that creaturely freedom is even possible. Aquinas confirms this by linking his understanding of free will with his theorem of divine transcendence:

> Free decision (*liberum arbitrium*) spells self-determination because man by his free decision moves himself into action. Freedom does not require that a thing is its own first cause, just as in order to be the cause of something else a thing does not have to be its first cause. God is the first cause on which both natural and free agents depend. And just as his initiative does not prevent natural causes from being natural, so it does not prevent voluntary action from being voluntary but rather makes it be precisely this. For God works in each according to its nature.[149]

The necessary movement of the will to the good of the end does not therefore impinge on human freedom because God moves the will in such a way it is able to act freely. Earlier we saw that conditional necessity in the cause can in no way imply absolute necessity in the effect and the same argument can be made for creaturely acts of will. In causing the will to will the good necessarily, God in no way coerces the will to act because God wills to cause it conditionally and not absolutely. In summary it is impossible for the will to be independent of God, just as it is impossible for the intellect to independently grasp the ultimate good. Thus creaturely free will only ever exists in relation to God and being in relation to God is not inimical to human freedom.

147. Burrell, *Freedom and Creation*, 90–91.

148. McCabe, *God Matters*, 14.

149. ST I. q83. a1 ad3.

The Surd of Sin

There remains one very important question: What then of moral evil—theologically, sin? To demonstrate the problem let us for a moment follow our argument through. Because God knows, wills and causes me to perform some act, I do that act—but with conditional necessity so the act I do is still understood to be free. God remains, of course, the principal cause of the act as without God I can do nothing, but nonetheless I am still a genuine secondary cause of that act. Furthermore, since God is universal cause, God is behind all the circumstances, conditions and motives that led me to doing that particular act.[150] Now it just so happens that the act in question was a sin. Because I am the free cause of the act, I am responsible and can be classified as a sinner. Yet God is still more a cause of my free act of sin than I am and therefore is not God more a sinner than me? Even if responsibility is limited somehow to the genuineness of the secondary cause, is it not still the case that God is the ultimate cause of evil? Such at any rate is the problem.

One possible solution is to affirm that God is, in fact, the cause of evil. This is what the early Reformers concluded since having denied any possibility of creaturely free will there was little choice but to respond to this problem by predicating all evil to God's operation in the reprobate.[151] Staunch Calvinist Gordon Clark does not hesitate in this regard: "Let it be unequivocally said that this view certainly makes God the cause of sin. God is the sole ultimate cause of everything."[152] Yet while God is heralded as the cause of sin there is much emphasis on the impossibility of God being tainted by its stain. Luther was insistent that God was not *sinful* in causing sin, because to claim that some action or event is sinful is to judge that action or event and humanity was (and is) in no position to judge the acts of its creator. Instead the duty of the creature was to afford God glory since the righteousness of God's judgments were revealed by the evilness of humanity's actions.[153] The fact that God caused those evil actions is more or less beside the point.

What this position achieves is a nullification of the problem of evil because it redefines the goodness of God to include evil's very cause. In other words, the goodness of God does not require the prevention of evil

---

150. Lonergan, *Grace and Freedom*, 339.
151. Luther, *The Bondage of the Will*, 51.
152. Clark, *Religion, Reason, and Revelation*, 221.
153. Luther, *The Bondage of the Will*, 204, 212–16.

but in fact the very opposite. Hence Hume's famous objection that if God were good there would be no evil is turned upside down.[154] God is shown to be good because there is evil for God to judge. Adherents of this view strenuously deny, of course, that God *does* evil but they acknowledge that God is good when God causes evil to be done by others.[155] Understandably, many struggle with this conclusion but its rejection does not so much lie in the moral revulsion to the thought that God can utilize evil to achieve God's purposes. In fact, the Scriptures confirm that God is able to do this very thing (Gen 50:20; Rom 8:28). Rather its rejection stems from the resulting theistic derivation that God operates with two seemingly counter opposed wills and, above all, because it fails to appreciate the true nature of evil.

But firstly, after arguing strongly that God is behind the evil actions of humanity, Luther is forced to reach the conclusion in his *Bondage of the Will* that God has a double will, even a double reality. There is the will of God that is revealed in the Scriptures (*deus revelatus*) and there is the will of the hidden God (*deus absconditus*) that remains inscrutable and beyond human comprehension.[156] The predication of two divine wills is necessary to explain the conclusion that God works to cause both good and evil since it is difficult to ascribe both actions to the one God at the one time. While Luther does his best to maintain that this difference is merely noetic he concedes that it may indeed be ontic and the will of the hidden God may in fact be diametrically opposed to that revealed in Scripture.[157] Thus we read that God "does not will the death of the sinner, that is according to his word; he does, however, will it according to his inscrutable will."[158] By appealing to a hidden God Luther inevitably makes theology an irrelevancy since any statements made on the basis of revelation can easily be refuted by what is, in effect, an argument from silence.[159] Thus the easy synthesis that predicates the causation of evil to the hidden God and the causation of good to the revealed God of love has no real foundation. Calvin sensed this but dismissed the problem as one of creaturely

---

154. Hume, *Dialogues Concerning Natural Religion*, part 10.

155. See for example, Calvin, *Institutes*, 1.16.5. Grudem, *Systematic Theology*, 328f.

156. Luther, *WA*, 18.684–86. Luther, *The Bondage of the Will*, 169–71.

157. McGrath, *Luther's Theology of the Cross*, 166–67.

158. Luther, *WA*, 18.685.28–29.

159. Paul Althaus details the difficulties of Luther's position at this point and we will not spend time on them here. Althaus, *The Theology of Martin Luther*, 274–80.

incapacity to understand the divine, and committed himself to the logical inconsistency.[160]

There is, however, one outcome of this position that is worth noting. That is, it attempts to make evil comprehensible. As caused by God, human acts of evil (and we could also include natural evils here as well) must be understood to fit within the providential plan of a sovereign God. And thus, despite the pain and suffering that evil entails, it nevertheless lends itself to some higher purpose. Hence, there is a kind of comforting intelligibility to the horror that scars the wickedness of humanity, even if it is difficult to deny that its intelligibility is somewhat grotesque.

But the theological consequences of a *deus absconditus*—the inherent tension with the *deus revelatus* and the ultimate irrelevancy of theological statements based on the latter—is a high price to pay for the possibility of an intelligible evil. There is, in any case, a considerable question as to the reality of human solace in the knowledge that evil suffered is caused by God for the purpose of enhancing the *gloria dei*. It would be a brave minister indeed who would try to explain to a grieving mother that her daughter was brutally murdered in order that God's glory might increase. But I would contend that such a conclusion would not be necessary if more emphasis were given to Augustine's notion of evil as privation and the inherent *unintelligibility* of evil that such a position entails. Of course, critics of privation theory contend that a denial of evil's intelligibility makes a mockery of evil suffered. It allows mitigating circumstances to be given that undermine the horror of the experience and fail to comfort the victims in the moment of their distress.[161] But this natural desire to know "why" arises out of the injustice of the evil event itself and not because there is something inherently within evil that can be understood.[162]

Indeed the fundamental horror of evil is the fact that there is no "why," that there is no rational or logical explanation to be uncovered.[163]

160. Calvin, *Institutes*, 1.18.3. See the discussion in George, *Theology of the Reformers*, 209–10.

161. Milbank, *Being Reconciled*, 6.

162. Kierkegaard is rather scathing: "To want to give a logical explanation of the coming of sin into the world is a stupidity that can occur only to people who are comically worried about finding an explanation" (Kierkegaard, *The Concept of Anxiety*, 49–50). Rather more soberly, Elie Wiesel in reflecting on the deaths of children during the Holocaust says, "I didn't understand, though I wanted to. Ask any survivor and you will hear the same thing: above all, we tried to understand. Why all these deaths?. . . Perhaps there was nothing to understand" (Wiesel, *All Rivers Run to the Sea*, 77–78).

163. Torrance, *Divine and Contingent Order*, 114.

Hence the problem with theodicies that give evil a cause, such as that proposed by the early reformers, is the unmerited compliment they give to evil in granting it intelligibility. On the contrary, evil is—in the most radical sense—unintelligible. It is not part of the intelligible order of the created universe, it is in fact a negation of that order even to the point of being *das Nichtige* in the Barthian sense.[164] Importantly, a conception of evil as "nothingness" is not meant to imply that the effects of evil are not real nor that evil itself should not be taken seriously. Barth's point was not the denial of evil but rather the affirmation that there could be no systematic theologizing of it. Evil is simply disruptive of grand theological schemes and totally resists comprehensive explanation.

> For this reason it is inexplicable, and can be affirmed only as that which is inherently inimical. . . . Being hostile before and against God, and also before and against His creature, it is outside the sphere of systematization. It cannot even be viewed dialectically, let alone resolved.[165]

In *Grace and Freedom* Lonergan makes the same emphasis in commenting that a unified synthesis is impossible on the grounds that the unintelligible cannot be related to the intelligible or else it would be rendered intelligible by virtue of that relation.[166] Hence we must speak of evil *apart* from divine causality because causality is an intelligible relation of dependence. For this reason it must be said that God can in no way plan evil, cause evil or otherwise bring evil about. Note that this is not to deny that God can utilize the evil acts of creatures to bring about some greater good. God remains sovereign. It is a simple statement that God neither causes evil nor does not cause evil but merely allows the incomprehensible to be perpetrated.

On what basis though can this conclusion be reached? The answer lies in the intelligibility of God's *actio* as universal cause. Earlier I outlined the Thomistic position of how God applies all things to act according to the divine intellect. The purpose of this application is not just to keep the universe in motion as would be the case in Aristotle's cosmic system, but to bring all things to their designated *telos*. Providence is thus an intelligible synthesis of finite acts that cohere towards an intelligible end and, as

164. For Barth's presentation of evil as *das Nichtige* (nothingness) see Barth, *CD*, III/3, 294f.

165. Ibid., III/3, 354. See also the excellent paper by McDowell, "Much Ado about Nothing," 319–23.

166. Lonergan, *Grace and Freedom*, 332. Lonergan, *Insight*, 690.

I have already argued, that end is the good that God necessarily directs the creature towards, an end the intellect appropriates and so specifies to the will. It is when the will acts under these circumstances that the act "fits" into the created order of the universe and can be considered intelligible on that basis. Acts of evil clearly do not fall under the same circumstances unless one considers the "good" that God applies to the intellect to include the sorts of acts that would be characterized as evil. Given our above rejection of this tenet something else must occur for evil to occur. And something else does occur, or rather does not occur since acts of evil do not result from decision itself but from a failure to decide.[167] So contrary to the desire of Milton's Satan, evil cannot be directly willed for its own sake but only occurs as a failure of the will to will the good that God presents to it.[168]

In fact for Aquinas, the evil of sin is said to occur when the creature exercises its own autonomy by *withdrawing from the ordering of divine understanding*.[169] Or in the words of von Balthasar, sin is "unmasked as man's wrenching himself loose from the divine power."[170] This "wrenching loose" or withdrawing can only be classed as nonconformity to the divine intellect, a non-participation in divine intelligibility and a gap in the providential order of the created universe. There is nothing rational or reasonable about it, it is the surd that blights the face of human freedom. Of course, the fact that evil occurs is intelligible, for there is objective truth to the statement that the sinner sins. But why the sinner sins is not. If there were a reason it would no longer be sin because it would then intelligibly pertain to the divine providential order.

The point that evil fundamentally has no intelligible antecedents does not, however, require the consequences of evil to be incomprehensible. Consider the following example:[171] A victim in a murder mystery novel is poisoned with anthrax while opening the mail. As the poison takes hold the victim predictably experiences cold and flu like symptoms before finally coming to the point of complete respiratory arrest. The victim's death is certainly a horrendous evil, but the manner by which it occurred

167. Hefling, "Christ and Evils," 876.

168. In book IV of *Paradise Lost* Satan concludes his soliloquy upon Mount Niphates with the verse "Farewell, remorse! all good to me is lost; / Evil, be thou my good" (Milton, *Paradise Lost*). Hannah Arendt provides a powerful critique of this position in her famous work on Adolf Eichmann, Arendt, *Eichmann in Jerusalem*.

169. ST I. q17. a1.

170. Balthasar, *Theo-Drama*, 4:175.

171. Modified from an example provided by Hefling, "Christ and Evils," 876–77.

is completely intelligible as any forensic scientist could demonstrate. Anthrax has certain effects on the human respiratory system that are readily recognized and identified post-mortem. What is not intelligible is that the villain who put the anthrax in the envelope did not decide against a course of action that would have such consequences. We can analyze this further and divide the action into three identifiable levels:

1. There is the fundamental evil, what Lonergan calls the "basic sin," which is the surd of failure to refuse a reprehensible course of action. In this example it is the failure to make the decision to not put the anthrax in the envelope.

2. There is the actual course of action: the sourcing and insertion of the anthrax into the envelope followed by its mailing to the victim. Such a deed constitutes the wrongdoing, moral evil or "sin" in its most obvious sense.

3. Having opened the mail and inhaled the poison, the victim experiences the physical evil of what anthrax does to a human respiratory system.

The second and third point, which correspond to moral and physical evils, are part of a causal train that can be effectively understood.[172] Not that they are in themselves intelligible but they are comprehensible when related to each other. Lonergan makes the point that a deficient cause will produce a deficient effect, there is a correlation between the two that can be followed.[173] However, the first point, the basic sin, is unique in the sense that it does not depend on any prior cause but is the irrational non-event that initiates the series. The really significant distinction then is between the first evil and the other two. Yet when we gauge the acts by virtue of our emotions the most horrendous evil is the third—the actual death of the victim. The first evil is considered minor in comparison. But this viewpoint needs to be inverted because the third evil is comprehensible on the basis of the first. The first evil, however, remains incomprehensible and is therefore the more horrendous of the three.[174]

172. For the division of evil into (a) basic sin; (b) moral evil; and (c) physical evil see Lonergan, *Insight*, 689–90.

173. Lonergan, *Grace and Freedom*, 332.

174. One thinks here of Jesus' statement that adultery occurs not just when a man sleeps with another man's wife (the actual act) but when he looks lustfully with his heart (the basic sin) (Matt 5:27–28).

So what then can be said in reference to the problem? What does God know of sin? Without a doubt God cannot be said to be the cause of sin but this does not mean that God does not know eternally and in detail all sins. The fact of sin is objective and therefore knowable. As was said, that the sinner sins is true and God knows the sin that the sinner commits. But God does not understand sin, for sin has no intelligibility to be understood. The conclusion to draw is that sin is not part of God's order of divine intellect, or a decree of divine governance, for these are both intelligible. Is God then morally bound to refrain from operating in the sinner when the sinner sins? This is the objection of Hume who partially defines the goodness of God by the willing ability to prevent evil. If God was truly omnipotent and good then evil should not occur. Indeed it should not! The fact it does occur points to its very absurdity and the need for a third category of divine operation. This is why Hume's argument is essentially irrelevant, for not only is there what God wills to take place and what God wills not to take place, there is a third category of what God permits to take place.[175] It is this third category that encompasses the sin for which the sinner is alone responsible. Furthermore in allowing the creature access to this third category God acts appropriately. Lonergan explains:

> Clearly, it is not evil but good to create a being so excellent that it possesses rational self-consciousness whence freedom naturally follows. It is not evil but good to leave that freedom intact, to command good indeed and to forbid evil, but to refrain from an interference that would reduce freedom to an illusory appearance. Consequently, it is not evil but good to conceive and choose and effect a world order, even though basic sins will and do occur; for it is only fallacy to argue that basic sins are entities or nonentities and that, if they are entities, they must be due to God's universal causality, or if they are non-entities, they must be due to God's unwillingness to cause the opposite entities.[176]

The fact that sin occurs then is not a reflection on God's character nor on God's (in)ability to prevent it. The creation of a rationally free creature is an excellent good and the good remains when the creature continues to have the ability to act freely. However, simply because the creature does not act according to the divine order does not require the conclusion that

175. Lonergan, *Grace and Freedom*, 330. Lonergan here makes reference to ST I. q19. a9. ad3m. "God neither wills evils to be nor wills evils not to be; he wills to allow them to happen. And this is good." For the reason why it is "good" see ST I. q23. a5. ad3m.

176. Lonergan, *Insight*, 690–91.

God is involved in or behind those evil acts. That evil occurs is due to the creature alone; why it occurs is beyond understanding and this not because we have a finite inability to comprehend but because there is nothing comprehensible to be comprehended.

Quite clearly this is not all that can or indeed should be said about this subject and pointedly nothing of the above should be read as a minimization of the fundamental horror of evil nor of the devastating impact that such acts have on individual lives. But enough has been said to allow us to proceed and this we will now do.

Divine Meaning and the Jesus of History

Over against recent attempts to sideline God in the action surrounding the death of Jesus of Nazareth, this chapter has emphasized God's ongoing operation in creation through both preservation and providence. Regardless of particular worldly events, the contingent nature of the created realm must be underpinned by the necessary work of God if it is to continue to exist at all. To some this emphasis will appear a little mundane, but it is a theological foundation that is often neglected in the contemporary effort to extricate God from the violence of the cross. Let me reiterate: the fact that the cross event occurred at all is only because of the ongoing preservation of God who continually and creatively acts in the created realm according to the divine universal order. If God fails to act, the world ceases to exist. There is no other conclusion that can be drawn unless the world is held to be ontologically independent of God. But a doctrine of creation *ex nihilo* fundamentally rules this out and so the utter dependence of the created realm upon its creator remains.

However, and as I have gone to some length to point out, God's continued operation in the created realm does not imply that all things occur necessarily, nor that creaturely free will is a chimera. The theorem of divine transcendence makes it possible to coherently understand that God can act in such a way that contingency and free will are not overruled. God creates with conditional necessity and in so doing gives room for creaturely free action, action that can either be understood to intelligently fit into the created order or action that unintelligibly does not. That God would create a world where the creature would have such freedom remains, as Kierkegaard put it, the cross that philosophy is still writhing on.[177] But come to terms with it we must, if we are to make any sense of the

177. Kierkegaard, JP, 1:1237 (1838).

action that surrounds the death of Jesus of Nazareth. The conclusion that I wish to draw is that unlike modern proposals that endeavor to divorce God from any involvement in the cross, the theorem of divine transcendence makes it possible to comprehend God's actions in the cross whilst the responsibility and inherent injustice of the event itself remains solely the responsibility of humanity. In fact, contrary to modern fears, the cross event is not a matter of divine violence at all, but rather a contingent event of the created realm that is given divine meaning by the transcendent God.

As a contingent event, two questions immediately come to the fore: (1) What are the historical circumstances surrounding Jesus' suffering and death? and (2) just how much is God behind them? The answer to the first is a considerable and often neglected task in theological analysis and we will begin our journey in the next chapter. But we have enough theological framework at this point to make some important conclusions about the second. Indeed, given our discussion, the answer should already be somewhat apparent.

To begin with we can schematically outline the historical circumstances that led to Jesus' death in terms familiar to us. (1) There was basic sin on the part of Judas, Pilate, the Jewish authorities, the crowd, the soldiers and probably others; (2) There was nothing that prevented their sin from taking effect; and (3) because nothing prevented it, it actually did take effect.[178] This is certainly overly simplified but it does serve to focus our attention on the pertinent question as to what extent these acts were due to God as transcendent first cause. Clearly in regard to the first point, the only conclusion that can be drawn is that there is no way that God could will the basic sin of those who brought about Jesus' death. As I have argued, the unintelligibility of sin requires that all acts of sin be considered apart from God's intelligible order of the universe. This means that sinful acts cannot be providentially framed and are therefore not caused by God, planned by God or otherwise enabled by God—except of course as they pertain to the divine preservation of the individual's very existence and their ability to act. But in any case this is a work of God that is always a causation to the good. The failure to achieve it—the withdrawing from divine intelligibility—is the responsibility of the creature alone.

For this reason the crucifixion of Jesus of Nazareth cannot be directly related to God's providential plan since the sinful actions of individuals that brought about that death are unintelligible to God. They have no reasoned basis within the intelligible order of the universe. God is thus

178. Hefling, "Christ and Evils," 879.

not behind Judas' betrayal of Jesus, any more than God is behind Pilate's action in handing an innocent Jesus over to the soldiers. These actions remain the responsibility of the individuals themselves (and are therefore open to historical and anthropological analysis on that basis). To some this will be a startling statement for it means that the historical event of the crucifixion cannot actually be willed by God. It remains entirely the result of sinful human actions and patently not the actions of an angry or vindictive God. If, post-Easter, faith is able to see in this terrible sequence of human hate the meaningful hand of God, then that reflection is not something that can be construed as divine determination.[179]

But what of the Scriptural texts that attribute the cross to the set purpose and foreknowledge of God? There does appear to be a paradox. On one hand the Scriptures confirm that it was God who set forth Jesus as the *hilestarion* (Rom 3:25), it was also by the direct plan and purpose of God that Jesus was handed over to "wicked men" to be crucified (Acts 2:23; 4:28). Yet on the other hand the surd of sin makes it impossible for God to will the death of Jesus since the act itself was sinful. Somehow God doesn't will it, yet God still wants it to happen. It is almost as if the crucifixion of Jesus is a good bad thing; good because it is part of God's purpose and yet bad because it is sinful. The two just do not go together. Indeed, they do not. The paradox expressed in this way misses the thrust of the theological point of the entire chapter.

The answer lies in the fact that the death of Jesus of Nazareth is not necessary in the same sense that we say that God is necessary. The reason for this is that God does not create with ontological necessity but with conditional necessity so that the events of this world always have an element of contingency about them. Indeed, Aquinas was insistent that the incarnation itself was not necessary for the restoration of humanity as God could have redeemed humanity in any number of ways.[180] That God did not, as Aquinas put it, is what makes the incarnation *"conveniens,"* but such fittingness arises not from the crucifixion's necessity but from the meaning that God gives to the event itself.[181] God can, of course, bring about events necessarily if God so chooses, but these events will always be aligned with the intelligible order of the created universe, which *ipso facto* rules out sinful acts. For this reason basic sin cannot in any way be consid-

179. Hall, *The Cross in Our Context*, 103.

180. ST III. q1. a2.

181. Ibid. Elsewhere Aquinas reaffirms that being *conveniens* in no way makes the cross event necessary. ST III. q46. a1–3.

ered necessary. Consequent sins do follow intelligibly from the basic sin but even so, the fact that the basic sin is a withdrawal from God's created order means that consequent sins cannot be part of God's providential plan either. Thus, the third point of our historical schematic, the actual event of Jesus' execution, cannot be willed by God even though it is intelligible insofar as it relates to the antecedent basic sin.

How, then, can the death of Jesus be part of God's set purpose for the salvation of the world if its origins are obscured in unintelligibility? The answer is that God knows eternally and in detail all sin. I have already made the point that the sinful event is an objective fact and can, therefore, be known by God. Being known does not mean that it must also be understood, it just means that it is known. For example, I can know that the sun rises in the East and sets in the West, but I do not have to understand why it does so in order to experientially know that it does.[182] However, unlike the sun's transit across the sky there is no intelligibility to sin that can be understood, but nonetheless, the event itself can be known and is known by God who knows all things. The point being that if an event is divinely known then it is *open to the creation of divine meaning*. This is why Aquinas was so forthright in his belief that evil acts can have divine meaning that is far from consonant with the evil of the event itself.[183] Importantly, the theorem of divine transcendence affirms that God's knowledge is not a means to causation either, so the fact that God knows an evil act does not override its contingency.

This conclusion in no way implies that there is a divine *requirement* for evil acts, as creation *ex nihilo* rules out any divine dependence on the created realm. But once such an act has occurred, God is not prevented from creating a divinely coherent meaning out of it. Furthermore, this meaning in no way justifies the evil act or the fact that the act should not have occurred. The fact that an evil act occurs remains unintelligible to God and beyond any kind of justification. But again, having occurred there is now an opportunity for meaning to be created from it. We can see this, for example, in the story of Joseph; his being sold into slavery was meant for evil yet God gave it a meaning that could never have been imagined (Gen 45:5; 50:20). This divine meaning was created *ex nihilo* because

---

182. Lonergan, *Grace and Freedom*, 330–32.

183. Julian of Norwich even goes so far as to suggest that sin is *conveniens* in the sense that it becomes fitting in the story that God is telling. The act itself remains unjustified but God is able to incorporate it into the divine narrative. See the discussion by Turner, "Sin Is Behovely."

the basic sin that Joseph's brothers engaged in was unintelligible in itself and it therefore could not have formed any basis for God's own intent.[184]

So what God does is to redeem the basic sin and its attendant consequences by creating redemptive meaning from them. As was said, this does not implicate God in the events themselves nor does it mean that God required or caused the events to be. But it does reveal that God's solution to the problem of evil is not to immediately eradicate the fallen creature in some dramatic act of destruction, but to act from *within* creation, creating it afresh even from the midst of its own fallen-ness.[185]

It follows then that the sinful execution of Jesus is also open to the creation of divine meaning. This is why the cross can be "good news *for* humankind," writes Douglas Hall, "even while it is a stark reiteration of the bad news *about* humankind."[186] The inevitable question to ask then, is just what meaning, what "good news" does God actually create out of the event of Jesus' death? The answer professed by the church is soteriological, but what exactly that means in the given context is something that must surely be based in the historical event. Indeed, the second point of our historical schematic is really the heart of the matter. The practical reason why Jesus dies is because nothing occurs to prevent the basic sin of Judas and others from moving to completion. There is no doubt that God could have prevented the crucifixion by an exercise of power, and in fact the Gospel

184. It could be argued that the statement "God creates meaning *ex nihilo*" is to suggest that meaning is a substance that God "makes." Clearly meaning does not exist on its own, it is the result of what someone does (meaning does not exist in itself, it is always expressed through various kinds of action (language, drama, art, symbols etc.)). It is a person or a subject that means, so meaning only ever arises when someone, somewhere understands and evaluates something to be meaningful. In this case God is "doing something" with this particular event of Joseph life, something that has no grounding in the event itself. It could equally be said that God *gave* the event meaning, in that God understood and evaluated the event to have a specific meaning that was not elsewhere intended by the event's participants. But I prefer to use the verb *create* because when God gives meaning to an event that has its origins in basic sin there is no intelligibility in the event itself for God to ground the meaning given. It is, in that sense, a *creatio ex nihilo* and highlights for us yet again, the meaninglessness that is inherent in the sinful event.

185. In this regard, N. T. Wright's small monograph, *Evil and the Justice of God* is illuminating since he emphasizes God's ongoing creative activity from within the narrative of Israel, climaxing as it does in the Christian story, with the death and resurrection of Jesus of Nazareth. The point being that God acts from within the world that God has created and we should therefore expect such activity to imbue historical events with divine significance. Hence the importance of examining the intention of Jesus from within his own historical context. Wright, *Evil and the Justice of God*, 42–44.

186. Hall, *The Cross in Our Context*, 99.

of Matthew records that Jesus had more than twelve legions of angels at his disposal if he so chose to call on them (Matt 26:53). We could therefore readily answer the question as to why Jesus suffered and died with the simple observation that Jesus neither fled nor resisted the consequence of the basic sins of others.[187] Such being the case there is significant implication for why Jesus chose the *via crucis* and did not take advantage of the natural or supernatural resources available to him. Why did Jesus not choose to flee? Why instead did he "resolutely set out for Jerusalem" as the Gospel of Luke records (9:51)? The inherent implication is that Jesus himself thought that his death would achieve *something*, and so there is a valid question as to what that something might actually be.

But on what basis can we conclude that the meaning with which Jesus of Nazareth imbued his death is the same meaning that God intended to create, and did create, out of Jesus' death? In other words, it is all well and good to propose that God created a redemptive meaning from the surd of Jesus' death but why would a historical analysis of Jesus' own vocational understanding reveal that meaning? After all, if as the Nicene creed says, Jesus was like us in all things apart from sin, then Jesus too was historically conditioned, that is, subject to human contingency. So even if we uphold that the Word became flesh, we cannot simply say that anything that Jesus did or thought, God also did or thought. That would be to say that all of Jesus' acts were divine, a conclusion the New Testament strongly resists.[188] On the other hand, if the Word did become flesh then it would be appropriate to expect some kind of relation between the divine and human natures of Christ by which the human Christ might know something of the divine. A closer examination of what might be concluded from a Chalcedonian affirmation is therefore required.

Chalcedonian Christology

At its heart, an explicit affirmation of Chalcedonian Christology demands that there be no discontinuity between God the Father and the words and actions of Jesus of Nazareth. That is, the two natures/one person doctrine of Chalcedon is the foundation for the connection between that which is divinely known and that which is humanly mediated. However,

187. It is on this basis that Aquinas understands Jesus to have laid his life down voluntarily. Jesus did not will his death directly, but indirectly since he did not resist it. ST III. q47. a1.

188. John 1:14; 1 John 1:1–4; 4:2–3.

trying to get a grasp on how the two natures of Christ function in the one hypostasis is fraught with theological difficulty. It is one thing to recognise the limits of the discussion (the two natures coexisting without confusion, without change, without division, without separation) but quite another to try and explain what that actually means. Fortunately, we can leave a full exploration of the incarnation to others. Here the (nonetheless) challenging task is to sketch an understanding of how Jesus might relate to, and be able in some sense to express, the knowledge of the divine.

And "sketch" is the word. Any conception of how the two natures relate will always be tentative and so, as in Trinitarian reflection, discussion tends to move by way of analogy. Two points are particularly suggestive: (a) An understanding that Christ's human nature acts as the instrumental cause of his divine nature; and (b) a reflection on the possible psychological constitution of Christ.

(a) We begin by returning to the theology of Thomas Aquinas. In both his *Summa Contra Gentiles* and *Summa Theologiae*, he unequivocally affirms the hypostatic union: the Word is both the bearer of divinity and, as incarnated, the bearer of humanity.[189] This much is to be expected, but what is of more interest to us is how Aquinas chooses to describe the relationship between the two natures. This he does in *SCG* by drawing upon the Athanasian creed in which the relation between the divine and human natures is compared with the relation between the soul and the body: "As the rational soul and flesh is one man, so God and man is one Christ."[190] Of course, Aquinas recognises that such comparisons are not without their dangers, the soul relates to the body as form relates to matter and this clearly cannot hold for the hypostatic union—divinity is not the form of humanity.[191] However, the soul also relates to the body in terms of an instrument, and Aquinas makes use of this relation to emphasise that in the same manner as the body is an instrument of the soul, so the human nature is an instrument of the divine nature.[192]

Thus, we find in the *tertia pars* of *Summa Theologiae* an explanation of how Jesus was able to perform miracles on the basis of instrumentality. Christ's human nature did not work the miracles independently, nor did

189. SCG 4.41; ST III. q2. a2.

190. SCG 4.41.

191. Ibid.

192. As Aquinas writes: "[The] human nature has been taken up in Christ to work as an instrument proper to God alone. . . . The human nature therefore of Christ stands to God as an instrument proper" (ibid.).

Christ's divine nature exercise power in abstract. On the contrary, "each [nature] communicates its actions to the other: in as far as the human nature is the instrument of the Divine action, and the human action receives power from the Divine Nature."[193] Hence, Christ's humanity was the instrumental cause of the miracles wrought by divine power.

In Aquinas' thought, such instrumentality was not limited to the performance of miracles but is present in other acts as well, perhaps seen nowhere more readily than in the salvific act itself:[194]

> There is a twofold efficient agency—namely, the principal and the instrumental. Now the principal efficient cause of man's salvation is God. But since Christ's humanity is the "instrument of the Godhead" . . . all Christ's actions and sufferings operate instrumentally in virtue of His Godhead for the salvation of men. Consequently, then, Christ's Passion accomplishes man's salvation efficiently.[195]

Here Aquinas confirms that all Christ's actions, including his sufferings, operate as an instrument of divinity for a salvific *telos*. Or as one commentator expressed it, here "the Word incarnate employs its humanity to bring about human salvation."[196]

What we can conclude for our present discussion then is that since God was involved in bringing about human salvation (2 Cor 5:18) the human acts of Jesus, especially those which are also oriented towards a salvific *telos*, cannot be considered mutually independent of the divine nature. Thus, there must be some connection between the meaning that God intended to create for the cross event and the acts of Christ related to that event. Indeed, because Christ's human nature is the instrumental cause of the divine nature, the human acts of Christ actually function to reveal that divine meaning. Again, this is not to say that everything that Christ did while on earth was divine, but that where divine significance or empowerment was mediated, the human acts of Christ functioned to carry that significance.

(b) Following the above discussion it is thus reasonable to ask the question: Could the human nature of Christ be aware—in some sense at least—of

---

193. ST III. q43. a2.

194. Aquinas also makes reference to such works as cleansing of sins, illumination of the mind by grace, and introduction to everlasting life (SCG 4.41).

195. *ST* III. q48. a6.

196. Wawrykow, *The Westminster Handbook to Thomas Aquinas*, 75.

the divine will? If so, then anything that Jesus said about his death might also be understood to similarly reflect God's will. Certainly, the New Testament makes it clear that Jesus was historically conditioned in that he did not seem to know everything that God the Father did. In a passage that has caused endless discussion, Jesus remarked that only the Father knew the exact time of the consummation of the age—the angels didn't know when it would be and neither did the Son (Matt 24:36; Mark 13:32). So we cannot simply conclude that the human Christ knew everything that God the Father knew. This limitation on Christ's knowledge is often explained in terms of kenosis, or the self-emptying of the Word that occurred in order for the Word to become flesh. But even if we accept that some form of kenosis did take place, it doesn't mean that the human Christ knew nothing at all of the divine will. Indeed, the Fourth Evangelist notes that Jesus expressly denied acting on his own accord, ministering instead according to the express will of the one who sent him (John 6:38; 12:50). So the question is therefore appropriate: in what sense did the human Christ mediate something of the divine will?

Here again, the work of Lonergan is helpful. In *The Ontological and Psychological Constitution of Christ*, Lonergan proposes an analogy: just as there is one divine person who subsists in two natures so there is one divine subject of two consciousnesses.[197] As a gross simplification, it might be said that Lonergan proposes this analogy on the basis that since Christ has a divine and human nature then he must also have two intellectual natures—one finite and one infinite. And since one who has an intellectual nature also has the potential to be conscious, Christ must have the potential of two consciousnesses—one human and one divine.[198] He writes:

> Since in Christ, God and man, the divine and human natures are neither changed nor mixed, the divine and human consciousnesses are likewise neither changed nor mixed as a result of the hypostatic union. Hence as the Son of God is aware of himself in his infinite perfection through his divine consciousness, so also the same Son of God is aware of himself through his human consciousness in the poverty of human nature.[199]

197. Lonergan, *Constitution of Christ*.

198. The flow of the argument is far more complex than that just described and is carefully constructed. For example, Lonergan spends the first two parts of *Constitution of Christ* just clarifying what is actually meant by the terms *person, subsistent, intellectual nature* and so on.

199. Ibid., 223.

What Lonergan has done here is to extend Chalcedon's ontological understanding of Christ by way of analogy into the psychological realm, thereby contending that Christ is aware of himself (i.e., conscious) as he relates to both natures. In other words, Christ who is one subject nevertheless has two consciousnesses that operate in accordance with their respective nature. So when he is the subject of a divine operation, Christ is divinely conscious and when he is the subject of a human operation, he is humanly conscious.[200] Such a statement is possible because at the incarnation the eternal Word did not cease being the eternal Word in order to become human flesh. This is contrary to some kenotic theories but in the words of the Athanasian creed, the incarnation was "not by conversion of the Godhead into flesh, but by taking of the Manhood into God." Thus in the incarnation the eternal Word remained aware of being the eternal Word while at the same time the human nature of Christ became aware of his own manhood. This is very much a conclusion derived from Chalcedon because it recognizes that both the divine and human consciousnesses of Christ are present in the one divine subject.

The analogy is incredibly rich, arguably orthodox[201], and can profitably be pursued in many directions.[202] We need, however, to limit our discussion to what this means for Christ's knowledge. In a later work, *De Verbo Incarnato*, Lonergan helpfully defines this further.[203] Thesis 12 states:

> In his earthly life, Christ had both effable and ineffable human knowledge, as well as his divine knowledge. As a beholder, he knew God immediately, by the ineffable knowledge that is also called beatific. In the same act, but mediately, he knew everything else that pertained to his work. As a pilgrim, however, he elicited by effable knowledge the cognitional acts, natural and supernatural, that constituted his human, historical life.[204]

200. Hefling, "Lonergan on Christ's (Self-)Knowledge," 139.

201. Lonergan vigorously defends the analogy's orthodoxy (Lonergan "Christ as Subject," 182–83).

202. For further details on the analogy and its application, in addition to *Constitution of Christ*, see the larger and more developed presentation of *De Verbo Incarnato* (the eagerly awaited English translation is forthcoming in CBWL). Commentary can also be found in Hefling, "Lonergan on Christ's (Self-)Knowledge"; Rosenberg, "Christ's Human Knowledge"; and Mongeau "Human and Divine Knowing."

203. Lonergan, *De Verbo incarnato*.

204. Ibid., 332. All translations are from Hefling, "Lonergan on Christ's (Self-) Knowledge."

As in all of Lonergan's work, much of the language used is technical but there are some conclusions that can be drawn without having to work through the detail. Of major importance is the three divisions of knowledge that Christ is said to have. There is:

1. Divine knowledge, that which is known by Christ as God and pertains to the divine life. This is any knowledge that is known by virtue of being God, such as the Trinitarian life that the Word shares with the Father and the Spirit. But since it is the eternal Word that becomes incarnate, Christ must also have . . .

2. Ineffable human knowledge, that which is known by Christ as man but which cannot be expressed. This is the beatific knowledge in which Christ knew God immediately (i.e., without the use of senses).[205] As a consequence, Christ must also know everything that pertains to his work, a conclusion that Lonergan grounds on the basis that "anyone who knows God's essence immediately also knows all those things to which the divine will extends."[206] And finally,

3. Effable human knowledge, that which can be expressed and mediated through normal acts of human consciousness.

The significant value of these three categories is found in the insight that the human Christ had both ineffable and effable knowledge.[207] These now-archaic terms describes two types of knowledge—that which can be expressed or mediated (effable) and that which cannot (ineffable). The divine knowledge which is immediately grasped (i.e., not known through sense data) is proper to Christ by virtue of being the incarnate Word. This knowledge cannot be directly expressed because it is by its very nature unutterable, it is simply known."[208] But the mystery of the incarnation is that the Word which became flesh also "grew in wisdom and stature" (Luke

205. The example that Lonergan gives to help explain what ineffable, inexpressible knowledge might be like is from Aquinas' discussion on rapture in *ST* II. q175. a4. Here Aquinas asks whether Paul, when in rapture was withdrawn from his senses or whether he saw what he saw "in the flesh" (2 Cor 12:1–6). Having argued in article 3 that Paul saw the essence of God, a vision of the blessed that cannot be uttered by any person, it is reasonable to conclude that such a vision was not according to the senses. Thus it must be ineffable knowledge since knowledge gained through the physical senses can be expressed. *De Verbo incarnato*, 386. C.f. John 8:19; 10:15; 17:25.

206. Rosenberg, "Christ's Human Knowledge," 834.

207. Detailed discussion on the three categories is available in ibid., 832–39; and Hefling, "Lonergan on Christ's (Self-)Knowledge," 149–64.

208. Hefling, "Lonergan on Christ's (Self-)Knowledge," 150–52.

3:52) and therefore like all humans gained effable knowledge by virtue of being historically conditioned. The relevant question therefore is whether Christ's ineffable knowledge could be expressed—however vaguely—in an effable way.

On this question, Rosenberg summarizes Lonergan's central argument as this: "the mystery of Christ demands ineffable knowledge for Christ to know the divine mystery and effable knowledge for him to reveal, manifest, and communicate the divine mystery in an incarnate way."[209] In other words, effable knowledge was needed for the very reason that it provided a framework in which ineffable knowledge could somehow find expression. In fact, Lonergan contends that "rendering in an effable and palpable way what in him was ineffable" was "the principal and original thing in the life of Christ the man."[210] This shouldn't really surprise us because it is just another way of saying that Christ is the mediator between God and humankind. For mediation to work there must be communication, defined theologically as revelation, that act of God to convey effably that which is ultimately ineffable.[211]

So how does Christ do this? Hefling writes:

> One thing he gave us was an expression of inexpressible insight. In order to give it, however, he had to know, effably, what he was giving. There had to be some kind of becoming-expressible, some transition from knowledge mediated by the divine essence to knowledge mediated by images, phantasms, diagrams, words in the sense of vocabulary items, gestures, intersubjectivity, and all the rest.[212]

So in order to mediate the ineffable knowledge that he grasped, Christ had to find "images, phantasms, diagrams" etc. in which such knowledge could be placed. Hefling again:

> Stated more concretely, it would seem that we can best think of Christ's *effable* self-knowledge as a transformation of existing, meaningful images and narratives and concepts that were available to him. To judge by the canonical gospels, the ones

209. Rosenberg, "Christ's Human Knowledge," 833.

210. Lonergan, *De Verbo incarnato*, 408.

211. In this regard, Meynell writes, "The object of [Christ's] human living was to express this knowledge in an effable form suitable to persons of that place and time, so that ultimately it could become available to those of other places and times" (*The Theology of Bernard Lonergan*, 114).

212. Hefling, "Lonergan on Christ's (Self-)Knowledge," 155.

> that proved to be most suitable were *bar-nasha*, "son of man,"
> the servant of Yahweh in the book of Isaiah, the notion of an
> eschatological prophet, and perhaps (though the point is hotly
> disputed) the notion of a, or the, messiah. These, it seems, each
> with its circle of connotations, were the "diagrams" that could
> and perhaps did convey, effably, Christ's ineffable knowledge of
> himself, both to himself and to others.[213]

Hefling's conclusion here is that the "diagram" that Christ found in which to place his ineffable knowledge is nothing other than his own life, expressed as it was through symbols, words, and actions. So the ineffable meaning that God created out of the unintelligibility of the cross event finds its effable expression in the very meaning that Christ himself gave to his death. Thus we can arguably conclude that whatever Jesus believed himself to be doing as he fulfilled his vocation in going to the cross will be coherent with the divine meaning that God intended to create for that unintelligible event.

To conclude then: In drawing upon the Chalcedonian doctrine of two natures/one person both in terms of what it means for human instrumentality and the knowledge of Christ, we can say the following: *Historical reconstruction of what Jesus of Nazareth thought his death would accomplish is a theologically important task in comprehending the story of salvation that God chooses to narrate out of that* event. It is important to point out that this is not to suggest that there is only one specific meaning or only one correct way to narrate the story that God is telling. The extent of what God works in the cross is not readily reduced to singular accounts. What I am saying here though is that the divine soteriological narrative—the divine meaning constituted for the cross event—is not arbitrarily imposed but is revealed and finds its ultimate expression in the intention of the one who endured it. And this conclusion requires that we come face-to-face with the Jesus of history.

Convergence

In many ways this discussion is an excursus to the main soteriological thrust of this work but it is a theological foundation that is sorely needed. The questions surrounding the atonement today and the critical evaluations of various atonement theories tend to be based in assumptions as to what God can and cannot do. God is a God of love, it is rightly said, and so

213. Ibid., 162–63.

it is concluded that God cannot in any way find value in the horrendous death of the Son. Moreover, if value or meaning was to be found in the death of Christ then it would imply that God was somehow behind the death and therefore responsible for it. The subsequent conclusion drawn is that human acts of violence are now justified since God has already demonstrated the possible value to be found in such acts. Yet this kind of criticism fails to be sustained theologically.

In classical theism God is certainly a necessary God but this understanding does not require that divine action be construed necessarily. Even as I have argued that God does work in secondary causes, the conditional nature of created humanity allows for the acts of secondary causes to be contingent. This conclusion carries over to the free actions of individuals who, while created by God to be necessarily aligned to the good, are nonetheless able to withdraw themselves from the divine order and do otherwise. This doing otherwise is basic sin since it is the unintelligible action of an individual who chooses to depart from divine purpose. As a consequence, sinful actions cannot be caused by God and are therefore not part of the providential order. Thus, the rejection and execution of Jesus of Nazareth was not willed by God and cannot in any way be justified. However, what is justified, and what is in fact divinely willed, is Jesus' own response to being rejected and executed. This is where the soteriological locus must be centered for it is the foundation of the meaning that is created in what is otherwise an unintelligible event. Therefore suggestions that there is no meaning in the cross event must be rejected. The existence of divine meaning does not implicate God in its violence nor does the cross' contingency deny the possibility of meaning. Does the divine meaning given then act to justify further acts of violence? In no way, for to draw this conclusion would be to justify and make intelligible the basic sin that preceded the evil act. But this is impossible and therefore the presence of divine meaning in no way permits this kind of conclusion.

Of course, atonement theology is not a matter of pointing to a meaning as "the" divine meaning because the New Testament makes no such claim. As we noted in the last chapter, the Scriptures do not give a definitive assessment of the cross but present instead a tapestry of symbols and typographical language from which the cross' soteriological meaning might be evidenced. What is crucial is to locate that soteriological meaning in the context that surrounds the cross, that context being naturally centered on Jesus himself. Hence, the meaning of the cross will correlate with the intention of Jesus who effably mediates what is ineffably known.

Jesus and the Cross

In this I wholeheartedly agree with Ben Meyer who well remarked that "Jesus did not aim to be repudiated and killed, he aimed to charge with meaning his being repudiated and killed."[214] The possible meaning in mind here and the impact that it might have on theories of atonement is what will occupy us from now on.

214. Meyer, *The Aims of Jesus*, 218.

3

Atonement, History, and Meaning

*The beginning is the end. That is, the end of one's theology
of the atonement is determined by where one begins.*[1]

—Scot McKnight

WHY SHOULD THE THEOLOGIAN CARE ABOUT WHAT JESUS OF NAZARETH thought of his impending death? The question becomes more potent if we phrase is slightly differently: Would it actually make any difference to the Christian faith if its doctrine of the atonement had no basis in the intention of Jesus and was merely a symbolic invention of the early church? An uncritical reaction to this type of question is to answer with an indignant affirmation, since there is more than a little audacity in the suggestion that Jesus' intention is irrelevant to the Christian proclamation of salvation. However, does the negative answer actually jar the foundations of Christian faith?

Indeed, if we restrict our investigation to the doctrine of the atonement we could easily be excused for concluding that it actually makes little difference. As we saw in the first chapter, theologies of atonement very rarely take into consideration the historical intention of Jesus of Nazareth in forming their soteriological accounts. It is generally assumed, of course, that Jesus knew his death would have universal atoning significance, but rarely is anything said as to *why* such an understanding would make sense for Jesus within his Palestinian first-century context. In fact, for the traditional motifs it matters very little what Jesus actually thought he was doing, since the cross' saving significance is found not in Jesus' intention *per se* but in God's overarching salvific narrative. Though somewhat unkind, it is perhaps not all that far from the truth to suggest that in traditional reflections, Jesus' life is merely the necessary prerequisite for his all-important

---

1. McKnight, *Jesus and His Death*, 371.

and all-conquering death. As N. T. Wright points out, if all we knew about Jesus' life came from the traditional atonement motifs it could readily be assumed that Jesus' ministry was simply designed to bring him up against the establishment in order to get himself crucified.[2] But does this really do justice to the importance of Jesus' kingdom preaching and praxis for the way we approach his death?

It seems to me that in much of our discussion on the atonement we have unintentionally divided the incarnation narrative into two separate and distinct acts. The first contains a nice moral story about right ethical living and neighborly love, while it is the second that provides the dramatic salvific moment of divine forgiveness. This division and emphasis on the second act is seen for example in Kähler's frequently repeated description of the Gospels as "passion narratives with extended introductions."[3] The phrase itself minimizes the value of the accounts of Jesus' life and ministry, and while such accounts may be both interesting and instructive, they appear to have little bearing on what is taken to be the key purpose of the incarnation—the death of Jesus.

History and Atonement Theology

Theologies of atonement do, of course, point back to particular sayings of Jesus to inform their presentations. Predominant is the ransom saying of Mark 10:45 as well as the heady symbolism of the last supper accounts. But discussion of these texts is usually read in a theological context apart from the first-century setting and worldview in which they were given. Proponents of the various traditional reflections certainly imply that their interpretations are coherent with Jesus' own self-understanding but little is given in the way of defensive argument. If, for example, there is any serious attempt to demonstrate that Jesus fully believed his death would restore God's honor in exactly the same way that Anselm framed it, it is unknown to me. But lest one feel I am unfairly singling out the traditional motifs, this criticism is equally valid for the current crop of contemporary motifs which tend to eschew the historical particulars of Jesus' death in favor of coherent contextualization. It is true that in accounts such as Mann's, Heim's and Milbank's, comment is made as to Jesus' intention for the cross. But as we saw, these appear within the framework of specific

2. Wright, *Jesus and the Victory of God*, 14.

3. Kähler originally made the comment with respect to Mark's gospel but the phrase has become more ubiquitous. Kähler, *The So-Called Historical Jesus*, 80 n. 11.

narratives rather than being particularly connected with Jesus' Jewish expectations and the eschatological context of the first-century.

Perhaps the reason this avenue is rarely pursued in theological accounts (both in traditional and contemporary versions) is that the Christian faith tends not to be so concerned with the exigencies of the cross event as to capturing some facet of the divine soteriological narrative. That is, we are not so concerned with what actually happened but are more interested in how it is that we can incorporate the cross into our various salvific models. Hence the oft-repeated notion that there are in fact two crosses: the theological symbol and the historical actuality. The former are always saving *interpretations* of the latter's significance and as such transform the historical event from mere history and into the power of religious symbol.[4] The benefit in doing so is found in the subsequent ease of transposing that symbolic meaning from one context to another but it must be said that the ultimate effect of this is to de-historicize the cross, emphasizing its eternal narrative or symbolic meaning at the expense of its historical context. Colin Gunton is critical of the Augustinian tradition particularly for this reason, commenting that it overvalues the "abstract logical connections" between ideas (i.e., death through Adam, life through Christ) and inevitably undervalues everything else.[5] Indeed the abstract, logical system that characterizes many atonement presentations *does* operate irrespective of the historical particulars of the death of Jesus of Nazareth.[6] Hence one could be forgiven for coming to the conclusion that Jesus' intention for his death, though no doubt a topic of considerable historical interest, nonetheless has little to say to the post-Easter theological interpretations.

But should the historical intention of Jesus be so minimized? In the epigraph above Scot McKnight points out that the final stopping point of our theologies of atonement will depend on where it is that we choose to begin. This might sound somewhat obvious but the point is nonetheless important. For if we begin with an ahistorical interpretation then it is doubtful that an appropriation of the life and ministry of Jesus of Nazareth will yield anything other than our own soteriological conception. This is readily evident in Mann's presentation because from the outset he claims

---

4. Trelstad, *Cross Examinations*, 3, 259.

5. Gunton, *The Actuality of Atonement*, 17.

6. For example, while seeking to remain within the Augustinian tradition, Hans Boersma is nonetheless critical of it at this point. See Boersma, *Violence, Hospitality and the Cross*, 169–70.

that the historical Jesus—the Jesus of historical research—is an "unnecessary distraction." Yet the very chapter in which he makes this claim is entitled "Jesus Narrates His Intent"![7] The intent narrated cannot then be the intent of the historical Jesus but rather the intent of the soteriological story that Mann himself is trying to narrate. In other words, Mann's purpose is not to investigate the historical context of Jesus' own self-understanding, but to demonstrate how the salvific story he is narrating can be read particularly in the Last Supper accounts. Here, as we saw, Jesus' self-narration of brokenness, for and on behalf of the other, is taken to be the pivotal offer of ontological coherence.[8] Such an account, while intriguing, is certainly in marked contrast to the Reformed tradition in which the purpose of the Last Supper is the revelation of Jesus' death as vicarious substitution in the context of a paschal sacrifice.[9]

The meaning of the cross does, of course, transcend any one view, but are we not in danger here of arbitrarily shaping its meaning along the specific lines of the theologian's soteriological conception? It has to be said that this is probably the case but, as Green and Baker argued, this is simply the theological cost of coherent contextualization.[10] Mann undoubtedly agrees and plainly states that his focus is not traditional fidelity but the ear of his target community.[11] What is important is not the particularities of a historical event long lost in the opaqueness of time but the saving invitation of a kerygma that confronts the individual in the here and now. I believe that this is the reason why a historically coherent conception of the self-understanding of Jesus of Nazareth (i.e., a conception that takes into consideration the first-century Jewish eschatological expectations and the place of the Jewish Messiah within it), is absent from the majority of theological works on the atonement today. The focus is not on getting the past narrative "right," but on transposing the soteriological story of the past into a coherent narrative for the present. It is no doubt important that Jesus really lived and died, but that, it seems, is as far as it goes.

As a consequence, the origins of our salvific musings tend to lie not in what Jesus thought he was doing but in the particular problems of our contemporary context. The logic here moves from identifying the contextual problem to a very specific and often creative appropriation of the

---

7. Mann, *Atonement for a "Sinless" Society*, 107f.

8. Ibid., 111–13.

9. Gruenler, "Atonement in the Synoptic Gospels and Acts," 103–4.

10. Green and Baker, *Recovering the Scandal*, 217–21.

11. Mann, *Atonement for a "Sinless" Society*, 11–12.

Christian hope for salvation to that problem. The danger in this, as Green and Baker along with others have recognised, is that there is no avoiding relativity in the presentations of the Gospel. On this reckoning, we simply have to accept that there is no normative Christian way of proclaiming salvation and to allow the context to dictate the theological appropriation of the Christian hope.[12]

The problem I have with this conception is not in the importance of contextualisation for that is the *sine qua non* of the theological task. The problem is that it predefines the divine soteriological narrative along the lines of the contemporary context rather than applying the divinely revealed narrative to that context. What I mean by this can be seen, for example, in some of the modern feminist proposals for a revised Christian understanding of the atonement. As we saw Brock and Parker outline in *Proverbs and Ashes*, oppressed and abused women only find salvation through the healing "restoration of presence," a presence free from suffering, power and domination.[13] Hence Christian salvation cannot be found at all in the suffering death of Jesus of Nazareth because such an example offers no hope to women already burdened by oppression. Contrary to many other motifs, then, the divine soteriological narrative is here redefined to *exclude* the cross in order to limit the narrative to the incarnational restoration of presence that the praxis of Jesus exemplified. Thus the contemporary context dictates to theology what should be, and what should not be, included in the telling of the salvific story.[14]

As we have already seen, Mann's presentation of salvation for the postmodern, post-industrialized self works similarly. Here the divine narrative is framed in terms of ontological coherence; salvation is found through the authentic unification of the real and ideal selves. But again, in what way is the importance of the divine willing of Jesus' response to his being rejected and executed captured by this understanding? Both presentations strongly minimise the historical mission of Jesus and completely negate any intention he might have had for his impending death. But this is to replace a crucial element of the divine narrative with constructions of

12. Green and Baker, *Recovering the Scandal*, 218.

13. Brock and Parker, *Proverbs of Ashes*, 116, 158.

14. The difficulty here is not in the particular desire to free women from abuse and oppression nor in the horror of a suffering savior but in the theological rejection of the divine freedom to create meaning out of sinful human events. As I argued in the last chapter, to suggest that divine justification is ascribed to sinful events once divine meaning is created for them is a fallacy. It misunderstands the nature and relationship between divine action and secondary causality.

our own making. The very reason for the detailed analysis of divine action in the last chapter was to justify the emphasis and importance of the divine response to the rejection of Jesus for our understanding of the atonement. The divine soteriological narrative must be located in that act or we inevitably misunderstand the nature of the redemptive story that God is telling. While we must be clear that this emphasis will not provide a normative answer to the question of how the cross brings about atonement, it may help prevent theological difficulties from creeping in uninvited. What it does do, however, is reintroduce the need for historical analysis as to the aims and intentions of Jesus and to the particular question of what narrative Jesus himself was creating for the cross.

Towards the Historical Jesus

But therein lies another problem for it can be, and quite often has been, cogently argued that the intention of Jesus is to all intents and purposes, unknowable. Rudolf Bultmann pragmatically accepted that we "know almost nothing concerning the life and personality of Jesus," and that which has been written on the topic is merely "fantastic and romantic."[15] Hence Bultmann turned all his attention to the proclamation of the kerygma and maintained a radical skepticism with regard to all things historical. The salvation-occurrence is found in the existential encounter with the preached word and therefore mere reminiscent accounts of the past do nothing to reveal that salvation.[16]

Admittedly, the ongoing debate within the then historical Jesus scholarship as to what might actually be the *right* past narrative of Jesus simply reinforced the conception that history had nothing positive to say to faith. It appeared to be far more theologically rewarding to float the kerygma free than to try and moor it to the uncertain and ever shifting sands of history that lay beneath. But even if, as Bultmann famously mused, the Christian understanding of Jesus *was* historically accurate and the traditional interpretations of his path to suffering and death *were* actually correct, what would be gained by it? "Would the result really be a legitimation of the kerygma which proclaims the historical Jesus as the Christ who died for us?"[17] The expected answer is no, and quite rightly so for history can never *prove* matters of faith. But is it then right to conclude as Bultmann

15. Bultmann, *Jesus and the Word*, 8.
16. Bultmann, *Theology of the New Testament*, 302.
17. Bultmann, "The Primitive Christian Kerygma," 24.

does that it is only the sheer existence, the "that" of the earthly Jesus, that matters for theology and faith?[18]

There are significant consequences of such a position, as Bultmann's students immediately realized. The problem is not that there is meaning to be found in the symbolic appropriation of the cross but in the separation of that meaning from the cross itself. Christianity is not simply an abstract ideal of human hope but a faith firmly rooted in actual historical events, events that must in some way bear on that faith or risk reducing the man Jesus of Nazareth to mere myth. The New Testament took a firm stance on this, strongly rejecting a docetic Jesus (1 John 1:1–3) and giving considerable importance to the events of his life. This was done, suggests Käsemann, not because the authors thought it interesting to record something for posterity, but because they saw his life-history as being *constitutive for faith* itself.[19] To simply ignore this central theme inevitably results in the creation of a lacuna at the heart of Christian theology, a point J. A. T. Robinson expresses well:

> I am not persuaded that it is possible to remain indifferent to the findings of the historian on how Jesus understood himself, nor that an ultimate skepticism is either tolerable or necessary. . . . In this sense the *self-knowledge* of Jesus is the indispensable heart of the mystery: to regard it as a matter of indifference or as a "no go" area is to leave a blank at the center of Christian theology.[20]

And blanks, unfortunately, do not remain vacant for long and what fills them is not necessarily healthy for Christian faith. But why allow a blank in the first place? The scandal of the incarnation is that the *Logos* did become flesh at a particular time and in a particular place and, if the incarnation is the decisive fulcrum in human history, as Christianity proclaims, do we have any choice but to be interested in those particular events? The Gospels clearly were interested, even if they are kerygmatic documents composed from a post-Easter vantage point. For far from contenting themselves with the "that" of Jesus' earthly existence they expend considerable energy outlining the "what" of Jesus' pre-Easter activity and it is the significance of this "what" in the Gospel's kerygma that highlights its constitutive character for Christian faith.[21]

18. Ibid., 20.

19. As the Gospel of John states quite clearly (20:31). Käsemann, "The Problem of the Historical Jesus," 15–47.

20. Robinson, "The Last Tabu?," 158–9, 161, italics original.

21. As Käsemann writes: "The Easter faith was the foundation of the Christian

Hence, I do not believe that it is theologically viable to blindly separate the Christological confession from the particulars of the Jesus of history (and hence his self-understanding), since this is to cut out precisely what it is that lies at the heart of the Christian proclamation. As Ben Meyer asked, "If Christology has no roots at all in the consciousness of the historical Jesus, how in the end could it claim to be other than and much more than mere ideology?"[22] The answer is that it cannot, which is why there is more than a little irony in the modern preoccupation with abandoning the historical Jesus for the purpose of constituting contextually coherent faith. The Gospels themselves demonstrate that coherent faith can only be found from within the constitutive framework of Jesus of Nazareth, his intention and meaning being paradigmatic for our own authentic appropriations. This means that Jesus' intention for the cross must inform our own understandings and articulations of the cross or our message will inevitably be reduced to a storied ideology.

But stating that the Jesus of history is significant for the Christian faith is one thing, explaining how it is so is something else entirely. The primary problem relates to exactly how one should approach the question of "who is the historical Jesus"? What methodology do we use to answer this question and furthermore, who are we actually looking for? Is it the Jesus *of* faith, or the Jesus *behind* faith? The liberal quest certainly assumed it was the latter, the "real" Jesus is the man unburdened by the later accretions of the Christian community. But as Martin Kähler pointed out, such a person is an illusion since the idea that we can see beyond the faith perspective of the New Testament writings to a Jesus who did not inspire faith is a rather fanciful notion. The Jesus behind the Jesus of faith is, simply put, the Jesus who inspired that faith and he cannot be understood apart from it. Indeed, efforts to develop a portrait of Jesus that went beyond this proved to be nothing more than "torturous" extrapolations, a state ably evidenced by the numerous "Jesuses" that emerged.[23] Even if Schleiermacher's post rationalist emphasis on religion as "the sum of all higher feelings" led the liberal quest to focus on Jesus' inner life and

---

kerygma but was not the first or only source of its content. Rather, it was the Easter faith which took cognizance of the fact that God acted before we became believers and which testified to this fact by encapsulating the earthly history of Jesus in its proclamation" (Käsemann, "The Problem of the Historical Jesus," 34).

22. Meyer, *Critical Realism*, 161.

23. Kähler, *The So-Called Historical Jesus*, 73. See also Dunn, *Jesus Remembered*, 126–27.

his religious persona, the results were hardly better.[24] The Jesus they discovered, bemoaned Kähler, was not Jesus as he really was but merely the creative artistry of the historian's own imagination.[25] Following the same line is George Tyrrell's famous criticism of Harnack which is now often paraphrased in reference to the entire enterprise: the Jesus of the historical quest is nothing more than the historian's own reflection at the bottom of the hermeneutical well.[26]

In light of the above, if we rephrase the question from "who" to "what is the historical Jesus"? the answer becomes the *Jesus constructed by historical research*.[27] But this acknowledgement immediately threatens the very viability of history in the theological task since it suggests that an objective answer to the question of Jesus' intention is, in fact, impossible. Part of the problem here is the modernist assumption of what "objectivity" actually is, but it is nonetheless true that if what we know about Jesus is merely the historian's own self-projections (however well intentioned), then we may as well embrace the narrative possibilities such a position makes available as theologians like Mann have in fact done. After all, what is the point of expending energy on historical investigation if Kähler and Tyrrell are right and the historian's understanding of Jesus of Nazareth tells us more about the historian than it actually does about Jesus? How can history deserve, let alone be given, any place at the table of theological discourse? The problem facing us is twofold: firstly there is the question of historiography, that is, the philosophy by which historical investigation is approached; and secondly, is the related question of the relative priority of faith over history when it comes to the role of history in matters of faith.

But firstly, all historians utilize a historiography, though not all historians are conscious of the one they appropriate.[28] The vast majority of previous investigations into the historical Jesus, for example, have been done

---

24. Schleiermacher, *On Religion*, 85.

25. "The Jesus of the 'Life of Jesus' is merely a modern variety of the products of human creative art, no better than the infamous dogmatic Christ of Byzantine Christology; they are both equally far removed from the true Christ" (Kähler, *The So-Called Historical Jesus*, 43). Alan Mann justifies his departure from the historical Jesus on the basis that we know nothing but the "abstractions of [our] own making" (Mann, *Atonement for a "Sinless" Society*, 107–8).

26. Tyrrell dismisses Harnack's historical reconstruction of Jesus as "the reflection of a Liberal Protestant face, seen at the bottom of a deep well" (Tyrrell, *Christianity at the Crossroads*, 49).

27. See Dunn, *Jesus Remembered*, 125.

28. A point well made by McKnight, *Jesus and His Death*, 4.

by way of common sense, an imbibing if you will of the current *zeitgeist* that provides the historian with a platform from which to work but at the same time exposes the results to significant criticism. As we will see shortly, postmodernism has strongly questioned the viability of this approach and emphasized the importance of the relationship between subject and object in the interpretation of that object. Modernist objectivity in which the subject (historian) is covered by a blanket in order to allow the object (historical data) to appear untouched is now recognized as a fallacy. Such accounts of history remain the construction of the historian's imagination. What is needed is a historiography that understands the relationship between subject and object and operates in conjunction with both. In this scheme history is still a reconstruction, but it is a reconstruction that can be judged on how well it understands that relationship and its various perspectives, rather than attempting to hide that perspective under the cover of modernist objectivity.

It is, of course, not just a matter of stating ones perspective and carrying on as usual. McKnight rightly remarks that "admission is not justification, what is needed is the willingness to let our presuppositions (subject) be challenged by the evidence (object)."[29] Such a historiography has emerged in historical Jesus studies under the name "critical realism," its primary benefit being the recognition that the subject can enter into dialogue with the object without either denying the subject's perspective, or subsuming the object within that perspective.[30] Such a method is critical if we are to have a genuine theological appropriation of history, an undertaking which inevitably raises our next point of concern.

The second problem turns on the question of how theological faith should relate to the historical task. Historical investigation into Jesus of Nazareth can be done, and is done, without any pre-commitment to a Christian faith perspective. In fact, it is quite possible that one can use historical investigation to assault the Christological elements of the Christian faith and both Reimarus and Strauss, to name just two, demonstrated how readily this could be done. However, it is important to point out that these assaults did not arise from some sort of "anti-theological" objectivity that is inherent in past events themselves but from their authors' particular

29. Ibid., 33.

30. See for example: Meyer, *The Aims of Jesus*, 16–21; Wright, *New Testament and the People of God*, 32–37; Dunn, *Jesus Remembered*, 110–11. Interestingly, Meyer appropriates his understanding of critical realism from Bernard Lonergan and we will have occasion to discuss the importance of Lonergan's contribution in more detail below.

interpretive framework. Schweitzer says as much when he remarks that what motivated the liberal quest was not an abstract historical interest but the desire to overcome "the tyranny of dogma."[31] It was felt necessary that this tyranny be "shattered" even before the quest itself could properly begin.[32] Such a prior commitment meant that the interpretations of history that followed were always going to set themselves apart from theology and so it proved to be. But to suggest that this arises as a result of the past events themselves overlooks that all historical knowledge is mediated through the narrative of the historian. As we will see, the idea that any historian can replace a theological perspective (or any other for that matter) with a supposedly neutral "look" is a fallacy. All one does is substitute the avoided perspective with an alternate construction of one's own making.[33] The point of this is not to pass judgment on the efforts of Reimarus and Strauss but to stress that historical investigation is not inevitably doomed to undermine theology.

Nor is there any reason to argue, as Bultmann did, that the historical quest is impossible or that its results are theologically irrelevant. Indeed, as long as we are talking about the Jesus of Christian faith we are always faced with questions that enfold both human and divine, both temporal and eternal elements. The human and temporal elements must in principle be objects open to historical investigation just as the divine and eternal elements are open to theological reflection.[34] We cannot then simply divorce history from theology as if the two never intersect, for the disciplines are inextricably drawn together in the person of Jesus of Nazareth who is called Christ (Matt 1:16).

What is needed then, from a theological perspective, is to relate the Christian belief in the risen Lord Jesus to the earthly reality investigated by historical research. As was said, the life-history of Jesus of Nazareth is proclaimed by the early church to be constitutive of faith itself and the task for the theologian is to ask how that history is constitutive of faith. What is the meaning that Jesus of Nazareth gave to his life, ministry and death and how does that meaning impact our understanding of what it means to be *Christ*-ian? This question goes far beyond that of the general historian and

31. Schweitzer, *The Quest of the Historical Jesus*, 4.

32. Ibid., 3.

33. As John Meier remarks, the "rejection of a traditional faith stance does not mean neutrality, it simply means a different philosophical view that is itself a 'faith stance' in the wide sense of the phrase" (Meier, *A Marginal Jew*, 5). See also Morgan, "The Historical Jesus," 196.

34. Gunton, *Yesterday and Today*, 74.

even that of the biblical scholar for it is not limited to "what did it mean then"? but extends to "what should it mean now"? in the context of the ecclesial community. The difference is not small and indicates the strong role of the theologian's faith in the historical task. It is not a question then of polarizing the dialectic of faith and history, but of moving forward to the foundation of a faith informed by history. Clearly much more needs to be said in this regard, but for now the point to be made is that the subject's faith has a role in the historical investigation of the object, which once again puts the onus back onto an appropriate historiography. For this reason we must pause to discuss these matters in more detail.

To summarize: I have been arguing that the intention of Jesus is not inimical to our understanding of the atonement and should in fact be constitutive of it. Recent works on the atonement, however, concerned as they are with the question of the doctrine's relativeness to various contemporary contexts, have found the need to take the opposite approach. What is important is the contemporary context's appropriation of the Christian hope of salvation and the particular means by which this might be found is neither here nor there. The problem with this direction is the subjection of theology to the context of the age in which it finds itself and the clear neglect of the historical framework of the salvific moment in question. Not only does this threaten to reduce the man Jesus of Nazareth to mere myth but it minimizes the constitutive nature of the life and ministry of Jesus for the Christian faith. Yes, the failure of the various quests for the historical Jesus is widely recognized but this does not mean that the instinctive compulsion to extract Jesus from his historical context is justified. Jesus the Christ is timelessly relevant as Christianity claims but that relevancy is based in the historical awareness of Jesus of Nazareth and not in an ahistorical, docetic Christ of faith.

Moreover, from a theological perspective the Easter story begins not with God willing the death of the Son but with the divine acceptance of humanity's rejection of the Son. The Gethsemane accounts indicate the difficult nature of this way forward and give impetus to the importance of discerning why this was so in our understanding of the cross. Significantly, the point here is not to discover some kind of historical proof for the hope of Christian salvation but to take into account the value of Jesus' own intention for our contextual presentations. If the Christian faith is to speak with more than just ideological fervor then it must demonstrate how its offer of salvation is connected to the historical reality of the man it claims as Christ, the Son of God. This connection between faith and history is something that theology cannot afford to lose, but having said that it does require careful presentation and appropriation. It is to this challenge that we now turn.

Faith Seeking Historical Understanding

The fundamental observation to make is that history is not an objective entity that can be scientifically dissected but an investigation and subsequent interpretation of the meaning of past events.[35] In fact our knowledge of history is not the mathematical knowledge of say, two plus two equals four, but the conditioned knowledge that arises through the data of the remembered past. In other words, historical knowledge does not come to us directly from the event itself but is mediated to us through the data of the event insofar as it is remembered. This view represents Collingwood's well known distinction: the actual "event" belongs to the irretrievable past, what is available to the historian is the "data" of the event.[36] This data comes down through time in diaries, oral traditions, external reports, archaeological artefacts etc., and from these the historian attempts to reconstruct the "facts" of what took place through arriving at a balanced judgment. This means that the data is not itself history but the information used to reconstruct history. "Facts," such that they are, are always interpretations of the data even if what is concluded can be considered to approximate the event itself.[37]

To be sure this distinction between data and fact is not always accepted, but it is becoming increasingly commonplace to utilize such a division for the express purpose of taking into consideration the interpretive factor in the construction of history. There is no such thing as "mere" history, or a perspective-less presentation of past events. Whether we like it or not, all history *is* interpretative and so we must dispense with the notion that historical investigation is just a matter of taking a diachronically equipped microscope and selecting a period of time to slide underneath. One cannot "just take a good hard look" and discover what is going on.

---

35. The literature here is extensive. From a theological perspective see particularly, Lonergan, *Method in Theology*, 175–234. Also Doran, *Theology and the Dialectics of History*. In relation to historical Jesus studies one need go no further than the excellent descriptions in Dunn, *Jesus Remembered*, 99–111; McKnight, *Jesus and His Death*, 4–28; Wright, *New Testament and the People of God*, 81–118.

36. Collingwood, *The Idea of History*.

37. For more on the differences between data and fact see Lonergan, *Method in Theology*, 201–3 and references therein.

The historical task is a menagerie (the wild connotations intended!) of selected data and interpretive fact that the historian must somehow order into a coherent and meaningful narrative that makes sense of not just what happened, but also why it happened in the way it did.

However, does this understanding of the relationship between event, data and fact not justify the postmodern incredulity towards historical truth? If it is true that all accounts of history are but narratives created in the head of the historian, then surely whatever meaning is portrayed can readily be reduced to the terms of that one perspective.[38] In such a case do we not need to accept that "getting the story right" is an impossibility—not because there is no story to tell but because there is a never-ending number of stories that can be told? For the postmodernist it is inevitable that the number of historical narratives is limited only by the number of historians willing to narrate them.[39] One narration will be different from another as a result of the different stories being told but neither can be judged "better" or "worse" since their stories have nothing to do with how well they cohere with the data of the event. In fact in postmodernism, while the past does exist, the data of any event are discrete, unrelated, un-interpreted and therefore meaningless in and of themselves.[40] As a consequence, when that data is woven into a meaningful narrative its meaning cannot have come from the discrete events but from the historian who imbued them with such significance.[41]

This is why the postmodernist decries any effort to claim one particular narrative as more correct or representative of the historical event than another. Such attempts are purely an effort to exert one's own power and dominance and are representative of the literary violence inherent in modernist notions of objectivity. This extends, of course, to all areas of truth, which for the postmodern is defined by the power-holders, the ones whose narrative (in whatever field that might actually be) can ultimately be enforced as the (singular) truth. In historical Jesus scholarship this is demonstrated in the statement that one presentation of Jesus better reflects the first-century worldview, or utilizes more appropriate "criteria"

38. Wright, *New Testament and the People of God*, 88.

39. Morna Hooker bemoaned this fact over thirty years ago in her discussion on the criteria of discontinuity. Hooker, "On Using the Wrong Tool," 581.

40. McKnight, *Jesus and His Death*, 9.

41. See particularly, Jenkins, *On "What is History?,"* 82–83, quoted in McKnight, *Jesus and His Death*, 9–10.

than another. In actual fact, one account is merely connected to persons in power while the other languishes due to lack of narratival privilege.[42]

But if this is all that can be said, then what is the point of historical investigation? It tells us nothing of the past; all we are left with it seems is various power games of pleasing narratives woven together from preselected data. Any relevance to an actual historical event is merely incidental (and truth be told, probably accidental as well). Ultimately the event has no genuine significance for the narrative being told.[43] Hence, in postmodernism the object of historical inquiry is gone forever, all that remains are polyvalent narratives that attract followers according to their various positions of power. No wonder Derrida calls the postmodern philosophy an "economy of war," it totally lays waste the possibility of knowing anything with certainty, probable or otherwise.[44]

Thankfully, however, this is not all that can be said. While postmodernism is right to point out the role of the subject in the interpretation of the object it goes too far when it subsumes the object into the subject. There actually is something "out there" that is separate and distinct from the historian, despite the fact that the historian's investigation cannot be done with complete impartiality. Objects and subjects are simply not the same thing even when what is known about the object is at the level of perception and representation.[45] So while it is true to say that all history is interpretative, it is not the case that all history is equivalent to the historian. This point can be made in part because past events do have a meaning that is independent of the historian's presuppositions. Note that this is not to say that the historian's knowledge of that meaning is independent of their presuppositions but that irrespective of whether a historian chooses to investigate a particular event or not, that event had an inherent meaning.

Why is this so? In the first place, the fact of the matter is that events themselves do not occur in a vacuum removed from the context of everyday life. They are part of human existence and are therefore *constituted* in some way by the narrative or meaning emplotted by the original participants. This means that the historical task is not about the recounting of sterile and isolated events but an investigation into the history of human beings and this requires us to "plot, uncover, and understand from the inside the interplay of human intentions and motivations present within

42. McKnight, *Jesus and His Death*, 10–11.

43. Frei, "Theological Reflections," 74.

44. Derrida, *Dissemination*, 44–45.

45. McKnight, *Jesus and His Death*, 20.

a given field of initial investigation."[46] That is, events are always motivated in some way, moving in some direction and significant in some context, and this dynamic correlation, which gives the event its "human and historical density," can only be described in terms of meaning."[47] This insight acknowledges that the meaning of an event is not dependent on historical afterthoughts but *already* exists insofar as it is intended by the original participants. It is simply inappropriate to consider events as just "one damn thing after another" to which the historian can arbitrarily attach meaning.[48] Contrary to postmodernism, events are never merely discrete, unrelated and un-interpreted, because they involve real people who consciously intend meaning, however inchoate, for that event.

As an example, I recently bought flowers for my wife and it is no doubt *possible* that one could describe the action as a meaningless transfer of organic material. Whilst such a description might be an accurate account of what physically took place it fails to recognize the intended meaning of the event, which in this case was to help celebrate her birthday. Indeed it is the intended meaning that actually imbues the event with a reality that transcends the mere physicality of what occurred. Thus, to limit the investigation to unrelated discrete moments does not tell us all that we could, or indeed should, know about what took place. For an example closer to our present theme consider Jesus' crucifixion. There is sufficient evidence to conclude that Jesus was crucified along with others, possibly two, on the eve of the Jewish Passover. But it stretches the realms of belief to insist that this event is a random combination of meaningless discrete occurrences. Even if we leave theological reflections far to one side, there still exists a meaning emplotted by the original participants that needs to be investigated. Why was Jesus handed over for crucifixion? Why did Pilate agree to crucify him? Why did Jesus not resist or flee? The point

46. Wright, *New Testament and the People of God*, 91, 109. Wright's use of the term "inside" here harks back to Collingwood's distinction between the "outside" and the "inside" of the event. The outside of the event can be described in terms of time, place and movement (i.e., such and such did this or that at some particular time). The inside of the event on the other hand moves beyond what took place to examine why it took place (i.e., why did such and such do this or that then?). Wright's point here is that it is all well and good to investigate the data of "what" happened but the real import of historical investigation is in the "why."

47. Meyer, *Critical Realism*, 167. Lonergan writes that meaning is a "constitutive element in the conscious flow that is the normally controlling side of human action." It is what "grounds the peculiarity of the historical field of investigation" (*Method in Theology*, 178).

48. Greene, *Christology in Cultural Perspective*, 164.

is, that if an original meaning (or meanings) exist then contrary to the postmodern deconstructionist agenda some narratives and meanings will be more truthful than others because some will better cohere with the original meaning(s) emplotted by the event's participants.

Referring back to my previous example, it is quite possible that years from now my grandchildren might find an entry in my wife's diary to the effect that she received flowers on that particular day. But unless they do further research and discover that it was also her birthday on that day, they could likely come to the conclusion that the flowers were my way of saying sorry to my wife for something that I had done (or had not done as the case may be). While this narrative would take into account the data of my gift of flowers it would also be incorrect, since it failed to adequately investigate the original intended meaning that motivated the gift. Again, the task of the historian is not just to ask what happened but to ask why it happened in the way it did, a process that involves close examination of the sources to get as near as possible to the event's original intended meaning.[49]

Of course, it would be naive to suggest that there is only one intended meaning for any particular event, especially when that event involves large numbers of people or has significant impact on a particular community. All participants will intend meaning in their own way and according to their own contexts and community expectations. The intention that Jesus had for his own death, for example, is unlikely to correlate with Caiaphas' religious expediency nor Pilate's political whim. Each of these, however, is a valid point for historical investigation into why Jesus died, even if they do not all contain the same theological merit. And this point brings us back again to the question of subjectivity and the historian's role in interpreting historical meaning. Or more specifically, is there a place for faith

---

49. McKnight, *Jesus and His Death*, 23. Lonergan remarks that while an investigation into original meaning is a necessary aspect of the historical task it is not the only task, nor indeed the major task of the historian. Because meaning will be different between communities and even individuals what is perhaps more important is to grasp what it is that is "going forward" in any particular group at any given time. In literary terms, what is meant by "going forward" is described by the whole drama of life. It is what results through the "characters, their decisions, their actions, and not only because of them but also because of their defects, their oversights, their failures to act." Hence the historical task is not complete with the discovery that "so and so" thought "this" about themselves, but continues into the wider impact of all associated meanings on the community's progress or decline. See Lonergan, *Method in Theology*, 178–89.

in the historical task or does it preclude any hope of objectivity as the postmodernist claims?

Objectivity in Authentic Subjectivity

Rather than ask in the face of postmodern criticism whether there is any hope for objectivity, perhaps the better question to ask is if there is anything about the object that can be known despite the fact that knowledge is inherently subjective? In other words, can we chart a path through the narrow straits of historical investigation with the Scylla of empiricism on one side and the Charybdis of idealism on the other? If there is such a path, it is clear that postmodernism did not take it, its efforts were quickly sucked down the Charybdis whirlpool. But not everyone has followed in its wake and there is now a significant push, at least in historical Jesus studies to take an alternate, though at times weaving course, between these two monsters. As I argued above, this alternate course bears the name *critical realism* and it affirms that the object is other than the subject, but at the same time it acknowledges that the subject's knowledge of the object lies along a spiraling path of dialogue between them both. As N.T. Wright defines it:

> This is a way of describing the process of "knowing" that acknowledges the *reality of the thing known, as something other than the knower* (hence "realism"), while also fully acknowledging that the only access we have to this reality lies along the spiralling path of *appropriate dialogue or conversation between the knower and the thing known* (hence "critical").[50]

The application of this methodology to historical Jesus studies is well defended here by Wright and his efforts find recent support in the works of both Dunn and McKnight.[51] The question then is not whether critical realism is a viable methodology—it clearly is—but just how it facilitates a theological appropriation of history. In other words, we are interested in how the subjectivity of the historian is able to dialogue with the object without compromising genuine knowledge of the object. If this is possible then there is significant potential for faith to enter into dialogue with history without reducing that history to mere ideology.

---

50. Wright, *New Testament and the People of God*, 35, italics original.

51. Dunn, *Jesus Remembered*, 110–11; McKnight, *Jesus and His Death*, 19–28.

Of considerable significance is the fact that Wright's presentation owes much, by way of Ben Meyer, to the philosophy of Bernard Lonergan and so there is value in engaging with Lonergan's contribution to this particular question.[52] To begin with, Lonergan insists that a critical realist approach requires a different perspective on the nature of knowledge from what one would have under an idealist or empiricist framework. Knowing something, in Lonergan's terminology, is not just a matter of "taking a look" but arises through a conjunction of experience, understanding, and judging.[53] At the center are two fundamental questions. The first Lonergan calls a "question for intelligence," which asks for possible descriptions or explanations of what is available in experience. The second is a "question for reflection," which asks whether or not the answer to the first question is appropriate or not. This is a cyclic two-stage process; the second question cannot be asked until the first is answered and the answer to the second may lead to further instances of the first.

Another way of looking at this is to describe it in terms of hypothesis and verification.[54] The hypothesis attempts to explain why something in experience is so, the verification is the act of judging whether or not that hypothesis is correct. If it is judged to be correct then something is known, if it is not then adjustments to the hypothesis will need to be made and the question for reflection asked again. Why is there smoke coming from under the bonnet of the car? Perhaps it is overheating (question of intelligence/hypothesis). Is it overheating (question of reflection/verification)? There is sufficient evidence to believe that it is and for eliminating other possibilities as much less likely.[55]

In this cognitional structure a dynamic and continuing interplay is needed between the object and subject. Knowledge of an object does not arise from an uninvolved subject but occurs as the result of ongoing dialogue. Data is gathered, a hypothesis that attempts to understand how that

---

52. See Wright, *New Testament and the People of God*, 32–37; Meyer, *The Aims of Jesus*, 16–21. Dunn also acknowledges Lonergan's influence (*Jesus Remembered*, 110–11).

53. Lonergan, *Method in Theology*, 238. In "Cognitional Structure" Lonergan is very clear that simply taking a look yields little in the way of knowledge: "An act of ocular vision may be perfect as ocular vision; yet if it occurs without any accompanying glimmer of understanding, it is mere gaping; and mere gaping, so far from being the beau ideal of human knowing, is just stupidity" (222).

54. These are the terms that Wright uses (*New Testament and the People of God*, 98–109).

55. Meynell, *The Theology of Bernard Lonergan*, 2.

data might fit together is proposed and questions of judgment are then asked of the hypothesis. This in turn drives further questions to be asked of the data and the hypothesis is subsequently fine-tuned. Much of this process is commonsense, yet it makes sure that the data is not understood uncritically and therefore mistakenly taken as fact.

Again, at this stage it is important to point out that no data comes to the attention of the historian discretely and un-interpreted. Data is imbued with a meaning that fits within the story or worldview of the original participants and any particular hypothesis must demonstrate how it fits that data within this larger framework of meaning. The process of verification must also ask questions of the hypothesis as to how well it incorporates the meaning of the event into its narrative.[56] Therefore throughout this cognitional process the key element that turns the understood data of experience into something *known* is judgment, and this is why it is judgment that provides the measure of objectivity in the subject's knowledge. In commenting on Lonergan's approach Hugo Meynell writes,

> According to the fully critical theory of knowledge as advanced by Lonergan, a truly objective account of human behaviour is one which examines all the relevant sensible evidence, in action, gesture, talk, documents, monuments and so on; which tried to envisage all the possible combinations of experience, understanding, judgments, and decisions by which it might be accounted for; and which judges that the one which best accounts for the available evidence is probably correct.[57]

Objectivity is therefore not found in taking an uncritical look at the object but is given in the subject's experience, organized and extrapolated by the subject's understanding and posited by the subject's judgment and belief.[58] To quote Meynell once more:

> [Objectivity] is not a matter of putting away one's imaginative capacities and taking a look at reality. Authentic subjectivity consists in attentiveness to experience, intelligence in theorising, reasonableness in judgment, and responsibility in decision. Each of us is conscious of these four operations, and of their more or less thorough exercise within ourselves. . . . History

56. Wright's emphasis on the importance and place of story is a classic example of this method done well.

57. Meynell, *The Theology of Bernard Lonergan*, 8. See too the discussion in Tracy, *The Achievement of Bernard Lonergan*, 223–24.

58. Lonergan, *Method in Theology*, 238.

and the human sciences are a matter of applying experience, intelligence, and reason as rigorously as possible in order to determine the degree of attention to experience, intelligence, reasonableness and responsibility immanent in the actions and products of other people and other societies.[59]

Therefore, a critical realist account does not claim that there is no objectivity to be had at all, but that there is no subject-less objectivity. What is needed is to bring subjectivity to full flower, to the point of self-transcendence, which Meynell here describes as being attentive, intelligent, reasonable and responsible. These terms are deliberately repeated because they constitute Lonergan's transcendental method, through which the knower truly comes to know that which can be known.[60] One must be *attentive* in gathering the data; be *intelligent* in asking the data questions; be *reasonable* in grasping the evidence as sufficient or insufficient; and be *responsible* in the decision one makes. To be sure the process is not easy. Objective knowledge is not just the fruit of subjectivity but of "authentic subjectivity" as Lonergan was apt to put it.[61] But due to the commonness of human bias, conscious and unconscious motivations, and the "illusory omnicompetence of commonsense," subjectivity is easily inauthentic.[62] However, just because it is easily inauthentic does not make it inevitably so; the onus is on the historian/theologian to approach the task of history well aware that the enduring value of their work will depend in large measure on the extent that they successfully adhere to the transcendental precepts. As Ben Meyer puts it, the purpose of critical realism is not to banish perspectivism in historical investigation but to respond constructively to the "subsurface in-authenticity in historical scholarship."[63] Meyer's complaint is aimed at uncritical historicism which assumes that objective knowing is co-ordinate with successful seeing. On the contrary, the critical realist perceives that objectivity requires considerable internal effort and is ultimately successful only insofar as one achieves authentic subjectivity.[64]

59. Meynell, *The Theology of Bernard Lonergan*, 11–12.

60. For more on Lonergan's transcendental precepts see Lonergan, *Method in Theology*, 6–20. If one has the time the full argument for the precepts can be found in Lonergan, *Insight*. In relation to historical Jesus research see particularly, Meyer, *Reality and Illusion*.

61. Lonergan, *Method in Theology*, 292.

62. Meyer, *Critical Realism*, 142.

63. Ibid.

64. Insofar as faith can be considered authentically subjective it too can engage in historical scholarship.

It can be concluded then, that an individual's religious experience or belief will not automatically render their investigation into historical events irretrievably biased. Certainly an adherence to religious belief can, and indeed, should impact how one responds to particular sets of data but this will not *inevitably* deem one's investigation any less valid than another who does not share such belief. It must be stressed that what makes any particular investigation more valid over against another is the extent to which the individual is able to achieve self-transcendence. That is, how successful they are with engaging with the data attentively, intelligently, reasonably and responsibly.

It is, in fact, this last term that is of utmost importance for the first three arrive in what Lonergan calls, cognitive self-transcendence in which the individual reaches a conclusion on whether a particular understanding is correct. This, unfortunately, is where much historical investigation stops. But true self-transcendence is only achieved when the final step is added and the understanding obtained is responsibly judged to have value. Lonegan writes,

> Still such self-transcendence [that which is achieved through being attentive, intelligent and reasonable] is only cognitive. It is in the order not of doing but only of knowing. But on the final level of questions for deliberation, self-transcendence becomes moral. When we ask whether this or that is worth while, whether it is not just apparently good but truly good, then we are inquiring . . . about objective value. Because we can ask such questions, and answer them, and live by the answers, we can effect in our living a moral self-transcendence.[65]

It is this concept of a moral self-transcendence that fully provides the capacity for authenticity because it results in action and not just knowledge. But what actualizes that capacity? For Lonergan, "That capacity becomes an actuality when one falls in love. Being-in-love is therefore the fulfilment of ones capacity for self-transcendence."[66] And since faith is the knowledge born of religious love, far from being a detriment to self-transcendence, it is actually its ultimate fulfilment.[67] We can therefore conclude that since

65. Lonergan, *Method in Theology*, 104.

66. Ibid., 105–6.

67. Ibid., 115. Referring to Pascal's famous remark that the heart has reasons which reason does not know, Lonergan contends that along with the factual knowledge reached by experiencing, understanding, and verifying, there is another kind of knowledge reached through the discernment of value and the judgments of value of a person in love. And faith, accordingly, is "such further knowledge when the love is

realized self-transcendence requires the experience of being-in-love to be authentic, and since faith is being-in-love with God, a faith perspective is not only possible but actually contributes to authentic subjectivity in the critical-realist enterprise. As a consequence, the theologian can rightly engage in matters of historical inquiry.

Bauckham on Testimony

Having defended objectivity as the fruit of authentic subjectivity, it becomes appropriate at this point to consider a recent and no doubt controversial contribution to the relationship between faith and history by Richard Bauckham.[68] In his recent work, *Jesus and the Eyewitnesses*, Bauckham contends that *testimony* is a reliable category for surmounting the "so called" dichotomy between the Jesus of history and the Christ of faith.[69] He makes this claim on the basis that testimony is a category that offers a reputable reading of the Gospels *as* history whilst at the same time being a reading that is *inclusive* of their theological elements.[70] Just how the Gospels can be considered historically reliable within their theological framework has its foundation in Bauckham's understanding of testimony, which he pre-eminently defines as a "genre that attempts to convey the fact and meaning of singular events of absolute significance."[71] While Bauckham identifies this as a special case of the more general definition (a speech act in which the witness' very act of stating *p* is offered as evidence for *p*) his identification of the Gospels as a narrative that expresses both fact and meaning requires this particular understanding to be at the fore.[72] The reason for this lies in the belief that the more exceptional the historical

---

God's love flooding our hearts" (ibid.).

68. Bauckham, *Jesus and the Eyewitnesses*.

69. Ibid., 5–6, quotation from 473.

70. Ibid., 473.

71. Ibid., quoting Vanhoozer, "The Hermeneutics of I-Witness Testimony," 269. Bauckham highlights the similarities with Ricoeur here. Ricoeur, "The Hermeneutics of Testimony," 119–20.

72. Bauckham identifies two other specialized definitions: First is the one perhaps most immediately expected: the testimony provided by a witness in a court of law; second, is the testimony that arises from historical evidence through which we come to know something of the past. Both these also have their place in the discussion of the Gospels as testimony to the history of Jesus but they remain subordinate to the one outlined in the text (Bauckham, *Jesus and the Eyewitnesses*, 473).

event proves to be, the more difficult it is for the historian to understand the event sans testimony.

The paradigmatic example that Bauckham uses is that of the Holocaust, for it is an event that could scarcely be imagined if it were not for the testimonies of its survivors. Giving due concern to its horror, Bauckham contends that the authentic testimonies of the Holocaust—an event that was undeniably "at the limits" of experience and representation—demonstrate the need and value of testimony in providing reliable historical knowledge of events that are similarly "at the limits."[73] Without testimony confronting us with the "sheer otherness of the event" we will necessarily reduce what occurred to the measure of our own experience and thus incorrectly reflect the event itself. Bauckham acknowledges that the content of testimony may readily "puzzle or provoke disbelief," but we must not allow our own experiences and expectations to reduce the testimony to something other than it is.[74]

But this is, of course, easier said than done. The problem is that the historian's preconceptions about what is possible and what is impossible will inevitably dictate the level of acceptance of witness testimony. If, for example, the historian's worldview excludes the possibility of miracles, then no matter how many witnesses testify to their occurrence, the historian will always conclude that somehow they were misled, dishonest or simply self-deceived. In this regard, Lonergan makes the interesting point that no amount of testimony can establish about the past what the historian does not find in the present.[75] This is not because particular testimony of the past is identifiably wrong, but because the historian cannot deal intelligibly with the past when that past is already taken to be unintelligible. Hence Lonergan wryly remarks that if scientists were suddenly to find a place for miracles in modern experience then there would be no shortage of historians willing to restore them to history.[76] And this is precisely Bauckham's point. Historical testimony is not generally discredited because the witness proved to be self-deceived but because the historian is unable to find a place for that testimony within their present worldview. The only way to overcome this preconception is for the historian to allow their worldview to be reconstructed on the basis of the testimony itself;

73. Ibid., 492, 499.

74. Ibid., 492.

75. Lonergan, *Method in Theology*, 222.

76. Ibid.

and this requires a fundamental shift in the acceptance of testimony as integral to the historical task.

Bauckham attempts to facilitate this shift by emphasizing the need to intentionally observe the primary requirement of testimony: that it be *trusted*. Drawing heavily on the hermeneutical work of Paul Ricoeur, Bauckham argues that the witness of testimony must be trusted in the first instance, its evidence being allowed to stand unless, of course, there prove to be valid reasons for its rejection.[77] Bauckham is quick to point out that this does not require *uncritical* acceptance of testimony, but it does require a predisposition to trust the sources over against one that loudly demands their independent verification. Bauckham is therefore critical of Collingwood in this regard, finding fault with the latter's insistence that testimony is not historical knowledge because it cannot be independently verified.[78] On the contrary;

> It has to be said, over and over, that historical rigor does not consist in fundamental skepticism toward historical testimony but in fundamental trust along with testing by critical questioning. Testimony may be mistaken and mislead, but this is not to be generally presumed but must be established in each case. Testimony should be treated as reliable until proved otherwise.[79]

Therefore, the question as to whether or not testimony should be accepted is fundamentally a question of that testimony's trustworthiness rather than an external ability to verify it independently as truth. In fact, such verification is ultimately impossible because the historian does not stand where the witness uniquely stood. This is why testimony demands to be trusted, a requirement that is even more important when the testimony in question relates events that are of exceptional significance.[80] So while very careful to maintain the stark contrast between the Holocaust and the life of Jesus of Nazareth, Bauckham nonetheless makes the point that an

---

77. Bauckham, *Jesus and the Eyewitnesses*, 479–93. In particular Ricoeur, *Memory, History, Forgetting*.

78. Bauckham, *Jesus and the Eyewitnesses*, 485. In particular reference to Collingwood, *The Idea of History*, 257.

79. Bauckham, *Jesus and the Eyewitnesses*, 486.

80. Again, this is not meant to be understood as uncritical acceptance but an acceptance that arises from critical tests of internal coherence and consistency along with tests of consistency with other historical evidence and from whatever else is known about the context.

exceptional historical event such as the life of Jesus requires its testimony to be trusted, just as, indeed, the Holocaust testimonies are trusted.

The significance of this for the Gospels is clear and certainly far reaching. It asserts that the Gospels be initially understood to provide valid and reliable testimony of actual historical events, their historicity only questioned when there proves to be adequate reason for doing so. This is without a doubt a far cry from the form-critical school, which although no longer at the center of the way historical studies into Jesus are done, still exerts enormous influence on the presumed lack of historicity of the Gospel accounts.

But can Testimony be Trusted?

Before we continue there is an obvious rejoinder to Bauckham's thesis. What of the reliability of human memory? It is all well and good to argue that testimony demands to be trusted but it can it actually *be* trusted? Writing in *Constructing Jesus,* Dale Allison argues that human memory is frail and all too fallible and is simply incapable of providing reliable accounts of historical events. In fact, the "fallibility of memory should profoundly unsettle us would be historians of Jesus. We have no cause to imagine that those who remembered him were at any moment immune to the usual deficiencies of recall."[81] The problem, says Allison, is not that the Gospel writers wilfully attempted to reconstruct the truth in order to suit their agenda, but that despite good intentions "[o]bservers habitually misperceive, and they unavoidably misremember."[82] To put it bluntly, we get it wrong and all too often for us to be able to treat memory as a reliable witness. Even the ancient Greeks realized this, comments Allison, and he quotes from the fourth-century BCE Greek philosopher, Thucydides, who remarked, "Different eyewitnesses give different accounts of the same events, speaking out of partiality for one side or the other or else from imperfect memories."[83] The point being that even if we think we are telling the truth, and even if our intentions are as pure as the driven snow, our memory is incapable of guaranteeing the accuracy of our retelling.

As a consequence, Allison contends that there can be no determination made on the reliability of individual events in the life of Jesus and so there is little point in trying to uncover the redactional layers to get at the

81. Allison, *Constructing Jesus,* 8.

82. Ibid., 1.

83. Ibid., 1–2, quoting Thucydides, *History of the Peloponnesian War* 1.22.

"untainted" data. For even if we could do what the various quests have found impossible, we would still be left with testimonial accounts from a writer whose sources also suffered from the frailty of memory. But this is not to say that all is lost, or that Bultmann was right, and we have to settle for the fact that Jesus lived and be done with it. On the contrary, Allison argues that the Gospels are more likely to be deeply true than superficially exact, in that there is an underlying current of discernible truth even if each recounted event cannot in themselves be accepted as historical.[84] Allison writes,

> The first-century traditions about Jesus are not an amorphous mess. On the contrary, certain themes, motifs, and rhetorical strategies recur again and again throughout the primary sources; and it must be in those themes and motifs and rhetorical strategies—which, taken together, leave some distinct impressions—if it is anywhere, that we will find memory.[85]

For example, Allison contends that we can confidently say that Jesus was an exorcist. This is not because there is one particular exorcism event that can be proved historically but because the literature as a whole has enough references to Jesus performing exorcisms to strongly suggest that Jesus was one.[86] So the value of testimony is not found, for Allison at least, in the individual telling of one particular story but in the weight of multiple "tellings." In other words, a singular testimony cannot be trusted but many testimonies that yield a consistent picture can be so trusted. He goes on to say:

> We are rightly more confident about the generalities than about the particulars. We are more sure that Jesus was a healer than that any account of him healing reflects a historical event, more sure that he was a prophet than that any one prophetic oracle goes back to him. When the evangelists generalize, in their editorial comments, that Jesus went about teaching and casting out demons, these are, notwithstanding the redactional agendas, the most reliable statements of all.[87]

In many ways this conclusion is the natural outcome from the failed attempts of the various quests to develop and apply specific criteria of

84. Allison, *Constructing Jesus*, 14.
85. Ibid., 15.
86. Ibid., 17.
87. Ibid., 19.

authenticity. If we cannot independently prove any particular event as true then all we have left is the general impression.

But I believe that this paradoxically serves to bolster Bauckham's point. The fact that we cannot get back "behind" the written testimony of the Gospels to prove or disprove their specific accounts means that we should, without evidence to the contrary, trust those accounts. Simply put, the authors of the Gospels did not believe that they were writing theological fiction in order to justify the memory of Jesus. On the contrary, they believed that they were representing the truth of what really happened when Jesus encountered sickness, disease and demons.[88] So if we are to say, as Allison does, that the general portrait of Jesus that is painted by the Gospels can be believed, then *contra* Allison, the specific elements that make up that portrait should also be believed. And this is precisely Bauckham's point. We can't choose to accept the overall testimony of the Gospels and yet deny individual elements on the basis that we cannot independently verify them. We either believe testimony or we don't.[89]

GOSPELS AS THEOLOGICAL TESTIMONY

Also of significant importance is how we should view the theological elements of the Gospel accounts vis-à-vis testimony. Bauckham contends that to define the Gospels as testimony is to insist that the theological elements of the Gospels be considered *as part of* that testimony and not merely later accretions of the Christian community. This is because testimony is constructed through the interaction of two elements, the "quasi-empirical" description (i.e., what actually happened) and the internal engagement that drives the witness's understanding (i.e., what the event means). Hence:

> Eyewitness testimony offers us insider knowledge from involved participants. It also offers us engaged interpretation, for in testimony fact and meaning coinhere, and witnesses who give testimony do so with the conviction of significance that requires to be told.[90]

88. A point that Allison makes in his own conclusion (*Constructing Jesus*, 458).

89. Bauckham laments the fact that in much of biblical scholarship, skepticism of testimony has somehow become equated with historical rigor. Such a view he believes to be "epistemological suicide" (Bauckham, *Jesus and the Eyewitnesses*, 506).

90. Bauckham here is again drawing from Ricoeur; Bauckham, *Jesus and the Eyewitnesses*, 505.

Faithful testimony is thus not accurate in its description of events alone but only insofar as it also attests to the event's meaning. In such a case an element of interpretive faith within the Gospel testimony does not prevent its history from being truthfully told, although what it undoubtedly does do is allow that history to be understood as the disclosure of God. Again, Bauckham does not view this as a theological imposition on the data of history but as a reflection of the faith that was evoked through the encounter with Jesus.

> Understanding the Gospels as testimony, we can recognize this theological meaning of the history not as an arbitrary imposition on the objective facts, but as the way the witnesses perceived the history, in an inextricable coinherence of observable event and perceptible meaning. Testimony is the category that enables us to read the Gospels in a properly historical way and a properly theological way. It is where history and theology meet.[91]

The coinherence of event and meaning within testimony is an appropriate reinforcement of our earlier point that meaning is present in the original participants' interpretation of the event and is not confined to later creations of individual historians. This understanding allows faith to stand alongside historical recollection without denying the historicity of the events expressed. Testimony thus fits in well with a critical-realist historiography because it does not attempt to hide the subjectivity of the witness from the objectivity of the event. Indeed, the objectivity of the event is found in the interaction between event and meaning, an engagement that takes place within the witness and expressed through subsequent testimony. The correlation here with Lonergan's idiom that objectivity is the fruit of authentic subjectivity is clear.

Of course, testimony in and of itself is not the be all and end all of the historical task for it requires to be critiqued and evaluated, just as, indeed, all other data must be. The value of testimony, however, is that it locates that coinherence between event and meaning in the eyewitnesses, which gives us a window into the inner reality of the event itself. To be sure there is a risk involved in trusting testimony, but in exceptional events it is the risk required by the quest for truth—both historical and theological.[92] If, indeed, the Gospels can be understood as testimony then they should be recognized for what they are—a fusion of event and meaning—an account of theologically understood history. No doubt Bauckham's thesis will

91. Ibid., 5–6.
92. Ibid., 506.

125

face continued challenges, but a reminder that history expressed through faith does not automatically relegate that history to the imagination is a welcome rejoinder to the historical skepticism rife in postmodern biblical scholarship.

Summary

I have been arguing that faith and history are not antithetical to each other and should in fact be seen to constructively relate. A critical realist historiography provides the foundation for this relationship because, in my view, it correctly takes into consideration the importance of authentic subjectivity in the coming to know of objective knowledge. One primary benefit is that it allows us to speak meaningfully of the past without giving constant caveats that we are merely speaking about our own constructed narrative. Past events can be scrutinized and we can discern something of their motivation, structure and overall impact without succumbing completely to the danger of self-narration. Historical accounts can therefore be judged; one narrative will be better or worse than another because there is something that can be known about the event that will provide a basis for such a judgment.

This methodology has certainty enabled a number of good studies on the historical Jesus to surface yet their impact on theology is, to the present time at least, barely discernible. Part of the reason for this is that many theologians are still stuck on either side of the strait wrestling with one or other of our epistemological monsters. Either they assume an empirical framework and are challenged by the apparent lack of objectivity in the historical process or they are so caught up in the whirlpool of subjectivity that history is regarded as more or less unknowable. The path between the two is no doubt a difficult one to travel, dependent as it is on the successful appropriation of the transcendental precepts.[93] However, difficulty

---

93. Adding to the difficulty is the increasing depth and complexity of the theological task that threatens to burden the theologian with the requirement to be omniscient and omni-competent. In *Method*, Lonergan attempts to overcome the problem by dividing the theological task into eight functional specialties that move the process from data to results. The purpose was to provide a clear method for theologians to maintain professionalism and concern for the entire process without succumbing to the need to competently master the whole range of theological operations. (On this see particularly, Lonergan, "An Interview with Fr. Bernard Lonergan, S.J.," 212–13.) The first four specialties constitute the positive or upward process from research, through interpretation, history and dialectics. The last four constitute the normative or downward movement from foundations, through doctrines, systematics and

does not necessitate avoidance and it is perhaps time that a critical realist presentation of the Jesus of history be allowed to influence the task of theology. I say this not only because there is something to be gained from an investigation into Jesus' own intention for his death but because a critical realist methodology enables theologians to approach history without the need to sideline their prior faith commitment. Conceptions of objectivity that require neutral observation are shown to have no viability and so the theologian does not need to pretend to come to history a-pathetically.

Bauckham's category of testimony is also of value because it acknowledges that both event and meaning coinhere and thus the Gospel witness does not have to be devoid of the interpretive element to be historically credible. So while the Gospels are undoubtedly religious testimony designed to inspire and strengthen the life of faith, they must be seen to refuse to reduce their accounts of Jesus' life to theological fiction. It is true that we must still read them with our eyes open for the evangelist's own perspective but as N. T. Wright points out, this "in no way cancels out the strong possibility that they are describing, in principle, events which actually took place."[94] If, as Wright goes on to say, we choose to reject this or that event, then we must do so on quite other grounds than that the evangelists were not neutral observers.[95] Bauckham would no doubt heartily agree. What critical realism and the category of testimony insist upon, is that objectivity does not require neutrality nor impartiality; what it requires is an understanding of authentic subjectivity in which the object is approached attentively, intelligently, reasonably and responsibly. This means that faith and history are not necessarily antithetical to each other

---

communication. The point at which the two phases meet is conversion, which is why according to Lonergan, it is conversion that proves to be the linchpin in authentic subjectivity. To detail this further will take us too far afield but for more information the reader is invited to consult Lonergan, *Method in Theology*, 125–48.

94. Wright, *New Testament and the People of God*, 91. This is in stark contrast with Crossan who dismisses any historical rooting of the passion in Christian memory. He remarks, "It seems to me most likely that those closest to Jesus knew almost nothing about the details of the [crucifixion]. They knew only that Jesus had been crucified, outside Jerusalem, at the time of Passover, and probably through some conjunction of imperial and sacerdotal authority" (Crossan, *The Cross That Spoke*, 405). Crossan does not explain why he thinks it "most likely," one can only assume that he understands it to be the case that the disciples who had followed Jesus around for such a long period of time suddenly had no interest in the events that took place. See the further critique in Brown, *The Death of the Messiah*, 15–16.

95. Wright, *New Testament and the People of God*, 91.

and an examination of history can be allowed to deepen faith just as faith, in turn, examines history.

We now come to a significant point of transition. Whereas the above discussion was aimed at defending the viability of both theology and history meeting in the historical Jesus, we must now face the question of what that meeting might actually entail. The crucial element of this discussion is the understanding that Jesus of Nazareth was *remembered in the way he transformed meaning*. It is the reality of pre-Easter faith that provides the evidence of this transformation, a reality that is usually marginalized because of its particular perspective yet it is this reality, I will argue, that provides a window into Jesus' self-understanding. For it is the *impact* that Jesus had on his disciples that reveals the world of meaning that Jesus constituted for his life, ministry and death. In what follows I will take my departure from a point made by James Dunn before delving into Bernard Lonergan's conception of constitutive meaning. What this line of argument will attempt to show is that Jesus' understanding of his death is revealed through the world of meaning that Jesus constituted for his life and ministry, a meaning evidenced in the faith response of the earliest disciples.

Impact, Meaning, and Intention

In *A New Perspective on Jesus*, James Dunn argues that the Jesus of history is only knowable within the context of the faith that he evoked.[96] To try and delve behind the Jesus of faith to a Jesus who did not engender faith is more or less an exercise in futility. The fact of the matter is that faith was present in the disciples' response to Jesus from the very first, which is why Dunn often points out that all we can access through the Gospels is Jesus as he is remembered and represented through faith.[97] We cannot

96. Dunn, *A New Perspective on Jesus*. This short book is a clarification on some of the methodological distinctions that underlie his much larger *Jesus Remembered*. The same point is made consistently in the larger work as well. See in particular pages 125–34.

97. Ibid., 16. It is therefore necessary that investigation into Jesus of Nazareth must somehow make sense of this faith, which in some respects gives a historian/theologian who begins with a faith perspective the upper hand over one who does otherwise. (See Lonergan, *Method in Theology*, 237–47.) This is not to say that historical investigation into Jesus is predominantly a theological task for that is not the case either. The question concerning the aims and intentions of Jesus is not formally theological insofar as one could easily ask the same question of any figure of history such as Julius Caesar or Socrates. However, we also need to recognize that in the case of Jesus of Nazareth the answers to those questions will always be theologically charged. As Ben Meyer

press back through the tradition to find a Jesus who did not make an impression or to find a Jesus who made a different (non-faith) impression. Such a man does not exist and while efforts to strip away faith from the tradition may aim at leaving behind a non-faith core, they in reality create an historical lacuna.[98] There is simply no faith-free or faith-neutral Jesus to be uncovered through historical research. Because of this, Dunn proposes a threefold thesis as to how we might investigate the Jesus of history: firstly, there is the recognition that Jesus made an impact on his disciples, an impact that was generative of faith; secondly, the initial formation of the oral tradition was based on the force of that impact and is therefore fundamentally expressive of it; and thirdly, the characteristic features of the Jesus tradition are reflective of the impression and impact that Jesus made on his first disciples. All three points are clearly interrelated and build upon the primary premise that Jesus impacted his disciples. This in itself is hardly contentious; the change in the life of the disciples is surely evident of the impact that Jesus had. As Dunn writes:

> The impact [of Jesus] was not a slight one—a memorable epigram, a good story, or an exciting event that caught their attention for a day or two and then sank below the surface of their everyday consciousness. His mission changed their lives. They became disciples. They gave up their jobs. They left their families. They committed themselves to him, to follow him. They were in his company day after day for many months. The impact of his mission turned their lives in a completely new direction; it lasted.[99]

The reality of this impact is evidenced by the faith that was generated in response to the encounter with Jesus. Now it is certainly a pre-Easter faith and one which had some way to go until it would be representative of later Christian belief, but even at this early stage, the element of faith evident in the actions of the disciples prevents us from postulating a Jesus who did not inspire faith.[100] Thus Dunn is very clear that we must start with the

phrased it, investigation into Jesus is an invitation to faith, hope and love just as an investigation into Caesar is an invitation to politics and an investigation into Socrates an invitation to wise ignorance (Meyer, *Critical Realism and the New Testament*, 153). One is naturally free to reject the invitation but that does not negate the genuineness of its offer.

98. Dunn, *New Perspective*, 29–30. Dunn is critical of the Quest's fixation with *criteria* for this very reason.

99. Ibid., 23.

100. Ibid., 26. See also Dunn, *Jesus Remembered*, 132.

historical *a priori* of a faith impact. However, the significance of this point is not that the disciples had faith, its significance lies in the fact that it is through their faith that we begin to see the Jesus of history.[101]

The second aspect concerns the use and development of the oral tradition in the transmission of the Gospels. Dunn elaborates on five features of oral transmission that he views as significant in supporting the reliability of the tradition, but the point of interest for us is found in his conclusion rather than in the detail. What Dunn is keen to stress is that the formation of the oral tradition did not arise from arbitrary reflections but was fundamentally constituted by the impact that Jesus had on his first disciples:

> What we have to imagine is that people like [Mary, Martha, Zacchaeus etc.] who had responded to Jesus and who had made some level of commitment to him would inevitably have expressed that commitment by meeting with others similarly impressed and committed. . . . That is to say, the impact made by Jesus would not be something that was only put into traditional form days, months, or years later. The impact would *include* the formation of the tradition to recall what had made that impact. In making its mark the impacting word or event *became* the tradition of that word or event.[102]

What Dunn is getting at here is that the tradition was constituted by the events and sayings that had significant impact on the disciples. As the proto-Christian community gathered together the topic of discussion would be the various events and sayings that each recalled having made a particular impact upon them. For this reason the tradition did not begin to coalesce post-Easter but was already being formed from the moment the first gatherings occurred. Indeed, Dunn concludes that the shape and character of the tradition was largely settled by the time it came to be penned in Mark and Q.[103] Hence what was subsequently selected and arranged into a unified written narrative was simply reflective of what was already considered constitutive of the Jesus tradition. This is why the Gospels cannot be characterized as a loose collection of arbitrary historical events concerning a first-century peasant Jew. The authors were not simply reminiscing but telling stories that were already considered significant within the Christian community. Therefore the Jesus the Gospels portray

101. Dunn, *Jesus Remembered*, 57, 129.

102. Dunn, *New Perspective*, 55, italics in original.

103. Ibid., 58.

is a Jesus who impacted the community, a Jesus who was specifically re-membered, discussed and proclaimed on the basis of that impact.

The third point is the most significant for us because it opens up a way in which we may approach the intention of Jesus concerning his life, ministry and death. The key feature is the desire to move historical investigation away from the distinctive Jesus and towards the characteristic Jesus. By this Dunn means that the Jesus we should be investigating is not a Jesus who is distinguished from his context, but a Jesus who characteristically fits within his context both as a Jew and as the founder of the Jesus tradition.[104] Hence if a particular saying or event is found to be characteristic of that tradition then the most obvious explanation for its presence within the tradition is that it is reflective of the impact that Jesus made on many of his followers. This is hardly surprising given the second point above, but its emphasis is appropriate because of what its reverse articulation implies. That is, the impression Jesus made on his disciples reflects the characteristic Jesus. And here Dunn is forthright, giving several examples from his larger *Jesus Remembered* as to exactly what that means for our understanding of the man from Galilee.[105]

One particular example is worth noting: the Jesus tradition is con-sistently presented as having a starting point in the mission of John the Baptist. Not only is this so in each of the four Gospels but it is also the case in Q, as well as in the *euangelion* presentations of Acts (1:21–22; 10:37). This multiple attestation suggests that the Jesus tradition always had a nar-rative shape with a particular starting point.[106] For Dunn,

> This in turn suggests that the gospel shape of the Jesus story actually reflects the shape both of Jesus' actual mission and of the earliest disciples' rememberings of it.[107]

This point is incredibly important not only because it implies that the Gos-pels intended actual historical events with a defined origin of significance,

---

104. Ibid., 68–69. Unsurprisingly, Dunn speaks favorably of Theissen and Winter's criteria of plausibility (Theissen and Winter, *The Quest for the Plausible Jesus*).

105. For example, the following are all considered authentic because they are re-flective of the impact Jesus made: Jesus' contention for the law; the Galilean setting of his parables; the future and present character of the kingdom of God; the Son of man sayings; the use of "amen" differently from the liturgical practice of the time, and there are, of course, others.

106. In this sense multiple attestation is not given as a criteria of authenticity but rather as a confirmation of what constitutes the characteristic Jesus.

107. Dunn, *New Perspective*, 76.

but also because it allows us to understand Jesus' mission *from within* the perspective of the disciples' impression. That is, the impact that Jesus made on his disciples functions to shape our knowledge of Jesus' mission. Dunn writes:

> And as we can tell the shape of the seal from the impression it makes on the page, so we can tell the shape of Jesus' mission from the indelible impression he left on the lives of his first disciples as attested by the teaching and memories of Jesus that they were already formulating during their initial discipleship.[108]

This direct correlation between impact and historical actuality is what enables Dunn to draw particular conclusions about the characteristic Jesus. Of course, exactly what can be known on the basis of impact remains a matter of considerable discussion, and Dunn certainly phrases his conclusions carefully. However, at this juncture the point to be made is that an emphasis on impact keeps the road open to Jesus' self-understanding. For in general the clearer the impression that Jesus made, the clearer the picture of Jesus becomes.[109] Caution must still be exercised and the temptation to conclude more than we ought rigorously resisted, but at least something can be said—and on this I concur with Dunn—it is the impact of Jesus that allows us to say it.

Our discussion, however, faces a challenge that Dunn did not address in detail, and that is to investigate the impact of Jesus for the express purpose of understanding his intentions in relation to the cross.[110] Now this should not be taken as a criticism of Dunn per se (his work is already long enough as it is), but as a simple recognition that understanding Jesus' intention for his death requires a more focused approach. This is perhaps why Dunn limits his conclusion to the characteristic expectations of suffering inherent in the motifs of both the righteous martyr and the Danielic son of man.[111] He contends that Jesus knew he would suffer in the same way the faithful and righteous had suffered before him, but stops short of concluding that such suffering was taken to be vicarious.[112] Even in his

108. Ibid., 30. Dunn here quotes Leander Keck: "The perception of Jesus that he catalyzed is part of who Jesus was" (Keck, *Who Is Jesus?*, 20). See also Jonge, *God's Final Envoy*, 4–5.

109. Dunn, *Jesus Remembered*, 616.

110. Dunn devotes 13 pages out of nearly 900 to the question of Jesus' intention for his death.

111. Dunn, *Jesus Remembered*, 806–7.

112. Although one can find in several places the suggestion that such overtones are

analysis of both Isaiah 53 and the paschal meal, Dunn is careful to avoid any overtones of atonement. The closest he comes to a theological interpretation is a brief acknowledgment of the possibility that Jesus saw his death as a covenantal sacrifice.[113] Yet after having made so much of what is revealed of Jesus' self-understanding through the impact he made on his disciples, it seems a little incongruous, for example, to now suggest that while Isaiah 53 was very influential in earliest Christian reflection, such use had little to do with Jesus himself.[114] Would it not be the case in Dunn's scheme that given the impact Jesus made, the symbols the early church appropriated would have been largely drawn from that impact?[115]

At this stage it is not my intention to challenge Dunn's conclusions but I am asking the question as to whether or not the impact that Jesus had on his followers is able to reveal any more about Jesus' own understanding of his death. It is possible, of course, that there simply is not enough evidence in the impact that Jesus made on his disciples to conclude that Jesus understood his death in an atoning way.[116] But from a theological perspective such a conclusion reinforces the existence of a significant gap between what the Church has proclaimed about Jesus' death and what we know of Jesus' self-understanding. It seems that Dunn has justified Marit Trelstad's contention that there are, in fact, two distinct crosses.[117]

However, I believe that this is not all that can be said, although if we are to make more sense of Jesus self-understanding in relation to his death it will be necessary to put forward a more focused description of impact than we have to this point. This conception would, in particular, take into consideration the impact engendered through the transformation of meaning. My contention is that something can be known of the self-understanding of Jesus through the way he transformed meaning, a transformation that challenges the existing world of meaning that constitutes the reality of those around him. As we might expect, the disciples' response to this challenge is evidence of the challenge and provides some insight into the new world of meaning that Jesus created for his death.

---

possible (e.g., 807, 809).

113. Dunn, *Jesus Remembered*, 817–18.

114. Ibid., 811. Dunn is, of course, agreeing with contemporary scholarship here although he is prepared to acknowledge that Jesus may have reflected on the servant passages. He contends, however, that we cannot draw this as a firm conclusion.

115. The point is not whether Jesus saw himself as the suffering servant, but whether such an attribution had anything to do with the impact Jesus made on his disciples.

116. As is, in fact, suggested. Dunn, *Jesus Remembered*, 817.

117. Trelstad, *Cross Examinations*, 3.

Exactly what I mean by this certainly requires further elaboration and we will do so in terms of Lonergan's description of constitutive meaning.

Impact as the Transformation of Meaning

It is a fundamental *a priori* that meaning is not simply given but is to a large extent intended. This is readily seen in language for example, because without intended meaning, speech is just articulated sound and words are merely a collection of characters. But when those particular sounds and collection of characters are given a certain meaning they become understandable and comprehensible by all those who share in that meaning. Thus in broad terms, meaning constitutes a level of reality in the human life, a reality that moves beyond the mere governance of language to our self-understanding and our place within the community. Indeed, the creation of community is itself an achievement of common meaning and therefore the point can be made that meaning is constitutive of our social reality and hence determinative of our actions.[118] But before we get too far ahead of ourselves we need to take our point of departure from Lonergan by dividing the known world into three. The first is described as the world of immediacy; the second as the world mediated by meaning; and the third as the world constituted by meaning.[119]

Unless one rejects all possible conceptions of realism in their entirety, there exists a world that is outside and beyond the individual. It is the world that can be known, and is there to be known, but it is a world that remains unchanged by being known. Lonergan defines this world as a world of immediacy: it is the world of immediate experience for it contains what there is to be known through empirical study, of what can be seen, heard, touched, tasted, smelt, and felt.[120] It is, in other words, the world of the senses, the world that is known by the infant, the world—as Lonergan was wont to put it—of the "empty head."[121] This last comment is not to denigrate that which can be known through the senses but is designed to draw attention to the world of immediacy's defining characteristic: that there is no "perceptible intrusion from insight or concept, reflection or

118. Lonergan, "Existenz and Aggiornamento," 245.

119. Ibid., 243–44. In addition one can consult the following: Lonergan, "Dimensions of Meaning"; Lonergan, "The Origins of Christian Realism," 240f; Lonergan, *Method in Theology*, 28, 76f.

120. Lonergan, *Philosophy of God, and Theology*, 1.

121. Lonergan, "Existenz and Aggiornamento," 243.

judgment, deliberation or choice."[122] The world of immediacy is simply given, its existence remains independent of the subject.

This is, however, not the only world we live in. Beyond the world we see, is the world that we mediate through meaning. To enter this world requires a cognitive act that moves us from what is known through sense experience to that which is known through the conjunction of experience, understanding and judgment. As Lonergan describes it:

> In entering the world mediated by meaning one moves out of one's immediate surroundings towards a world revealed through the memories of other men, through the common sense of community, through the pages of literature, through the labors of scholars, through the investigations of scientists, through the experience of saints, through the mediation of philosophers and theologians.[123]

This is clearly a much larger world for its content surpasses that of the immediate physical realm to include that which is intended by questions, organized by intelligence, described by language, and enriched by tradition.[124] In other words, the criteria of reality in the world mediated by meaning transcend that of immediate experience to include that which is known through both understanding and judgment.[125]

The addition of these cognitive activities is crucial because the world mediated by meaning is fundamentally insecure. It does not remain constant for it is continually subject to both positive and negative change. Besides fact there is fiction, besides truth there is error, besides honesty there is deceit. Yet contrary to the naive realist, this does not mean that the world mediated by meaning is just an abstraction, it remains real. But its criteria of reality are dependent upon the operations of both understanding and judgment.[126]

The third world that Lonergan describes is not only mediated but also *constituted* by meaning. This is certainly related to what we have

122. Ibid.

123. Lonergan, "Dimensions of Meaning," 253.

124. Lonergan, "The Origins of Christian Realism," 241.

125. The parallels here with critical realism are intentional. In fact, Lonergan disparagingly remarks that those who maintain that knowing arises from taking a good look are merely reaching back to an infantile solution of reducing everything to immediate experience. Such an endeavor "empties the world mediated by meaning of everything that is not given to immediate experience" (ibid.).

126. Ibid.

just discussed but also transcends it, since meaning is not just mediated but is, in fact, constituted through its acts. "Beyond the world we know about is the further world we make," writes Lonergan, a world constituted through the human act of intended meaning.[127] The example of language has already been given but language is not the only feature of human life that is constituted by meaning. Other examples abound including those of money, property, governments and marriages. None of these are mere products of nature nor do they exist outside the realm of human understanding.[128] In the world of immediacy, for example, a fifty dollar note is just a piece of colored paper, but in the world constituted by meaning it has a fiscal value and can be exchanged for material goods. Of course, the precise exchange value of the note is also subject to acts of meaning as anyone who has ever experienced the effects of inflation knows. Thus there is a radical difference between the data of natural science and the data of human science. In the natural sciences the data is taken and dealt with as given, but in the human sciences the data can only be verified in terms of corporate meaning.

The example that Lonergan gives is that of a court of law. A physicist, chemist, and engineer might enter a court of law but even after making all sorts of measurements and calculations there is no way they could declare that it was, in fact, a court of law. All they can conclude is that it is a building of certain dimensions with characteristics appropriate to its design.[129] What actually defines it as a court of law is the community intention that this particular building would be used for the express purpose of applying the rule of law to members of the community according to the accepted code of conduct. A code, we might add, which is itself constituted through a corporate act of meaning. Therefore what is meant through various acts of meaning becomes real for the community and is, in fact, constitutive of the community. The community is thus defined by the way it intends meaning:

> Community is not just an aggregate of individuals within a frontier, for that overlooks its formal constituent, which is common meaning. . . . Such common meaning is doubly constitutive. In each individual it is constitutive of the individual as a member

127. Lonergan, "Dimensions of Meaning," 253–54.

128. In contrast to the world of immediacy which requires no human institution for its existence. See Searle, *The Construction of Social Reality*, 2.

129. Lonergan, "Existenz and Aggiornamento," 244.

of the community. In the group of individuals it is constitutive of the community.[130]

Hence it should come as no surprise that the key feature of the world constituted by meaning is human agreement, a *collective intentionality* in which the boundaries and frameworks of authentic living are agreed upon.[131] Just why this is important for our discussion is something that will become clearer as we proceed.

The designation of "three worlds" is clearly of heuristic value only, for one does not physically move out of one world in order to move into another but simultaneously experiences all three.[132] However, the distinction is important because it emphasizes the constitutive role of meaning in the formation of the community. As individuals we live in a world of immediacy, but when we come into contact with others there is the potential to form a community to the extent that there is an accepted set of meanings and values that is able to be shared by those concerned.[133] Meaning is thus constitutive of the community and its content defines, controls and characterizes the community itself.

To help explain this further Lonergan defines four functions of meaning: the cognitive, constitutive, effective and communicative functions. These are again heuristic devices designed to make it easier to comprehend what is occurring when individuals and communities intend meaning. I have already mentioned that it is the cognitive act that moves one from the world of immediacy and into the world mediated by meaning. It is then the *cognitive* function of meaning that understands that what is meant by an individual or community is actually real for that individual or community. But for meaning to have a reality it must also be meant and that is the role of the *constitutive* function. Here the world of meaning that defines the community is intended and over time that common meaning is clarified, enriched and deepened to the extent that it becomes all-constituting for the members of the community. This results in what is known as "worldviews," which in the words of N. T. Wright are "the basic

---

130. Lonergan, *Method in Theology*, 356–57.

131. The term is from Searle, *The Construction of Reality*, 23–26.

132. One does not always operate in all three worlds since a dreamless sleep or unconsciousness removes one from the world mediated by meaning. However, insofar as we remain an aware and conscious entity we simultaneously move in all three worlds. There is an interesting discussion of consciousness in terms of Lonergan's ontology of meaning in Matustik, *Mediation of Deconstruction*, 51–73.

133. Lonergan, *Method in Theology*, 298. See also Lonergan, "Existenz and Aggiornamento," 245.

stuff of human existence, the lens through which the world is seen, the blueprint for how one should live in it, and above all the sense of identity and place which enables human beings to be what they are."[134] Worldviews are therefore the result of the constitutive function of meaning and become the filter through which humans organize reality.

An important point to draw from this is that individual members of the community are required to accept and conform to that reality if they wish to remain a member of the community. What this means is that authentic existence within a particular community is defined by the meaning corporately constituted and hence an individual who desires to remain an authentic member has their freedom limited by the accepted meanings of that community.[135] This does not necessarily imply that an individual is required or forced to accept the meaning constituted by the larger community, just that they must do so if they wish to remain an authentic member. Indeed, it is quite possible for the meaning constituted by the community to be challenged, debated and even its truth-value called into question.[136] Lonergan identifies that in constitutive meaning, there is an enforced moment of existential crisis for each individual who must decide for themselves whether or not they wish to accept and conform to the values corporately intended.[137]

This moment of existential crisis becomes even more important when an individual is faced with the third function, that of *effective* meaning. The effective function of meaning describes what occurs when meaning persuades or commands others to modify their own world mediated by meaning according to the new world of meaning encountering them. It is primarily an ethical challenge and one that requires judgment. It occurs most commonly when individuals change communities but can also arise from within communities as individuals rebel or challenge the status quo. The effective function is therefore both challenging and transformative, the latter inasmuch as its changes in value are accepted. It is clear then that it is the constitutive and effective functions of meaning that are of particular importance in comprehending the impact inherent within the transformation of meaning. Finally, the *communicative* function induces in the hearer some share in the cognitive, constitutive, or effective

134. Wright, *New Testament and the People of God*, 124.

135. Lonergan, "Existenz and Aggiornamento," 245.

136. See Wright, *New Testament and the People of God*, 125. Wright makes particular reference here to Meyer's drawing on Lonergan. Meyer, *The Aims of Jesus*, 17.

137. Lonergan, "Dimensions of Meaning," 264.

meaning of the speaker.[138] The point here is that common meaning is only common insofar as it is communicated to others.

So how do these designations help us proceed? There are two points of significance. Firstly, the necessity of human agreement, or collective intentionality for the existence of this world entails that it will always remain insecure, because there is nothing fixed or immutable about the reality we construct through the constitutive function of meaning.[139] Culturally and socially our worlds are always in transition, as Lonergan explains:

> The family, the state, the law, the economy are not fixed and immutable entities. They adapt to changing circumstances; they can be reconceived in the light of new ideas; they can be subjected to revolutionary change. But all such change involves change of meaning—a change of idea or concept, a change of judgment or evaluation, a change of the order or request.[140]

The fluidity of corporate intentionality means that a community constituted by meaning is never stagnant but is always in a state of motion. These corporate changes in meaning can be slow to be effected and communicated, though they can also be incredibly fast. The rate of change fundamentally depends on how quickly the changes in meaning are grasped and accepted as constitutive of the redefined community.

And herein lies our second point of significance. The effective function of meaning requires a corresponding response from the individual to judge and decide whether or not they wish to be part of the newly constituted community. For while judgments and decisions can be made collectively (i.e., mob mentality), this does not excuse each individual from within that community from necessarily judging for themselves. As it happens, more often than not this judgment will reinforce the collective intentionality and the individual will remain an authentic member of the community. But on occasion, the individual will make a judgment that goes against the collective intention of the majority and unauthenticity results.[141] What occurs then is rather predictable: either immediate social

138. Lonergan, *Method in Theology*, 356.

139. Lonergan, "Dimensions of Meaning," 255.

140. Lonergan, *Method in Theology*, 78.

141. With respect to the community and not necessarily oneself. Indeed one can grow in authenticity (particularly through conversion, see ibid., 52.), but it might be a growth that puts one at odds with the present community's constitutively defined meaning. Lonergan distinguishes between the two by using the terms minor and major authenticity. Minor authenticity has to do with the subject in respect to the

alienation for the dissenting individual or if they are able to garner suffi-cient support for their differing judgment, the community might split into factions. In such a case authentic existence will have been redefined for the segregated community and conflict between the two groups will entail. Eventually one side will gain the upper hand and will either reinforce the status quo through assimilation or exclusion, or a new reality will take shape on the basis of the opposing judgment. On a larger scale the same principle is seen in the change of national governments and ultimately the rise and fall of different cultural epochs.[142] Yet the cause of all this is, at root, the judgment of the individual.

Given the above, it should now be clear that impact occurs through the transformation of meaning in three recognizable stages. Firstly, in-dividuals are confronted with a challenge to their existing worldview, a challenge that is also an invitation to transformation. Secondly, individu-als must judge for themselves the value of the newly constituted meaning over against the common meaning previously accepted. Finally, the result-ing judgment will go one of two ways; individuals will either be impacted through the transformation of their constituted meaning and redefine what it means to live authentically, or they will reject the challenge and remain within their previously accepted world of meaning.

These three stages are readily applicable to the disciples' response to the challenge presented in the encounter with Jesus of Nazareth. As a Jew, there is little doubt that Jesus was brought up thoroughly enmeshed in the traditions of the Israelite people.[143] While it is true that the precise nature of Second Temple Judaism during the first-century is still a mat-ter of considerable debate, there are enough commonalities to allow us to define a "common meaning" that both unifies and distinguishes Juda-ism *as* Judaism. Works from Wright, Vermes and Sanders, to name just three, expend considerable energy in identifying the common meaning that constitutes authentic existence within the Israelite community.[144] The exceptional element about Jesus, of course, was that he did not remain within the accepted common meaning, redefining such sacred institutions

---

tradition that nourishes them and major authenticity has to do with the justification or condemnation of the tradition itself. Here I am using the term in the former sense, to describe an individual who is successfully conforming to the meaning constituted by their community (ibid., 79–80).

142. Lonergan, "Dimensions of Meaning," 256.

143. See the discussion for example in Evans, "Context, Family and Formation."

144. Wright, *New Testament and the People of God*, 215–44; Vermes, *Jesus in His Jewish Context*; Sanders, *Jesus and Judaism*.

as the Sabbath, ceremonial purity laws and, perhaps most provocatively, the temple. An encounter with Jesus therefore entailed a stark challenge to the prevailing common meaning and brought with it an invitation to re-constitute one's life according to a new criteria of authenticity.

The New Testament accounts certainly indicate that this change of meaning, this new reality that Jesus intended, had what could only be described as the expected results. On the one hand it caused Jesus to become alienated from the world of meaning accepted and enforced by the leadership of the existing community, and on the other hand a new community was formed that found an authentic existence in that reality. Hence we could say that Jesus was *creative* in his existential judgment about the larger world he intended to create despite the alienating consequences. His disciples were therefore *responsive* as they encountered the new judgment of Jesus and existentially judged for themselves the importance of this new reality. Those who remained opposed to this change in meaning were also reactive, but in a negative sense, remaining within their existing constituted world. It can therefore be said that Jesus had both a positive and negative impact on people as they encountered the meaning he constituted for his life and ministry. However, it is the positive impact that is of particular importance, for the transformation of authentic existence that was engendered in the disciples reflects the meaning that Jesus constituted.

This statement goes further than what Dunn was prepared to allow impact to disclose because it links meaning rather than just cause and effect. Dunn emphasized that the disciples were affected by the ministry of Jesus and that effect allows us to view Jesus' activities as the cause of that effect. But what motivated that cause remains more or less unknown. In constitutive meaning, however, the transformation engendered by the change of meaning constituted is evidence of the meaning that constituted the change. It still does not completely define self-understanding but it does allow a correlation to be drawn that is both meaningful and instructive. The question remains though as to how that meaning constituted by Jesus is known through the impact it made and the answer lies in the various ways that meaning is conveyed.

Carriers of Meaning

If meaning is to be transformative it must be appropriately carried and to this end Lonergan identifies five carriers of meaning: the intersubjective, artistic, symbolic, linguistic and incarnate carriers.[145] It will become

145. Lonergan, *Method in Theology*, 57–73.

clear that the first two are of limited applicability, but the remaining three are of considerable importance and will help define our approach in the following chapter. At present though, perhaps the best way to introduce these terms is to provide an immediate example of them in action, and an appropriate one is found in Anthony Kelly's discussion on the way meaning is conveyed within the Gospel of John. Given that the incarnation itself predicates that the Word (*Logos*) enters into the world of human meaning, we would expect to see the divine intention conveyed through the various carriers of meaning. And so we do:

> In the course of the Gospel narrative, the meaning of the Word incarnate is expressed *linguistically* as, say, a question (Jn 1:38), a conversation (Jn 1:47–51), a command (Jn 13:34), judgement (Jn 5:27) and prayer (Jn 17). It is carried in *symbols* such as light (Jn 8:12), bread (Jn 6:35), the good shepherd (Jn 10:11), the true vine (Jn 15:1), to name but some. It is *dramatically* instanced in works of healing as with the man born blind (Jn 9:13–39) and in *interpersonal* gestures such as Jesus washing the disciples' feet (Jn 13:1–11). It generates its own *art* as in the prologue to the Gospel and in the discerning arrangement of Gospel narrative itself. This complex of meaning culminates in the subversive glory of the Cross as it *incarnates* the meanings of all the words, gestures, relationships and symbols that anticipated it.[146]

Here I have highlighted the carriers of interest and Kelly provides us with good examples of them in action.[147] It is, however, the purpose of the next chapter to examine how these carriers convey the meaning that Jesus constituted for his death, for now we need merely to introduce their distinctive features.

Intersubjective Carrier

Lonergan begins with the intersubjective carrier because it is the one that arises most naturally and in many cases, spontaneously. The primary example is that of a smile, for it is not just the wilful synchronization of particular facial movements but the natural and spontaneous embodiment of a particular meaning conveyed from one to another. Of course, as we all know, the meaning of a smile is not fixed; it can certainly differ from

146. Kelly, "Dimensions of Meaning," 43–44.

147. I have highlighted six terms here, though there are only five carriers identified. The artistic and dramatic carriers can be categorized similarly.

context to context and just as there is the smile of recognition, friendship, joy, and contentment, there is the smile of sarcasm, belittlement and resignation. But whatever the precise meaning actually carried, the point is that the smile does in fact carry meaning, which is why "we do not go about the streets smiling at everyone we meet."[148]

However, given that this is Lonergan's primary example of the intersubjective carrier of meaning, one could be forgiven for wondering just how it could possibly be applicable to historical investigation. No doubt Jesus smiled from time to time as the occasion warranted, but surely there is no historical access to the meaning that motivated each of these acts. Indeed, in general, the meaning of such intersubjective acts is momentary and meaningful only to those involved.[149] The only time such meaning becomes available to others outside the initial context is when it is carried in additional ways, such as through linguistic or symbolic carriers, as is the case in the example given by Kelly—that of Jesus washing his disciples' feet. This is clearly an interpersonal gesture, an expression of intersubjective meaning, but it is only known to us because it was carried beyond its initial manifestation. Because of this, the intersubjective carrier will be of minimal use to us and our attention will be given more to the other carriers of meaning.

ARTISTIC CARRIER

Lonergan's single sentence, though rather dense definition of art as the "objectification of a purely experiential pattern," helps guide our understanding of art as a carrier of meaning.[150] Primarily it draws attention to the fact that art takes the form of either an abstract or concrete pattern, a pattern that is designed or created by the artist to be experienced. But art is never an arbitrary experience because the pattern is imbued by the artist with a meaning, and meaning intends something meant. Indeed, the artist consciously controls and expresses meaning through the elaboration of carefully determined aesthetic forms.[151] These forms, be they pictures, musical scores, dance, drama, or vocals, transports the subject into the

---

148. Lonergan, *Method in Theology*, 59.

149. Lonergan makes the observation that intersubjective meaning is not about some object, but reveals (or even betrays) the subject to another who immediately responds to the meaning carried (ibid., 60, 357).

150. Ibid., 61.

151. Tracy, *The Achievement of Bernard Lonergan*, 215.

world of the artist. It is in that world that the art then conveys the meaning with which it has been imbued and it is only from within that world that its meaning can be comprehended.

As David Tracy points out in regard to the art of poetry: through prose one may be able to describe and discuss the meaning of the poem but one cannot capture, let alone express, its "mysterious power."[152] To comprehend the power one must accept art's invitation to participate, to try it, and to see for oneself. We will return to this point in a later chapter when we come to discuss the relationship between Jesus' intended meaning and contemporary articulations of the cross' salvific significance. However, in a similar manner to the intersubjective carrier, the artistic carrier of meaning does not readily lend itself to historical investigation. It is present, in that the entirety of Jesus' actions can be understood as a dramatic work of art, but we are better served in the first instance by examining the other carriers of meaning.

Symbolic Carrier

A symbol, for Lonergan, has a very precise definition—it is an image of a real or imaginary object that evokes a feeling or is evoked by a feeling.[153] This element of affectivity is why symbols are able to explain that which is linguistically inexpressible (such as a deep seated feeling) or at least that which is difficult to describe logically. Indeed, symbols have "the power of recognizing and expressing what logical discourse abhors: the existence of internal tensions, incompatibilities, conflicts, struggles, destructions."[154] Symbols, in other words, are not bound by the laws of logic but are governed instead by the freedom of image and feeling. Thus, the revelatory power of a symbol is not found in its ability to describe comprehensibly

---

152. Ibid. Lonergan describes the same point this way: "Art criticism and art history are like the thermodynamic equations, which guide our control of heat but, of themselves, cannot make us feel warmer or cooler" (Lonergan, *Method in Theology*, 63).

153. Lonergan, *Method in Theology*, 64. It is recognized that Lonergan's understanding of symbol is underdeveloped and certainly lacks the rigor of, for example, Paul Ricoeur. Having said that, Neil Ormerod points out that Lonergan's position can be constructively developed (a task attempted most notably by Robert Doran), but the point here is not to evaluate Lonergan's depth of understanding but to point towards the importance of affectivity in the symbolic carrier of meaning. Any more than this takes us too far afield. Ormerod, *Method, Meaning and Revelation*, 128, n. 29 and n.32.

154. Lonergan, *Method in Theology*, 66.

or prove what it represents, but in its ability to convey something of the affect-laden depth of the individual.[155]

Indeed, it is the evocation of affectivity that successfully carries the symbolic meaning. This is a two stage process. Firstly as a symbol is invoked, either for the first time or for the first time in a new way, meaning is also constituted for it. The symbol is therefore not the meaning constituted, but the carrier of the meaning inasmuch as it successfully engenders the second stage; and that is, the symbol evokes an internal communication that yields an understanding that correlates with the intended meaning. The key affective element is found in the subject's response to the symbol, which Lonergan describes as an internal communication between mind and body, mind and heart, and heart and body.[156] Hence Lonergan writes,

> It is a meaning that has its proper context in the process of internal communication in which it occurs, and it is to that context with its associated images and feelings, memories and tendencies that the interpreter has to appeal if he would explain the symbol.[157]

Thus, according to Lonergan, the contextual meaning of a symbol is found in the affective response to the symbol, a response that is evidence of the symbol's impact. This is a significant point, for it implies that the common meaning of a symbol is reflective of the intention of the individual who first constituted that symbol's meaning.[158]

As Kelly demonstrates in the above example, Jesus made extensive use of symbols throughout his ministry and we find them particularly evident when it comes to the meaning that Jesus intended for his death. Some of the symbols were already available to him (such as the sign of Jonah and baptism), but Jesus also felt free to reappropriate other symbols for his own use (most notably the Paschal meal). The potential meaning that Jesus may have constituted for these symbols is something that we will address in the next chapter.

155. Matustik, *Mediation*, 107.

156. Lonergan, *Method in Theology*, 67.

157. Ibid.

158. This by no means implies that there is only one meaning to be found in a symbol. Symbols are inherently polyvalent and this is to be expected given their affective character. Yet there will be a primary meaning discernible within a given context because such symbolic use evokes a particular orientation and disposition (ibid., 65).

LINGUISTIC CARRIER

Meaning as it comes to be embodied through language is a complex field and much given to philosophic discourse. However, how language comes into being and the difficulties associated with how individual words obtain their collective intentionality is not of particular concern. What is of interest is the simple recognition that words are not unintelligible vocal sounds or incomprehensible markings on a piece of paper but have a common meaning that is agreed upon and intended by the community. Thus on the basis of common meaning, the individual can convey through the linguistic carrier a meaning that is expected to be understood by the hearers/readers.

In Lonergan's terms, this can occur as ordinary, technical or literary language. Ordinary language, the language of commonsense, is the "vehicle in which the human community conducts its collaboration in the day-to-day pursuit of the human good."[159] It is transient, it expresses the "thought of the moment at the moment, for the moment."[160] It has no particular lasting value other than to enable the day-to-day living of life. In contrast, technical language is the language of the specialist, it moves beyond the language of the ordinary to provide special meaning to words used in a particular context. Finally, meaning can be expressed through literary language. Here the language is permanent, learnt by heart or written out for all to read. The meaning conveyed then has permanent value for not only is it recorded and subsequently understood but also because it is particularly intended to be felt. It is language that intentionally desires to change the heart and therefore "floats" somewhere between logic and symbol.[161] This is undoubtedly where the Gospels need to be classified as the examples given by Kelly would suggest.

INCARNATE CARRIER

The final carrier of meaning to be discussed here is the incarnate carrier. By this Lonergan is implying that meaning can be incarnated through one's life and deeds. In other words, praxis conveys meaning. Hence incarnate meaning incorporates all the other carriers; it is at once intersubjective, artistic, symbolic and linguistic. This is why Lonergan writes that the

159. Ibid., 71.
160. Ibid.
161. Ibid., 72.

incarnate carrier can be characterized as, "the meaning of a person, of his way of life, of his words, or of his deeds."[162] Everything a person does in self-constitution can be seen in some way through the incarnate carrier. In relation then to the life of Jesus, Kelly makes the point that all the meanings that were identified as previously carried now culminate in the subversive glory of the cross, since it is the cross that primarily incarnates the meanings that foreshadowed it. This is certainly a theological statement, but it is one based on the understanding of how meaning is constituted and carried throughout one's life. The point is that Jesus did, in fact, constitute meaning for his life and this meaning finds its clearest expression in the time of his death when all that Jesus intended is incarnated at one climatic moment.

This completes our brief introduction to the five carriers of meaning that Lonergan identifies in *Method in Theology*.[163] This list is by no means exhaustive (and Lonergan never claims as much) but it does suffice to demonstrate the ways in which meaning can be embodied, a division that is far more nuanced than that which usually accompanies theological discourse.[164] The reason for their inclusion here was to again highlight the viability of identifying the meaning that was constituted by Jesus for the new world of meaning he created—a world of meaning that was constituted for Jesus' entire ministry including that of his approaching death. Therefore to make the claim that Jesus failed to imbue his death with meaning is to deny the constitutive function of meaning and its role in the formation of community.

Indeed, the very existence of the proto-Christian community is evidence itself that there was a meaning constituted, a meaning that could be existentially judged and appropriated. Hence, in the next chapter, I will argue that Jesus did in fact create meaning for his death, a meaning that stemmed from, but enlarged upon, the corporate intentionality that constructed the community's expectation. This challenge to the community's accepted world of meaning required the disciples to respond existentially. Again, their response to that challenge is evidence of the meaning that was constituted by Jesus and this must surely give theological impetus to the following questions: what world of meaning did Jesus constitute for his

162. Ibid., 73.

163. Other carriers of meaning can be identified, such as for example, the historical carrier. Yet Lonergan would no doubt include these within the incarnate carrier, which does function as a kind of "catch-all" carrier of meaning. In any case, the five carriers identified are sufficiently specialized to enable the point to be made.

164. Ormerod, *Method, Meaning and Revelation*, 93.

death and how should that meaning impact our approach to the doctrine of the atonement?

Collecting the Threads

I ended the last chapter with a quote from Ben Meyer who stated that Jesus did not aim to be repudiated and killed, but purposely charged with meaning his being repudiated and killed. This chapter has been a defense of theology's right to engage with history in the determination of that meaning. Initially the point was made that atonement theology tends to focus more on the cross' divine soteriological narrative than on the particular meaning with which Jesus may have imbued it. Certainly, given the Gethsemane accounts and such kenotic passages as Philippians 2:5–12, traditional interpretations are right to emphasize the obedience of Jesus of Nazareth in going to the cross. Yet to limit Jesus' understanding of his death to the necessity of obedience is to neglect the meaning that Jesus himself constituted for his life and ministry. Without a doubt there is a divine narrative to be told, but it is a narrative that has its telling *in the praxis* of Jesus of Nazareth and not apart from it.

This is why I have argued so strongly for the theological right to engage in matters of history. The theological story begins with Jesus and thus the kerygma that proclaims him is inextricably linked to the particular exigencies of those days. For this reason the doctrine of the atonement must incorporate these historical particulars or risk dividing the cross into historical and theological components as has so often been the case. But again such a distinction, even if it is only heuristic, fails to do justice to the life of Jesus and to the ministry he so boldly incarnated. As J. A. T. Robinson put so well, the self-knowledge of Jesus is the indispensable heart of theology and it cannot remain within some kind of enforced theological exclusion zone. Quite simply, the meaning that Jesus constituted for his life and ministry is an integral element of theology, not just for today but from the very beginning of Christian reflection.

If this is indeed true, then it makes no sense to postulate that reflection on Jesus' death, which necessarily began post-Easter, occurred in total isolation from the meaning that Jesus constituted. On the contrary, Dunn's emphasis on the role and importance of impact demonstrates that what Jesus said and did immediately began to have a bearing on the lives of the disciples. This is clearly comprehensible when impact is viewed as the transformation of meaning, for then the effective function of meaning challenges individuals to transform their world of meaning to match the world being constituted by the one making the impact. Hence a recognizable change in the disciples' world of meaning is reflective of the meaning constituted by Jesus. The result of this is that there is no *a priori* reason to conclude that such an impact was devoid of any reference to the approaching death of Jesus. We will need to discuss this further in the next chapter, but if it can be shown that Jesus created meaning for his death, and that meaning impacted the disciples before his death (whether they initially understood what Jesus was on about is, of course, another matter), then the post-Easter reflections are more than likely going to take the shape of that initial impact.

Moreover, this means that the Gospels' theological perspectives do not automatically negate the historical accuracy of their narratives. Indeed, if Bauckham's emphasis on testimony is accepted, then the very fact that event and meaning coinhere in the Gospels is precisely what makes their accounts all the more trustworthy. But even if Bauckham is perhaps overly optimistic, Dunn's emphasis on the characteristic Jesus being reflected in the Gospels as the result of the impact that Jesus made, does give further credence to the accounts themselves. What this allows us to conclude is that the Gospels' testimony to the impact that Jesus made contains sufficient evidence to allow us to approach the question as to what meaning Jesus might have actually constituted for his life and impending death. As to what that meaning might entail is the subject of the next chapter.

4

The Meaning of Jesus' Death

One of the great mistakes of Christian theology has been our attempt to understand the death and resurrection of Jesus apart from his life.[1]

—Stephen Patterson

IN THE PREVIOUS CHAPTER I ARGUED FOR THE VIABILITY OF A THEOLOGI-cal engagement with history for the purpose of informing our theology of the atonement with the historical intention of Jesus of Nazareth. The task now is to discuss what can be known of the world of meaning that Jesus constituted for his death and then, in the next chapter, to bring these results to bear on our understanding of Christian atonement. Easy enough perhaps to state, a rather more difficult task in practice. Indeed, the endeavor threatens to become all-consuming; John Meier's four-volume work is ample evidence of the sheer amount of data that can be brought to bear on matters concerning the Jesus of history.[2] Of course, the current project's limitations make it altogether impossible for us to engage at such a level, but happily there is no need for us to do so. The focus here is deliberately theological, that is, we are not attempting to paint a new portrait of the historical Jesus but to utilize the results of existing research to contribute to our understanding of the atonement. But this in itself raises a further problem because scholarship's answer to the question of Jesus' own intention is at least as diverse as atonement theology itself. It is, therefore, necessary to give some brief comment as to the logic behind the following selection of material.

The determination of what research to draw upon was made on the basis of the conclusions reached at the end of the previous chapter. There I

---

1. Patterson, *Beyond the Passion*, 2.
2. Meier, *A Marginal Jew*.

argued that Jesus constituted a world of meaning for his life and ministry and that meaning was reflected in the impact it made upon the disciples. Furthermore, there is no immediate consideration that prevents that newly constituted world of meaning from also including a coherent narrative for Jesus' death, and so we can justifiably ask whether that narrative had a soteriological element. It is this assertion that actually removes a large part of historical Jesus scholarship from the table, since very few works include a significant discussion on Jesus' intention for his death,[3] and even those that do are not all that inclined to relate that intention to the understanding of the early church.[4]

Part of the problem has been the past skepticism within scholarship that equates any correlation between the early church and Jesus as historically untenable. The criteria of double dissimilarity practically guaranteed a Jesus who could not be associated with the faith of the early church, so it made very little sense to actively pursue such directions. It is only relatively recently that the criteria of plausibility (Theissen and Winter) and of double similarity (Wright) have begun to make an impact on scholarship, opening the way for the re-tabling of the question of Jesus' self-understanding. Works such as McKnight's *Jesus and His Death* and Bauckham's *Jesus and the Eyewitnesses* are examples of the revitalization of this question within scholarship.[5]

But significant in the context of our previous discussion is the fact that the works which do attempt to integrate Jesus' understanding of his death within his overall mission are penned by those who embrace a critical realist historiography. As I argued earlier, this method of doing history opens the door to the question of Jesus' self-understanding in ways other methodologies cannot and therefore it should come as no surprise that the works which will predominate here are those of McKnight, Wright, Dunn and Meyer.[6] All of these authors utilize a critical realist historiography

---

3. Many works on the historical Jesus simply fail to address the question. By way of example see Crossan, *The Historical Jesus*; Horsley, *Jesus and the Spiral of Violence*. A few years later Horsley evaluated the state of current research on the topic of Jesus' death for *New Testament Tools and Studies*. Once again we look in vain for any discussion as to what Jesus thought his death might achieve. Horsley, "The Death of Jesus."

4. Aside from those mentioned herein, see Balla, "What did Jesus Think?," 239–58; Stuhlmacher, *Jesus of Nazareth*, 49–54; Theissen and Mertz, *The Historical Jesus*, 429–30.

5. McKnight, *Jesus and His Death*; Bauckham, *Jesus and the Eyewitnesses*.

6. McKnight, *Jesus and His Death*; Wright, *Jesus and the Victory of God*; Dunn, *Jesus Remembered*; Meyer, *The Aims of Jesus*.

in their attempt to place Jesus' intention for his death within the context of his overall mission and are therefore of primary importance in asking whether Jesus did, in fact, imbue his death with soteriological meaning.

However, the following does not take the form of a comparative analysis, for while such a discussion may be interesting, it is not sufficiently focused on the world of meaning that Jesus constituted for his death. To address this question we need to demonstrate how that constituted meaning is conveyed through the various carriers of meaning. For it is only once meaning is carried that it can be effective and it is the effective function of meaning that reveals the constituted world. Hence, while we will utilize the various insights of the above authors, our discussion will be structured on the basis of the carriers of meaning.

Now as I argued in the last chapter, not all the carriers are particularly open to historical investigation and I suggested that it was the incarnate, linguistic and symbolic carriers that held the most applicability.[7] Our discussion will therefore be divided into these three categories with a constant focus directed towards what meaning Jesus may have conveyed through these carriers in regard to his death. But before embarking on the discussion proper, there is one final point that needs to be addressed.

Did Jesus Anticipate a Premature Death?

The expectation that Jesus did actually constitute meaning for his death requires that Jesus also anticipated that he would die prematurely and therefore had the time to constitute meaning for it. This point is not all that contentious although there continues to be those who suggest that Jesus was more or less unprepared for the possibility of an early death.[8] But

7. It is true that the artistic carrier can be seen in such areas as liturgy and the Last Supper is an obvious candidate for its expression. But given the symbolic nature of the Last Supper and the fact that at the time of Jesus the Christian meal had not yet been imbued with liturgical meaning (such meaning is developed through repetition), we will examine the meaning of the meal through an analysis of the symbolic carrier.

8. Paula Fredriksen seems to suggest this when she postulates that Jesus only became aware of the possibility of a premature death in the last week of his life as he sensed that he had "lost control of the situation," the cause of his trouble being the over-enthusiastic crowds whose messianic hope had gotten out of hand, their heightened excitement threatening to spark incendiary action in the heart of the city thereby prompting his quick arrest. For Fredriksen, Jesus at no point charges his death with soteriological meaning, he merely takes the opportunity at the Last Supper to reinforce to his disciples that despite the unexpected turn of events, the truth about the coming of the kingdom stands. To her credit, Fredriksen makes an excellent historical case for

it seems to me that regardless of how one understands Jesus' mission, the fact that his forerunner John the Baptist was executed would have alerted Jesus to the possibility that he too could suffer the same fate. Indeed, the close parallels between John's and Jesus' ministries lead scholars to comment that fundamentally, Jesus' own perception of his life and death was anchored in the experience of his mentor.[9] This being the case, John's death would inevitably result in Jesus' own reflections, even if to that point in time it was not something he had consciously dwelt upon.

If we then throw into the mix the historically defensible position that Jesus saw himself operating within the prophetic tradition, it becomes even more probable that an early death was to be expected.[10] Certainly, by the time of Jesus, the idea that the prophets suffered to the point of death was common place, evidenced not just by the many logia in the New Testament but by the deep roots going back through the biblical tradition.[11] Furthermore, Jesus' prophetic action in the Temple could not have been undertaken without some realization that he was "throwing down a gauntlet to the Temple authorities," and he would have been extraordinarily naïve if he had not anticipated the likely results of such an action.[12]

I would point out that none of this relies upon the hotly contested passion predictions (on which see below), but is instead drawn from natural inferences that are fully comprehensible within the first century Jewish context. There is, of course, considerably more that can be argued on this point but further defense will not be given here.[13] The point to be made is that if it is historically probable that Jesus did in fact predict his death prior

---

why Jesus was executed and particularly crucified (i.e., to visually quell the excitement of the crowd), but her reconstruction does struggle to adequately explain just why Jesus remained in Jerusalem in the first place, especially given the danger he was in (Fredriksen, *Jesus of Nazareth*, 252).

9. McKnight, *Jesus and His Death*, 132; Wright, *Jesus and the Victory of God*, 579; Meier, *A Marginal Jew*, 2:175–76; Brown, *Death of the Messiah*, 2:1486.

10. See Matt 23:29–36; Mark 12:1–12; Luke 9:59; 12:27–31; 12:49–50. Scholarship is relatively settled on this point. Dunn, *Jesus Remembered*, 797 and citations within.

11. In the New Testament: Matt 5:11–12/Luke 6:22–23; Matt 23:29–36/Luke 11:47–51; Matt 23:37/Luke 13:33–34; Acts 7:52. In the Hebrew Scriptures: 2 Chr 36:15f; Neh 9:26; Jer 2:30; 26:20–23; 38:4–6; 1 Kgs 19:10; 22:8; Ezra 9:10f. On the prophetic fate see Dunn, *Jesus Remembered*, 417f, 797.

12. Dunn, *Jesus Remembered*, 798.

13. For example there is evidence that Jesus expected his presence with the disciples to be temporary (Mark 2:19–20; 10:38; 14:3–9) and that he had a strong sense of destiny. See Keck, *Who Is Jesus?*, 117–18. McKnight also provides extensive discussion on this point. McKnight, *Jesus and His Death*, 105–56.

to that last week in Jerusalem (and I certainly believe it is), then there is no reason why he could not have also created meaning for that death in line with his overall mission.

We begin then, with the incarnate carrier because the context and framework of Jesus' own mission is fundamentally crucial to the determination of the meaning that was constituted. So what did Jesus think he was doing? What meaning was being embodied through his life and death? The answer has to do, of course, with the establishment of the kingdom of God and we must not forget that Jesus died in the context of this mission. As always the debate that surrounds us is complex, but it is nonetheless a vital waypoint on our journey to the cross.

Jesus and the Kingdom: The Incarnate Carrier

There are two facts about Jesus that command universal assent among scholars. One is that he was crucified, the other is that he was baptized by John the Baptist.[14] The importance of John's baptism for Jesus' understanding of his own mission cannot really be over emphasized. Prior to that day at the Jordan, Jesus was an unknown carpenter from an obscure town in Galilee. After his baptism Jesus begins a public ministry, first as disciple of John and then subsequently in his own right.[15] This transition, centered as it is on a purificatory water rite,[16] marks not only Jesus' identification with the sinful Jewish people,[17] but also his identification with the message of John the Baptist.[18] Indeed, Matthew records that Jesus' initial preaching after his baptism mirrored exactly that of John's ("Repent, for the kingdom of heaven is near," Matt 3:2 = Matt 4:17), a correlation that

14. Dunn, *Jesus Remembered*, 339.

15. While the theophany at Jesus' baptism is understood by most scholars to be a Christian "midrash," there is no reason historically to deny that Jesus received his calling or at least a confirmation of his calling at his baptism. Wright, *Jesus*, 537; Dunn, *Jesus Remembered*, 376.

16. On the nature of the rite see the comprehensive discussion in Meier, *A Marginal Jew*, 2:49–53.

17. Meyer makes an excellent case for understanding baptism as an identifying marker for those who were preparing themselves for the coming judgment of God (*The Aims of Jesus*, 116–19).

18. Wright comments that "Jesus regarded his ministry as in continuity with, and bringing to a climax, the work of the great prophets of the Old Testament, culminating in John the Baptist, whose initiative he had used as his launching-pad" (Wright, *Jesus and the Victory of God*, 167. See also: Meier, *A Marginal Jew*, 2:109; Fredriksen, *Jesus of Nazareth*, 197; Meyer, *The Aims of Jesus*, 123.

provides a recognizable and appropriate starting point. But even then, the sheer amount of literature concerning the kingdom of God requires that our approach be selective, and we will therefore limit the discussion to five particular elements that help frame the constituted world of meaning that Jesus created for his death. We begin with the expectation that the coming of the kingdom brings with it eschatological judgment.

Eschatological Judgment

In John's preaching the coming of the kingdom is strongly associated with eschatological judgment. It is a coming day of "wrath" (Luke 3:7) in which the unrepentant would be separated from the righteous and doomed to "unquenchable fire" (Luke 3:17). In fact, the axe was already at the base of the tree and unless the tree began to produce fruit in keeping with repentance it would be cut down and thrown into the fire (Luke 3:9). Schweitzer famously interpreted this eschatological vision as an expectation that the end of the world was near, but recent scholarship contends that such a view is an inadequate reflection of the Jewish understanding.

There is actually very little in the relevant literature that suggests that the coming day of judgment would involve the end of the space-time universe. Accounts of the sun, moon and stars being shaken and darkened are meant to imply that something cataclysmic and life-changing would occur, but Wright argues strongly that such events were expected to occur *within* history and did not actually signal the end of history.[19] Indeed, John's dire call to repentance sounds an appropriate tone of urgency but his reference to raising up other children to Abraham hardly envisages the end of the Jewish line and in Luke, John is clearly remembered to have this-worldly concerns (Luke 3:10–14). Hence, Dunn concludes that "John's warning [of impending judgment] could equally have been to the current generation, with the implication that it was a final *warning* for them, rather than a warning of universal and temporal *finality*."[20] What we need to observe then, is that the heralding of eschatological judgment does not automatically require the negation of ongoing existence. It proclaims that something climactic, and undoubtedly life-changing is about to happen, but whatever is about to occur will take place *within* the current space-time continuum.

---

19. Wright, *New Testament and the People of God*, 208, 285–86. Wright, *Jesus and the Victory of God*, 208–9.

20. Dunn, *Jesus Remembered*, 365, emphasis original.

And for John, what was about to occur would be directed at Israel herself. The imagery he used reflects the judgments prophesied by some of Israel's greatest prophets (Isa 10:33–34; Ezek 31; Dan 4), but whereas the prophets of old directed their invective at Israel's enemies, John took direct aim at the covenant nation (Luke 3:8).[21] Israel had once again failed to be the "light to the nations" that God had called them to be (Isa 49:6) and for John, even their Abrahamic lineage would not be able to protect them from the kingdom's fiery coming. The question that arises then, is how is that judgment to be realized? Did John expect fire to fall from the sky to consume the unrepentant or was the prophesied judgment to be effected in another way altogether? The Gospels, of course, do not outline what John thought, but they hardly needed to:

> Just as the wrath of YHWH, within the Hebrew scriptures, consisted as often as not of military conquest and consequent social disaster, so we may assume that John's hearers would have heard, and John would have intended, a reference to a great national disaster, to be interpreted as the judgment of the covenant god.[22]

In other words, warnings of divine judgment are to be taken in a thoroughly historical sense. Thus, John's pronouncement was not made in the expectation that God was about to suddenly strike the unrepentant dead, his warning was directed to the nation because her current sinfulness and unrepentant attitude was propelling her headlong towards national disaster. A disaster like that of the Babylonian exile of old, which would be rightly interpreted as the judgment of God against the nation.[23]

Hence, it is quite likely that when John pronounced the coming of imminent judgment the people at the Jordan would have looked over their shoulder at the might of Rome and began to wonder just what might be around the corner. This is a crucial point for it helps locate Jesus' understanding of divine judgment in terms of what might occur historically. That is, when Jesus followed John the Baptist in pronouncing the coming of eschatological judgment he was not referring to some future post-mortem judgment as is prophesied in later Christian texts (i.e., Rev 20:11–15).

21. Meyer, *The Aims of Jesus*, 117–18.

22. Wright, *Jesus and the Victory of God*, 326. See for example: Jos 2:14; 2 Chr 36:16f; Dan 9:16; Isa 40:1–2. It is very interesting to compare such verses with Rom 1:18f. See the discussion in Schwager, *Jesus in the Drama of Salvation*, 164–65.

23. In this regard we can also note that the Maccabean tradition demonstrates that national suffering was readily experienced and interpreted as divine judgment. E.g., 2 Macc 7:37–38.

Jesus' warnings were about a coming national disaster that would be effected historically and within this generation (Matt 24:34; Mark 13:30; Luke 11:51).[24] The contemporary nature of the warning cannot be over-emphasized. However, if it is true that divine judgment was a well-known theme in Jewish literature, so too was the theme of divine restoration. And if the coming of the kingdom would dramatically judge the nation, would it not also restore it?

The Coming of the Kingdom

The answer is an expected "yes," though there is little doubt that Jesus' expectation proved to differ markedly from that of his contemporaries.[25] But as members of the nation of Israel they at least shared the same starting point. The Babylonian exile might be over and the daily sacrifices may once again be taking place in Herod's Temple but still Israel as a nation had yet to be restored in the way long hoped. Despite brief periods of self-determination, Rome was most definitely her current master and this situation made a mockery of Israel's claim to be the covenant people of God. At some point, God would surely have to act against her oppressors if the covenantal promises were to be fulfilled. A day was therefore coming in which Israel would be restored to her rightful place on the center of the world's stage.

This was not necessarily a vain hope. There was a long tradition of prophetic announcement in which it was heralded that God would act to preserve both the covenant and election of Israel. The prophets, though, were convinced that this action would not return Israel to the old ways, because God was undertaking something new (i.e., Jer 31:31–34), something ultimately eschatological.[26] This new action was, of course, expressed in terms of the old saving traditions, but there was nevertheless a growing expectation that the time would soon come when God would

24. Wright, *Jesus and the Victory of God*, 322–23.

25. Of course his contemporaries also had competing visions, which is one of the reasons why scholars refer to the existence of Second-Temple "Judaisms" rather than a homogenous "Judaism." Nevertheless, Wright argues that there remains a standard Jewish story common to all. See for example: Wright, *New Testament and the People of God*, 145–214.

26. "The eschatological phenomenon is . . . the extremely revolutionary fact that the prophets saw Jahweh approaching Israel with a new action which made the old saving institutions increasingly invalid since from then on life or death for Israel was determined by this future event" (Rad, *Old Testament Theology*, 2:118).

dramatically inaugurate a new phase of Israel's story.[27] The question is what exactly would that new phase look like? Scholarship continues to debate the extent of the narrative but Wright strongly argues that it takes a threefold structure, which when viewed together would point towards the climax of Israel's story, the fulfilment of her covenantal promise. Again, the three elements are not without their controversy, but Wright contends that "return from exile," "the defeat of evil," and the "return of YHWH to Zion," essentially reflect the eschatological hope of the first-century Jew.[28] Moreover, this threefold hope is exactly what would be understood by the phrase, *kingdom of God*:

> We must stress, again, that this message [about the kingdom] is part of a story, and only makes sense as such. And there is only one story that will do. Israel would at last 'return from exile'; evil would be defeated; YHWH would at last return to 'visit' his people. Anyone wishing to evoke and affirm all this at once, in first-century Palestine, could not have chosen a more appropriate and ready-made slogan than 'kingdom of god'.[29]

27. "Hosea foretells a new entry into the land, for Isaiah a new David and a new Zion, for Jeremiah a new covenant, and Deutero-Isaiah a new Exodus" (ibid., 2:117). The key element here is that the act of Yahweh would be "new," previously unseen and unknown in the history of the covenantal relationship. For the Psalmist's call see Psalms 74, 79, and esp. 137.

28. Dunn criticizes Wright for being too narrow in his threefold analysis listing instead seven motifs that were characteristic of the Jewish expectation. To be fair to Wright, it seems to me that many of those found in Dunn's list could be folded into one of his three categories. Dunn, *Jesus Remembered*, 475.

29. Wright, *Jesus and the Victory of God*, 227, c.f. 204, 206. Criticism is often brought to bear on Wright's use of the "return from exile" motif, and perhaps rightly so, for there is no *clear* evidence in the literature that the Jews who lived in Palestine during the first half of the first-century believed that they were *still* in exile. (See particularly Dunn, *Jesus Remembered*, 473f.). So too, Wright's use of this motif as a grid through which to view all the parables and sayings of Jesus appears from time to time to be a little forced. However, having said this, it is true that the "return from exile" motif does have an important place in the eschatological restoration movement as Wright's ample references attest. Craig Evans agrees that there is a strong sense of ongoing bondage even within geographical Israel in which "return from exile" would be seen as an appropriate liberating motif. In my view Wright was correct to draw our attention to the eschatological hope of a renewed Israel through the exilic metaphor but I do question whether everything that Jesus' said or did has to be viewed so strictly through such a grid. In other words, I accept Wright's threefold taxonomy of the Jewish eschatological hope but am wary of its over reading. See the further discussion in Evans, "Jesus and the Continuing Exile of Israel"; Bryan, *Jesus and Israel's Traditions*, 12–20; Snodgrass, "Reading and Overreading the Parables."

Thus, to invoke the phrase "kingdom of God" was to call Israel's attention to the coming salvific work of God, who would at last fulfil the covenantal promises, vindicating Israel and defeating her enemies. In Wright's view, this is the eschatological world of meaning constituted by the Jewish community, a world of meaning that longs not just for political and social justice but for the theological fulfilment of her covenantal relationship. Hence, when John the Baptist appeared on the banks of the Jordan summoning people to repentance in preparation for the coming of the kingdom, one can sense the excitement that was generated. If the kingdom of God is in fact near, then God is about to return, evil will be judged and Israel will finally be restored. The covenantal promise will at last be fulfilled and God's promised new age would begin. That at least would be the corporate Jewish hope; the question is to what extent Jesus appropriated the same understanding.

The Kingdom Has Come

Immediately it must be said that Jesus' acceptance of John's baptism requires us to acknowledge that Jesus also accepted John's basic eschatological outlook.[30] So like John, Jesus expected imminent judgment to befall Israel and like John he called upon the nation to repent. But as Jesus' ministry progressed, it became increasingly clear that he also expected God to act in such a way that Israel would be restored to its true calling. There is, in other words, a strong sense of restoration in Jesus' actions and preaching but it must be said that it would be a restoration that fundamentally subverted the standard Jewish expectations. At the risk of simplicity we can highlight two particular themes.

Firstly, in Jesus' preaching there is no escaping the fact that the kingdom of God is *already partially realized*. Somehow, and despite the fact that Israel's historical situation had not changed, the kingdom of God was already breaking into the world even as it remained, at the same time, a future hope.[31] We see this clearly in the third Gospel because here Jesus

---

30. Meier, *A Marginal Jew*, 2:31–32; Meyer, *The Aims of Jesus*, 123. Even Crossan accepts this point although he argues, of course, that Jesus later changed his mind. Crossan, *The Historical Jesus*, 259.

31. Hence the difficulty in coming to terms with Jesus' expectation of national judgment when already national restoration was occurring. Bryan, *Jesus' and Israel's Traditions*, 3–6. Yet it is clear that neither aspect can be removed from Jesus' understanding. The tradition is consistent in its emphasis that Jesus spoke about the kingdom in future terms (Mark 1:15; 13:1–37; 14:25; Matt 4:17; 5:3–6; 6:10; Luke 6:20–23;

begins his ministry with the claim that the time of redemption is now (Luke 4:21); the coming of the kingdom *is* the great divine invitation to the miracle of salvation and it is already being made manifest in and through the ministry of Jesus.[32] This is the essential difference between Jesus and John. Whereas both John and Jesus proclaimed that God's kingdom was imminent, Jesus also insisted to John's disciples that the kingdom was already here (Luke 7:22).[33] The new time of salvation was already effective—the blind see, the lame walk, the deaf hear and the dead are raised. This is not just a future hope but a present reality; through the ministry of Jesus the restoration of Israel had already begun.

But it must be stressed—and John the Baptist's own bewilderment and questioning of Jesus provides ample evidence of this point—the restoration that Jesus inaugurated was decidedly different to anything generally expected by the first-century Jew. And herein lies our second theme because Jesus fundamentally subverts the nationalistic expectation by enacting a program that *did not lead* to political victory over the pagans but was aimed at making Israel what she was called to be—the light of the world. To be sure, the coming of the kingdom was focused on restoring Israel, but it was not to be at the expense of the nations. Israel was to be the people of God *for the world*, not in isolation from the world.[34] As Dunn notes, Jesus was certain that God had a purpose for all of creation, and that his mission was an "expression of that purpose and a vital agency towards its fulfilment."[35] In other words, Jesus not only announced the kingdom to Israel but *embodied* it to the world, with the various healings and exorcisms in Gentile territory ably demonstrating that point. So while Jesus did, in fact, embody the renewal of Israel he did so in such a way that it broke the boundaries and the wineskins of the nationalistic expectation.

This does not mean, however, that Jesus abandoned the threefold eschatological expectation (i.e., the return from exile, the defeat of evil and the return of YHWH to Zion). What it means is that he appropriated it in such a way that its fulfilment looked totally unlike the meaning corporately

---

10:9; 13:28–29; 22:18), and it is equally consistent that Jesus understood himself to be inaugurating the kingdom in the here and now (Matt 12:27–28, 41–42; 13:16–17, 44–46; Luke 4:21; 11:19–20). For a comprehensive survey see Dunn, *Jesus Remembered*, 406–65.

32. Betz, "Jesus' Gospel of the Kingdom," 58–59.

33. Meier argues strongly for the historicity of this pericope (*A Marginal Jew*, 2:130f).

34. Wright, *Jesus and the Victory of God*, 595–96.

35. Dunn, *Jesus Remembered*, 465.

intended.[36] Jesus certainly shared in Israel's eschatological hope but he dramatically weaved the strands of the community's expectation into a striking new pattern.[37]

Jesus and the Final Ordeal

Wright expends considerable energy detailing the shape, color and texture of that new pattern and we simply do not have the opportunity to examine the totality of his argument here. But a crucial element of Wright's presentation along with that of both Meyer and McKnight, is that the coming of the kingdom also entailed an expectation of the Final Ordeal; that great period of tribulation that would befall the saints prior to the final victory of God. To those not familiar with works on the historical Jesus it is no doubt somewhat surprising to discover that discussion concerning Jesus' expectation of the Final Ordeal begins with the Lord's Prayer.[38]

Traditionally, of course, the meaning of the Lord's Prayer has been understood to reflect immediate concerns. The disciples were to ask God to take care of their daily needs, to seek God's forgiveness in the present and to request God's help in trying situations.[39] Given that Matthew has Jesus prefacing the prayer with a comment about the Father's knowledge of the disciple's physical needs (Matt 6:8) such an interpretation is certainly warranted. Yet recent scholarship, while not denigrating the importance of this understanding, contends that there is also a striking element of eschatology to the Lord's Prayer that should not be ignored.[40] Indeed, the undisputed first petition, "thy kingdom come," places the entire prayer into an eschatological framework within which the other petitions function.[41] But it is the sixth petition, "lead us not into temptation (*peirasmos*)" that is of specific importance, for here is a clear indication that Jesus was looking ahead to a time of imminent testing. The question is whether *peirasmos* signifies any "test or trial" in general or whether it particularly

36. See Wright, *Jesus and the Victory of God*, 481.

37. Ibid., 538.

38. The tradition is strong that Jesus taught his disciples to pray and while the Gospel form of the Lord's Prayer reflects later liturgical tradition most are nonetheless prepared to accept its elements as authentic. McKnight, *Jesus and His Death*, 106–10. See also Dunn, *Jesus Remembered*, 226–28.

39. Davies and Allison, *Matthew*, 594.

40. McKnight, *Jesus and His Death*, 106–15; Meyer, *The Aims of Jesus*, 206–8.

41. See the discussion in Davies and Allison, *Matthew*, 593–94.

looks forward to the great tribulation that was widely expected to precede the age to come.[42] Jeremias famously, and (time has demonstrated) rather successfully argued for the latter, and the term is now generally accepted to refer to the Final Ordeal.[43] Importantly, such an understanding fits the prayer's eschatological framework and, moreover, allows the inference to be drawn that Jesus was aware that the final testing was imminent.[44] But what exactly was expected? Jeremias describes it with typical flourish:

> [It is] the final great Testing which stands at the door and will extend over the whole earth—the disclosure of the mystery of evil, the revelation of the Antichrist, the abomination of desolation (when Satan stands in God's place), the final persecution and testing of God's saints by pseudo-prophets and false saviours. What is in danger, is not moral integrity, but faith itself. The final trial at the end is—apostasy! Who can escape?[45]

In other words, the Final Ordeal was not just any kind of trial but the final encounter between God and the evil one, in which the ultimate danger for the believer was to fall away.[46] Given this context the early Christian gloss which adds to the sixth petition an invocation for God to "deliver us from [the] evil [one]" becomes readily understandable.[47] The thrust of the request is not that God would keep the disciples from daily moral failure but that God would spare the disciples from the battle to come. Hence, McKnight argues that the sixth petition should be interpreted as a petition of avoidance, it is a prayer of escape from an ordeal "that will utterly test us."[48]

But, if this is the prayer that Jesus taught his disciples to pray, is it not also reflective of what Jesus prayed himself? McKnight certainly thinks so, arguing that if Jesus did not want his disciples to face the Final Ordeal then it is more than likely that Jesus sought to avoid it as well.[49] The account of Jesus in the garden of Gethsemane seems to indicate this, his apparent

---

42. Dunn, *Jesus Remembered*, 411.

43. Jeremias, *The Prayers of Jesus*, 105–6. For a strong defense of this position see Pitre, *Jesus, the Tribulation, and the End of Exile*.

44. In fact, Meyer argues that the setting and context for the prayer *is* the Final Ordeal. Meyer, *The Aims of Jesus*, 208.

45. Jeremias, *The Prayers of Jesus*, 105–6.

46. Ibid. See also Brown, "The Pater Noster as an Eschatological Prayer," 314–16.

47. Given the eschatological context, Brown favors the personal interpretation. Ibid.

48. McKnight, *Jesus and His Death*, 115.

49. Ibid.

anguish about the immediate future provides sufficient evidence to con-clude that Jesus sought to avoid or at least postpone his suffering.[50] Here too, Jesus' exhortation to the disciples to watch in order that they might avoid the *peirasmos* (Mark 14:38), directly links this account to the Lord's Prayer and is highly suggestive of an expectation that the Final Ordeal was near. Indeed, Jesus' request to be preserved from the hour to come itself echoes the sixth petition and highlights the eschatological frame-work within which Jesus approached his death. Hence, Pitre argues that if Jesus perceived his ministry as standing in the "morning-glow of the dawn of the kingdom of God," he also perceived it to stand "under the shadow of the eschatological tribulation."[51] In other words, Jesus considered his impending suffering and death to be elements of the Final Ordeal that he would have to endure according to the will of God (Mark 14:36).

This conclusion is strengthened by the fact that Jesus was repeatedly remembered to have associated his own death with the coming Ordeal and there is a strong sense that the kingdom would not come until the Ordeal had been endured.[52] In such a case, the Ordeal was not just an "evil to be reversed, it was a good somehow intrinsically designed to generate the reversal."[53] This is perhaps why Jesus was occasionally remembered to have expressed a longing for its inevitable coming (particularly Luke 12:49–50). Here Jesus' willing of "fire" and "baptism" should not be read as a counter to the sixth petition but as an expectation of the Ordeal's inevitability.[54] For Meyer, this means that Jesus expected an enduring of the Final Ordeal to dramatically mediate "the dawn of the new age, the consummation and restoration, the reign of God."[55] Despite its horror, the enduring of evil would somehow result in ultimate victory, a victory that was already in evidence, as we will now see, in and through the praxis of Jesus' ministry.[56]

50. "[A]lmost no one questions the anguish of Jesus in the garden of Gethsemane" (ibid., 117).

51. Pitre, *Jesus, the Tribulation, and the End of Exile*, 218.

52. Mark 10:39; 14:27; Matt 23:29–32; Luke 12:49–59; 22:35–38.

53. Meyer, *The Aims of Jesus*, 216.

54. McKnight, *Jesus and His Death*, 145.

55. Meyer, *The Aims of Jesus*, 216.

56. A willingness to endure the Final Ordeal fits in well with our earlier argument that what God willed was not the death of Jesus but Jesus' willingness to endure the consequences of the creature's freedom to withdraw from the good. We will have more to say about this below.

The Victory of the Kingdom

Finally, there is one further element that falls within the incarnate carrier and that is Jesus' confrontation with the powers of evil. The Gospels make it very clear that Jesus was not only up against the machinations of humanity but the powers of darkness that operate at a supra-personal level. The exorcisms that were a consistent expression of his ministry were not just random acts of mercy for a few tormented souls but were "part of the very fabric of his mission."[57] The inauguration of the kingdom brought with it God's judgment on evil which was being defeated in and through the events of Jesus' ministry; Satan had already fallen like lightning (Luke 10:18), the strong man had been bound (Matt 12:29) and the kingdom of God was being made manifest in the lives of those released from the bondage of demonic oppression (Luke 11:20). Inevitably this brought him into conflict with the authorities, who having already rejected Jesus' re-definition of the kingdom had no choice but to conclude that there was a dark power at work in him (Luke 11:15). Jesus responded, of course, with logic[58] and counter-claim[59] but as Wright emphasizes, the real conflict was not with the Jewish authorities or even with the Roman occupation, but the power that stood behind them.

> [From] Jesus' perspective the battle for the kingdom was being classically redefined . . . the story was being radically retold, so as to focus on the climatic conflict not with Rome, but with the satan. Jesus had already won a decisive victory in this battle; his exorcisms were the implementation of that victory. Acting on his own authority, he was demonstrating the fact that the kingdom was already in some sense present; . . . Israel's god was already becoming king, in the events of Jesus' ministry.[60]

Such a theme parallels nicely the salvation proclaimed by Isaiah 51–52, in which the expected enthronement of God (Isa 52:7) is announced as a victory over both the powers of chaos (51:9) and the rulers of the world (52:5).[61] Hence the triumphant "Your God reigns" of Isaiah 52:7 proclaims

---

57. Wright, *Jesus*, 452; Meier, *A Marginal Jew*, 2:406–7.

58. "If Satan is divided against himself, how can his kingdom stand?" (Luke 11:18).

59. "Now if I drive out demons by Beelzebub, by whom do your followers drive them out?" (Luke 11:19).

60. Wright, *Jesus and the Victory of God*, 454.

61. Betz, "Jesus' Gospel of the Kingdom," 59.

not just YHWH's return to Zion but the victory that accompanies that return. In this context, Jesus' healings, exorcisms and even his table fellowship with "sinners," decisively demonstrates the reality of that victory. Perhaps more than in any other way, it is here in the conflict with evil, that we find Jesus embodying the threefold eschatological expectation. The key question that arises from all this then, is how was Jesus' death connected to the conflict with evil? An expectation that Jesus would endure the Final Ordeal is clearly relevant, but from an incarnational perspective there is little more that can be said at this point. As such, how Jesus understood his death to contribute to the restoration of Israel and the victory of the kingdom requires further investigation into both the linguistic and symbolic carriers of meaning.

Conclusion

We have only begun to scratch the surface here and yet already we have come as far as we are able in the context of our discussion. By submitting to John's baptism, Jesus accepts not just John's call for national repentance but also the eschatological tenor of that call. God is about to dramatically judge the nation via the might of Rome if Jesus' proclamation of the kingdom is rejected. But Jesus is also convinced that the coming of the kingdom will bring restoration to the covenant community. True, the eschatological expectation of return from exile, victory over evil and the enthronement of YHWH will not take place according to the nationalistic hope that was corporately intended, but the extent of Jesus' praxis indicated that restoration was nonetheless already taking place. But the final victory of God awaited the Final Ordeal, and Jesus soon came to realize that his own suffering and death would be caught up in its coming. What Jesus may have made of this is something to which we will have to return, but for now Jesus' exorcisms and healings are suggestive of an expectation that the ultimate victory had already been won. Evil would not triumph even if it was allowed its day in the sun. So how then, does Jesus' death fit within such a context? The answer must await our following discussion into both the linguistic and symbolic carriers of meaning.

Jesus and His Death: The Linguistic Carrier

There is no doubt that the Gospel tradition remembers Jesus to have openly talked about his death. Perhaps the most obvious examples are the passion predictions, the ransom saying of Mark 10:45 and the words of the institution, but many other logia are arguably connected.[62] In fact, McKnight comments that the potential evidence for Jesus thinking and reflecting upon his death is "broader and deeper" than scholarship usually admits. There is a strong and recognizable thread running throughout the Jesus tradition that Jesus openly anticipated and perhaps even interpreted his coming demise.[63]

However, in the history of historical Jesus scholarship very little has been made of such logia, primarily because of the various criteria of authenticity which viewed these sayings with significant suspicion. Because the church proclaimed the death of Christ was "for us," any hint of this redemptive value from within the Gospel witness must have been redacted. As a consequence, each logia was dissected almost beyond recognition in the hope of reaching the holy grail of the *ipsissima verba Jesu*, the very words of Jesus. But what resulted from such endeavors was ever only abstract analyses that proved to have little value, historical or otherwise. For his part, McKnight is strongly critical of such attempts because they inevitably failed to recognize the strong connection between the sayings and moreover, how those sayings might actually function to reveal Jesus' own understanding of his mission.[64]

In fact, if Jesus was to constitute meaning through the linguistic carrier as I have argued, then such meaning would only be coherent if it added to, and reinforced, whatever meaning was also constituted by the other carriers. In other words, constituted meaning must be coherent if it is to be judged to have value. Thus the meaning constituted by the incarnate carrier functions to provide the requisite context for understanding the meaning of the other carriers, particularly the linguistic and symbolic. We cannot then take the sayings of Jesus in relation to his death in isolation but must view them as a whole and do so within the context of his life and mission.

As a first reflection then, it could be suggested that a mission to embody the kingdom of God required more than just teaching and preaching with the odd kingdom miracle thrown in. There is seemingly a genuine expectation that inaugurating the kingdom would somehow result in suffering and death. Why Jesus would have such an expectation is something

62. By my count McKnight identifies 37 relevant logia (*Jesus and His Death*, 79–81).
63. Ibid., 79.
64. Ibid.

to be discussed below but it is clear that enduring it was very real prospect of carrying out his mission.

A second observation presents more of a challenge, for it becomes very clear as one reads through the relevant logia that Jesus very rarely gave his death an explicit soteriological significance. The passion predictions, for example, provide a prime opportunity for Jesus to explain just how his death would atone for the community, yet any sort of explanation is notably absent. Jesus simply indicates that he is to suffer at the hands of men before being vindicated by God, a common hope among martyrs of the period.[65] Indeed, it is remarkable that the evangelists and subsequent redactors eschewed every opportunity to insert something like a "for us," or "on our behalf" clause to these predictions and it can only be concluded that the reason they did not do so, was because Jesus was not remembered to have used them on such occasions. But this does not rule the passion predictions out from our discussion because it is here that Jesus implies a definite sense of *necessity* to the suffering of the Son of man, and one can, therefore, justifiably ask whether this necessity had a soteriological motivation. However, before we continue some initial comments on the passion predictions and Mark 10:45 are required.[66]

Initial Observations: Passion Predictions

Whether or not Jesus actually made the passion predictions as recorded in the synoptic Gospels (Mark 8:31 pars.; 9:31 pars.; 10:33-34 pars.) continues to be debated. Bultmann was convinced they were all prophecies after the event (*vaticinia ex eventu*) and the various members of the Jesus Seminar all concurred, voting the sayings black (inauthentic).[67] Yet if it can be accepted that Jesus was not oblivious to the possibility of a premature death, then there is no *a priori* reason to consider such predictions impossible. To be sure, the highly detailed prediction in Matthew 20:18 betrays traces of later Christian redaction but this does not mean that the core elements of suffering, death and vindication do not go back to Jesus

---

65. See, for example, 4 Macc 9:8; 10:21; 12:18 which is commonly dated around the first half of the first century. For the dating of 4 Maccabees see Williams, *Jesus' Death as Saving Event*, 197–202.

66. The relevant sayings at the Lord's Supper will be left for a later section.

67. Bultmann, *Theology of the New Testament*, 1:29; Funk and Hoover, *The Five Gospels*, 75–78.

himself.[68] Such a core may be found in the second prediction (Mark 9:31 pars.)—which is arguably the least developed—but the authenticity of the first prediction (Mark 8:31 pars.) also finds support in scholarship, and indeed, both may independently reflect the teaching of Jesus.[69] In any case, it is readily clear that the predictions themselves provide another indication that Jesus expected a premature death. While we earlier argued that this was so even without such evidence, the passion predictions do support the conclusion that Jesus was well aware that he was not to live his full three-score and ten.

Beyond this though, there are three points worth noting. Clearly significant for evaluating Jesus' understanding of his death is the appellation of "Son of man" in all the passion predictions bar one (Matt 16:21). Why Jesus uses this phrase and exactly what he meant by invoking it, remains a contentious point in historical Jesus scholarship. However, because Jesus chose to refer to himself in this way, and did so repeatedly in the context of his suffering and death, it remains a question of considerable importance. Secondly, in the first prediction there is a marked sense of necessity given to that suffering. Here it is said that the Son of man "must" suffer and this emphasis leads some to conclude that there is a divine soteriological necessity to Jesus' death, in that God is unable to forgive fallen humanity unless Jesus' blood is shed. Yet there is a significant question mark over whether Jesus himself had this understanding since he was remembered to have directly conferred forgiveness during his ministry, and moreover, claimed divine authority to do so (Mark 2:10). The question then of why Jesus understood his death to be necessary is something to which we will have to return. Finally, as was mentioned briefly above, there is no hint of direct soteriological significance in the passion predictions *per se*. One may look for it in the "Son of man" typology but it is clear that Jesus does not give an explicit atoning interpretation to his death at this point. All we can say for the moment is that the passion predictions demonstrate that

---

68. McKnight, *Jesus and His Death*, 226f; Wright, *Jesus and the Victory of God*, 574–76; Brown, *Death of the Messiah*, 2:1487.

69. As argued by Beasley-Murray, *Jesus and the Kingdom of God*, 238–40. Similar to Jeremias, Dunn prefers a shortened form of Mark 9:31 ("The son of man is (about) to be handed over into the hands of men") as the core of the tradition (*Jesus Remembered*, 801 n. 192); Jeremias, *New Testament Theology*, 282. McKnight rejects this shortened form on the basis that an appearance of vindication in such a context is completely coherent and should, in fact, be expected (*Jesus and His Death*, 229–30). Here we agree with McKnight as the forthcoming discussion on the Son of man will make clear.

Jesus expected a premature death and that through being raised he would also be vindicated.

Initial Observations: Mark 10:45

The importance of this verse for determining the world of meaning that Jesus constituted for his death is matched only by the Eucharistic words of the institution. Nowhere else in the Synoptic Gospels does Jesus give such a clear soteriological inference to his death, decisively connecting his purpose (to serve rather than be served) with a suffering that leads to deliverance. Small wonder then that this verse has been subjected to enormous scrutiny—both historical and theological—and much ink has been spilt about its origins, influence and atoning significance. The minutiae of the debate are, perhaps thankfully, beyond our purview. The question of interest is how the verse contributes to the world of meaning that Jesus was constituting for his forthcoming death.

In this regard there are two major points of note: again Jesus' choice of the "Son of man" appellation; and the crucial though somewhat curious addendum of "ransom for many." In relation to this latter point we can initially note that the precise meaning of *lutron* is not in doubt. It represents the purchase price for manumitting slaves. The question is why was Jesus remembered to have used the term here, and in such an unusual context, to point towards the meaning of his death?[70] Indeed, it is immediately apparent that the discussion Jesus is having with his disciples is not at all centered on his death. The emphasis is on how Jesus resolves the heated discussion that was occasioned by the disciples' discovery of James and John's attempt to reserve their seats at the kingdom table. Instructing them to abandon the Gentile lust for power, Jesus exhorts them to serve each other in love just as he himself is doing in offering his life as a ransom for many. The soteriological comment is, therefore, an aside to the major thrust of the teaching, a point that makes understanding Jesus' intention here all the more difficult.[71]

---

70. The point is often made that the phrase does not appear in Luke's parallel account and given that the author is quite willing to employ other soteriological language it is difficult to understand its omission here. Dunn, *Jesus Remembered*, 813–14. But it must be said that omission in one Gospel is not proof of in-authenticity in another and it can be argued that Mark's witness has historical merit. Hooker, *The Son of Man in Mark*, 144–47; Wright, *Jesus and the Victory of God*, 575, 602.

71. For the narrative context of this passage see particularly, Dowd and Malbon, "The Significance of Jesus' Death in Mark."

However, at one level it is readily apparent that giving his life as a ransom is, in fact, what happened. Jesus devoted his life to the service of the kingdom and at some point that mission demanded his life. His followers, however, were not arrested nor was their life demanded from them, they were allowed to go free, their lives in one sense being ransomed by the death of their leader.[72] It is possible then to interpret this verse purely from an anthropological perspective; Jesus dies as the scapegoat for the community (John 11:50), his death ransoms them from the violence that threatens and peace is restored for a period of time.[73]

The Girardian insight here is certainly appropriate even if the question can be asked as to whether such a perspective adequately takes into account Jesus' eschatological vision. This is essentially the nub of the issue. How does the soteriological idea of "ransom for many" fit within the eschatological coming of the kingdom and Jesus' expectation of the coming Final Ordeal? A link is often made with the suffering Servant of Yahweh and there is certainly an apparent linguistic connection between Mark 10:45b and the "many" of Isaiah 53:11.[74] But as Morna Hooker and C. K. Barrett have rightly warned, the textual connections are open to significant debate and so if there is to be a connection argued, it must be done on other grounds.[75] But even if, like Wright, one does attempt to find alternative footing, we must still not lose sight of the fact that it is not the Servant of Yahweh that gives his life as a ransom for many but the Son of man. Here then, should be our starting point.

These introductory observations lead us then to three crucial discussion questions: Firstly, what soteriological hints are there in Jesus' self-reference as the Son of man? Secondly, how should the apparently soteriological phrase "ransom for many" be understood? Thirdly, what did Jesus mean when he said that his suffering and death were necessary?

The (Saving?) Son of Man

Almost all commentators acknowledge that it is particularly striking that the phrase "the Son of man" only appears in the Gospels on the lips of

72. Fredriksen, *Jesus of Nazareth*, 235–59.

73. The most extensive analysis from this perspective can be found in Girard, *The Scapegoat*, 112–24. See also Girard, *Things Hidden*.

74. A recent argument for the connection between Mark 10:45 and Isaiah 53 can be found in Watts, "Jesus' Death."

75. Hooker, *Jesus and the Servant*; Barrett, "The Background of Mark 10:45."

Jesus. He is not called "the Son of man" by anyone else, nor is he worshipped as "the Son of man" by the disciples or by the burgeoning church.[76] It is an appellation that Jesus alone appropriates. At the very least then, this suggests that Jesus found the self-designation relevant, if not constitutively significant for his self-understanding. This much is generally agreed. However, the question that continues to haunt scholarship is exactly what significance did the term actually have? Broadly speaking there are two alternatives offered, principally characterized by the distinction between the heavenly Son of man and the human son of man. The former gives particular emphasis to the apocalyptic imagery of the "one like a son of man" found in Daniel 7.[77] The latter suggests Jesus merely found in the appellation an appropriate way to refer to himself and his own humanity.[78]

Scholarship remains utterly divided on the issue and whichever answer is to be preferred depends, for the most part, on other contributing factors. For example, those who view Jesus as an eschatological prophet have little difficulty in contending that Jesus utilized the term as a fulfilment of the Danielic tradition, those who do not obviously prefer the circumlocutory alternative. It is an understatement to say that the debate is overly complex and more than a little passionate and we are certainly not about to enter into its abyssal depths here. However, given that we have heretofore argued for an eschatological Jesus we will also accept it as likely that Jesus utilized the title in a self-referential way, drawing particularly from the context of Daniel 7.[79] With such a starting point, the question of interest is whether Jesus deliberately utilized the apocalyptic Son of man appellation in his passion predictions to intentionally create salvific meaning for his death. And if so, what shape does that meaning take?

Immediately, we can note that there is no explicit salvific interpretation given to the suffering of the "one like a son of man" in the text of Daniel 7 for Jesus to directly appropriate. In verse 25 the saints of the Most

76. Dunn, *Jesus Remembered*, 737.

77. See for example: Wright, *Jesus and the Victory of God*, 517–18. McKnight (following Hooker) prefers to understand the term as a "role" rather than a "title" but this subtlety does not affect the titular usage (*Jesus and His Death*, 173–75). Davies and Allison, *Matthew*, 43–53. And somewhat tentatively in Dunn, *Jesus Remembered*, 759–61.

78. On the circumlocutory interpretation see Casey, "General, Generic and Indefinite." The remaining possibility that Jesus was referring to a third party has little currency today.

79. For an overview of the history of the debate see Burkett, *The Son of Man Debate*. For a defense of Daniel 7 as background see Wright, *Jesus and the Victory of God*, 517–18; McKnight, *Jesus and His Death*, 173–75; Davies and Allison, *Matthew*, 43–53.

High (understood in terms of a corporate Son of man) are said to suffer for a "time, times and half a time," but there is no explanation given to their suffering, nor is their later vindication said to atone for others.[80] Likewise, the exaltation and enthronement of the "one like a son of man" in verse 13 does not directly redeem. The emphasis in Daniel is not salvation through suffering but vindication for those who endure that suffering (c.f. 7:27; 12:1-2).[81] Consequently, Wright cautions us against attempting to force the narrative to generate a comprehensive soteriological picture as has sometimes been attempted.[82]

But even heeding such a caution there are still two important features of Daniel's vision that remain suggestive. The first is that suffering prior to God's ultimate victory had an aura of inevitability, which raises the question as to whether that suffering in any way contributed to that victory. The second feature is the expectation that the Son of man would suffer corporately, that is, his suffering would be equivalent to the suffering of the saints.[83] Both these points are related and can be argued to be indicative of a salvific framework, even if they are not themselves soteriologically focused.

It should be readily apparent that the language of the passion predictions does not depict the exalted Son of man. Jesus clearly expects the Son of man to suffer and to do so necessarily. But why is the Son of man, a figure usually associated with glory and exaltation (Mark 8:38; 13:26-27; 14:62; Luke 17:22) now expected to suffer? Morna Hooker provides a very plausible explanation:

> [T]he Son of man can—and will—suffer when his rightful position and God's authority are denied: this is the situation in Daniel 7, where the 'beasts' have revolted against God and have crushed Israel who, as the Son of man, should be ruling the earth with the authority granted by God. Given this situation of the nations' revolt and their rejection of the claims of the one who is intended to exercise authority, it is true to say that the Son of man not only can but must suffer.[84]

80. Dunn provides an appropriate defense of the Son of man as a corporate figure. Dunn, *Jesus Remembered*, 729. Contra e.g., Collins, "The Son of Man in First-Century Judaism," 451.

81. Wright, *Jesus*, 361.

82. Ibid., 599.

83. See again, Dunn, *Jesus Remembered*, 729.

84. Hooker, *The Son of Man in Mark*, 108–9.

So if Jesus did understand his mission in the light of the Son of man of Daniel 7 then it would be readily apparent that he would face suffering if his claims of God-given authority were to be rejected. The parable of the vineyard suggests that this is, in fact, exactly what Jesus thought to be happening (Mark 12:1–9). After having his servants beaten and killed, the owner of the vineyard ultimately sends his son to collect a share of the fruit, but the tenants reject the son's authority as well, murdering him and taking the vineyard for themselves. The meaning of the parable (including, no doubt, its final threat of judgment) was not lost on the Jewish leadership since the reader discovers that they immediately looked for a way to arrest him. The narrative's omniscient conclusion functions to stress the nation's rejection of Jesus, and adequately reinforces the thrust of the parable.

We find this theme of rejection again in Luke 11:47–51 in which Jesus condemns the Pharisees and teachers of the law for their failure to accept the prophets whom God had sent. They build the tombs for the martyred prophets thus testifying that they approve of what their forefathers did and thus become jointly responsible for their deaths. Indeed, Jesus claims that this very generation will pay the supreme price for their rejection of God's representatives because ultimately they failed, suggests Meyer, to recognize "God's climactic and definitive revealer."[85] There is no doubt that the distinct emphasis on judgment in both these logia is an appropriate response to such rejection, but there is quite possibly more to Jesus' comments than just abstract condemnation. As we will shortly see, Jesus' expectation of judgment may actually provide a possible basis for a salvific inference in his actions. For the moment though, the point to be made here is that like the rejected prophets of old, Jesus expected to suffer because of the nation's apostasy.

An important element of this whole line of argument is the point raised earlier about Jesus' conflict with the powers of evil. The Markan narrative makes it quite clear that Jesus was not rejected because the Jewish and Gentile leadership thought he was merely a Galilean upstart. He is rejected because it is the powers of evil that ultimately lie behind the worldly forces that usurp Jesus' authority. Morna Hooker comments:

> It is obvious that [the Jewish leaders] do refuse to recognize the authority of Jesus, and that they are instrumental in bringing about his death, but they are scarcely great enough for the role of powers which rule the world. . . . There are numerous indications

85. Meyer, *The Aims of Jesus*, 207.

in the gospel narratives that Jesus saw the whole of his life and ministry as a battle against Satan; it would be surprising if he had not regarded his death also in the same light.[86]

Hence, it is this *present rule of evil* that ultimately makes the Son of man's suffering and death certain, a point confirmed in the Danielic vision with the suffering of the saints caused not by God but by the powers of evil that were allowed to reign for a period of time. Thus, it is quite likely that Jesus perceived that his suffering and death would occur because of the powers of evil which God permitted to reign for a short time prior to the coming of the kingdom and the final victory of God.

Given that Daniel 7 provided a background to Jesus' self-understanding as the Son of man, the above conclusion is more than tenable and does adequately explain why Jesus would contend that his rejection would also necessitate his suffering. However, whether Jesus thought that suffering as the Son of man would in some way be *efficacious* remains, as yet, inconclusive. However, the interpretation of the Son of man offered in 7:25 provides a possible clue. Here the Son of man is likened to the "saints of the Most High" and thus the suffering of the Son of man corresponds to the suffering of the saints. In such a case, it would be possible for Jesus to perceive himself as representing Israel, his suffering thereby endured on their behalf. But is this a realistic suggestion? In other words, would a contemporary Jew accept that someone could suffer on behalf of the nation? There is some evidence to suggest that it would be accepted and I speak, of course, of the Maccabean tradition.

Wright is correct to point out that what is important about these accounts is not their particular historicity, but the way in which the death of the martyrs is understood during this period to be significant for the community.[87] It is clear that as loyal members of the community the martyrs endured persecution not because God had divinely ordained their destruction, but because the nation as a whole was being disciplined for its sins (2 Macc 6:12–17). Indeed, the martyrs actually recognized that they shared in the sins and punishment of the people (2 Macc 7:18, 32), which means they should not be understood to be the nation's substitute for they too are part of the nation's sinfulness. "[We suffer] because of our own sins," remarks one of the seven brothers (2 Macc 7:32). They, therefore, do not suffer in the place of the nation but endure it in solidarity with the

---

86. Hooker, *The Son of Man in Mark*, 110–11.

87. Wright, *Jesus and the Victory of God*, 582.

nation.[88] However, such is their vision for the community that they nevertheless request that God accept their suffering *on behalf of them all*. This is seen especially in the youngest brother, who in summing up the hope of the six martyred brothers before him, contends that their suffering will in fact bring an end to God's wrath:

> I [the youngest of the seven sons], like my brothers, give up body and life for the laws of our ancestors, appealing to God to show mercy soon to our nation and by trials and plagues to make you confess that he alone is God, and through me and my brothers to bring to an end the wrath of the Almighty that has justly fallen on our whole nation.[89]

For the author of 2 Maccabees that mercy is demonstrated in the very next chapter through the successful military actions of Judas and his army, who found success precisely because God's wrath had now turned into mercy (8:5). The death of the martyrs is therefore understood to effect a decisive change for Israel.[90]

This emphasis continues in 4 Maccabees, and indeed, we find the atoning value of the martyrs suffering and death articulated with even more force. Here it is expressed in such terms as "ransom" (*antipyschon*) and "atoning sacrifice" (*hilasterion*), their deaths said to even "move divine providence" to redeem the covenant people (4 Macc 6:27–29; 17:20–22). Hence, for the author of 4 Maccabees the death of the martyrs is clearly effective, and moreover, there is some indication that the martyrs suffer on behalf of the nation rather than in solidarity with the nation as in 2 Maccabees.[91] In other words, they do not actually suffer because of their own sins but because of the sins of the community.

Whether this demonstrates a development of the Maccabean tradition remains a matter of debate, but it seems likely that the death of a righteous person came to be understood in either way. What the Maccabean literature therefore demonstrates, is that by the time of the composition of 4 Maccabees (middle of the first century), not only was a vicarious death readily comprehensible within the Jewish tradition but that it was quite

88. Dunn, *Jesus Remembered*, 806 n. 209.

89. 2 Maccabees 7:37–38.

90. C.f. de Jonge: "The martyrs die in solidarity with Israel as the people of God, because of their own sins and those of their people. The result of their death is that God is indeed reconciled with Israel and shows his mercy" (Jonge, "Jesus' Death for Others," 148).

91. Williams, *Jesus' Death as Saving Event*, 165–82, 195–96.

plausible for someone approaching martyrdom to believe that God would make their suffering redemptive for the community.

This does not mean, of course, that Jesus must have perceived his death as being redemptive for others, merely that it is plausibly Jewish for him to have done so.[92] But when we add the appropriation of the corporate Son of man figure to such a context, there is potential for the suffering of the Son of man to be understood as redemptive because it was considered to be equivalent to the suffering of the nation. In other words, the Son of man suffers so that the nation might not have to.[93]

To explain this further we need to note two points. Firstly, as was just argued, the suffering of the Son of man arises ultimately from the reign of evil which rejects both God and God's messenger. Hence, if Jesus did draw upon Daniel 7 to inform his own sense of mission, he would not have entered the garden of Gethsemane unaware that the strong opposition he faced actually reflected the present reign of evil. And it is also quite likely that Jesus would have expected to endure that opposition and consequent oppression until God convened the heavenly court (Dan 7:25). No wonder he instructed the disciples to pray that they might not fall into the *peri-asmon*! The great time of eschatological tribulation was imminent and it would be almost too much to bear.

Furthermore, as the *representative* Son of man, what confronted Jesus that night was not just the horror of his own death but the sufferings of the nation itself. Sufferings, to draw from our earlier discussion, which would ultimately be understood as the judgment of God.[94] And this is the second point, for it is quite possible for Jesus to have interpreted the suffering that results from the nation's rejection of his God-given authority (i.e., the suffering that results from the present reign of evil) to be the judgment of God upon the nation. In fact, this is precisely what Wright contends to be the case. Jesus took upon himself the "wrath" of God which was coming upon Israel (that is, the sufferings of the tribulation), not only because she had compromised with paganism but because she had refused his offer

92. The point is made well in McKnight, *Jesus and His Death*, 168–70.

93. But again, it must be emphasized that here in Daniel the enduring of the Final Ordeal does not explicitly result in salvation but vindication. The righteous Son of man suffers for a limited period of time after which God exercises sovereign power and vindicates the one(s) who had suffered. This too is the sequence of the passion predictions, which helps explain why there is no direct soteriological reference to be found therein.

94. See also Wright, "Jesus," 54; Wright, *Jesus and the Victory of God*, 97, 184–85, 596. C.f. Schwager, *Jesus in the Drama of Salvation*, 164–65.

of the kingdom.[95] And with that, of course, he believed that God would vindicate him as Daniel had also prophesied. It is on this basis that Wright argues that Jesus not only suffers at the hands of evil as an individual but does so on behalf of the nation as a whole:

> The death [Jesus] dies is Israel's death, and the pattern of healings and welcomes which make up so much of the gospel narratives indicates the motive: he dies Israel's death in order that Israel may not die it. He takes the wrath of Rome (which is, like the wrath of Assyria or Babylon, the historical embodiment of the wrath of God) upon himself so that, in his vindication, Israel may find herself brought through the judgment and into the true Kingdom, may see at last the way to life and follow it while there is yet time.[96]

In Wright's view then, Jesus chooses to take upon himself the eschatological judgment about to befall Israel because of her rejection of God's way of announcing salvation, not just for Israel but for the world. In enduring that judgment Jesus ushers in the victory of the kingdom, an outcome which would be ably demonstrated through his subsequent vindication.

Further suggestive is Jesus' promise to his followers that the vindication that he himself expected would also be extended to them. The Gospels consistently emphasize that those who followed Jesus would not go unrewarded.[97] The Son of man would repay everyone for the works that they had done (Matt 16:27) and no one who left property or family for his sake would fail to be rewarded a hundredfold, inheriting even eternal life (Matt 19:29). Jesus could promise this because ultimately it would be him who vindicated his followers before his Father, just as he will also deny those who rejected him (Matt 10:32). These verses leave little doubt that Jesus expected his followers to experience the future of the kingdom. His death, which if Meyer is right would launch the Final Ordeal is not the end of the story.[98] Evil would be overcome, the disciples would be enthroned (Matt 19:28), and the temple would be rebuilt (Mark 14:58). Jesus' vindication would be the sure sign that all of this would occur and his hope in this is further evidence that Jesus created redemptive significance for his death.

---

95. Wright, *Jesus and the Victory of God*, 596.

96. Wright, "Jesus, Israel, and the Cross," 90.

97. Wright, *Jesus and the Victory of God*, 336.

98. Meyer, *The Aims of Jesus*, 209.

SUMMARY

To conclude this section it will be helpful to simply outline the relevant points and I do so here without further comment:

1. As the Son of man, Jesus viewed his forthcoming suffering and death to be necessary because of the rejection of his authority by the powers of evil that presently rule the world.

2. The rejection of Jesus dramatically brings the powers of evil into conflict with God.

3. According to Daniel 7, those powers are allowed to oppress the Saints for a short period of time. That oppression is understood by Jesus to be the long awaited Final Ordeal. In fact, Jesus' rejection ushers in the Final Ordeal.

4. Jesus interprets the Final Ordeal as the judgment of God against the nation for its failure to recognize and respond to him and his message.

5. However, as the Son of man, Jesus fully intends to suffer for and on behalf of the nation. In other words, Jesus intends to endure the judgment of God upon the nation so that his follows might not have to endure it.

6. Jesus fully expects to be vindicated by God when the forces of evil are defeated. That vindication would also extend to those who followed him.

A Ransom for Many

So then, what meaning did Jesus constitute for his death in Mark 10:45? In the first place, it is another "Son of man" saying and therefore the above discussion needs to be kept in mind here. In the second place, it must be insisted that "ransom" is *kingdom language* and is therefore not arbitrarily plucked out of the air to provide some abstract soteriological motif. Jesus speaks of his death as a "ransom for many" because in terms of the coming of the kingdom that is exactly what Jesus expected his death to do. It is true that ransom itself refers to the price paid in order to redeem another from their current situation and in Mark's Gospel it is made clear that it is the forces of evil that oppress and enslave the nation. But Jesus does not here insinuate that he offers his life *to* those hostile powers, nor is it in any way suggested that his death is offered to God. Later theological attempts to argue for either one of these possibilities suffered terminal difficulties. The fact is, Jesus does not offer his life *to* anyone, the emphasis is on the redemption for many that arises through his death.

In light of our kingdom discussion and the recognized element of suffering that always precedes the victory and enthronement of God, Jesus here confirms that his suffering would be redemptive for others not because of some needed fiscal exchange but because it is through suffering that redemption would be effected.[99] This makes good sense too in terms of the context of Mark 10:45 in which Jesus' primary concern is the correct attitude of the heart to service. The Son of man, who according to Daniel, is to be enthroned in power and majesty does not promote his own exalted position but recognizes that as Israel's representative he must serve the nation by suffering in its place. The result, of course, is that through that service the Son of man would be vindicated and exalted but this is not the primary motivation. As Mark's Gospel makes clear, the Son of man did not come to be served, but to serve and to give his life as a ransom for many.

Could there be a further connection with the Suffering Servant of Isaiah 52:13—53:12?[100] Certainly, there is no doubt that Mark 10:45 *can* be understood with Isaiah 53 as its background and one often finds such statements in the relevant literature.[101] Of course, just because Christian tradition has read the passage in this way does not necessarily mean that Jesus himself actively had the Suffering Servant in mind when he spoke about giving his life as a "ransom for many." Indeed, this may very well be one of those instances when the distinction between judgment and theological understanding is most apparent.

If we assume, just for one moment, that Jesus did judge the figure of the Suffering Servant appropriate for his own self-understanding, it does not follow that everything later Christian reflection has seen in Isaiah 53 can automatically be ascribed to Jesus' self-understanding.[102] Gerald

99. For the Jewish expectation of great suffering prior to restoration see the discussion in Wright, *Jesus and the Victory of God,* 577. And earlier in Wright, *New Testament and the People of God,* 277f. This point can also be read from within the context of Mark as Dowd and Malbon demonstrate ("Jesus' Death in Mark," 283–85).

100. Hereafter Isaiah 53.

101. A recent and thorough defense of this position can be found in Watts, "Jesus' Death."

102. This is not to imply, contra the Bultmanian school, that the early Christian community *created* such a judgment in the first place. It is to say that it is an intrinsic element of the theological task to open up such judgments to further understanding.

O'Collins reminds us that "there could have been much more meaning in [Jesus'] death than he fully and clearly realised."[103] However, as I have taken pains to argue, our theological understanding must be based in Jesus' constituted meaning and so the question of what Jesus actually intended remains paramount.

And here, of course, Jesus does not directly speak about the Servant of YHWH but of the Son of man. This fact should initially direct us towards Daniel 7 rather than Isaiah 53 and Morna Hooker has famously attempted to demonstrate the sufficiency of the former text. Noting that the purpose of Daniel's vision is to provide comfort to those who are suffering for their faith, she contends that such suffering is always endured on behalf of the nation as a whole. Not everyone will be called upon to suffer in this way and so it can be said of those who do, that they give their lives as a ransom for the rest of the community.[104] Hooker's point certainly needs to be acknowledged, although it must be said that such a connection between the suffering Son of man and a "ransom for many" remains far from satisfying. Wright agrees, wryly appropriating Schweitzer when he suggests that efforts to limit Jesus' self-understanding to Daniel 7 here is like watering the garden with a leaky bucket when a stream runs right alongside.[105] There is simply no need to do so.

That wider stream is, of course, Isaiah 40–55 which is well recognized as the primary source of inspiration for Jesus' mission to Israel.[106] The chapters themselves are concerned with Israel's return from exile (understood as forgiveness of sins) and Yahweh's return to Zion, which we will remember encompasses the threefold Jewish eschatological hope (where Yahweh's return also presupposes victory).[107] The thematic center of these chapters is undoubtedly Isaiah 52:7–12, which not only proclaims Yahweh's triumphant return but the peace and salvation that such a return evokes. The good news is that "Your God reigns"! The exile is over, Israel's sins have been forgiven and restoration is assured. It is small wonder then that these few verses became thematic for Jesus' own ministry, and indeed, they lie behind his announcement of the kingdom.[108]

103. O'Collins, *Interpreting Jesus*, 79.

104. Hooker, *The Son of Man in Mark*, 142.

105. Wright, *Jesus and the Victory of God*, 599.

106. Ibid., 601–4; McKnight, *Jesus and His Death*, 209.

107. Childs, *Isaiah*, 410–11.

108. For Isa 52:7–12 as the central theme of Isa 40–55 see Wright, *Jesus and the Victory of God*, 588–89. As background to Jesus' pronouncement of the kingdom see

So far, so good. But the point that Wright contends is obscured in much of scholarship today is how that message of Isaiah 52:7–12 was to be put into effect. The prophecy itself has a clear answer: "The arm of Yahweh, which will be unveiled to redeem Israel from exile and to put evil to flight, is revealed, according to Isaiah 53:1, in and through the work of the Servant of Yahweh."[109] In other words, the return from exile and enthronement of Yahweh was somehow brought to fruition through the servant's suffering. Hence, if Isaiah prophesied that the good news of the kingdom would be made manifest through the suffering of the servant we can comfortably conclude that such significance was not lost on Jesus himself. To root one's entire teaching, ministry and mission in the great Isaian traditions and then to somehow overlook or forget how such a hope was to be realized simply defies imagination. Hence, if as has been argued, Jesus was aware of Isaiah 53, then there is a strong possibility that the servant tradition played a part in shaping Jesus' own intention for his death.[110]

However, this does not mean that we can simply extract Isaiah 53 from its broader context in order to use it as a basis for an abstract theory of atonement, and *ipso facto* read such a theory by way of "ransom for many" back into Jesus' self-understanding.[111] Jesus did not constitute his world of meaning by removing particular passages from their context and then arbitrarily applying them to himself. The reason why Isaiah 53 is determinative for Jesus is because of its *place in Isaiah 40–55 as a whole*, and in particular because it is the way the hope of 52:7–12 is to be realized.

This is not to deny that there are important theological considerations about the way in which that suffering is deemed by God to be

---

Betz, "Jesus' Gospel of the Kingdom," 58–59.

109. Wright, "The Servant and Jesus," 293.

110. I readily acknowledge that this does not mean that we can conclude Jesus understood himself as "the Servant." Nor can we simply point to a text such as Luke 22:37 and draw the conclusion that Jesus intended to imbue his death with the soteriological significance inherent in the Servant tradition. Even if the quotation of Isa 53:12 therein is accepted as Jesus' own (and the debate here is legion), it could be as McKnight suggests, that Jesus merely found it to be a ready figure for his own fate (numbered with the transgressors) rather than a direct reference to the soteriological significance of the Servant's death (McKnight, *Jesus and His Death*, 215–17). However, the quotation here does suggest that Jesus was remembered to have at least been *aware* of the tradition, and hence, Wright's insistence that Jesus did in fact reflect upon it should not be summarily dismissed. The point being that the potential for the tradition to have influenced Jesus should be accepted, even if its overall importance needs to be seen in the light of the entire study.

111. Wright, *Jesus and the Victory of God*, 604. Cf. O'Collins, *Interpreting Jesus*, 92.

redemptive, but such considerations are borne out of later understanding rather than being inherent in the initial judgment. It is, for instance, folly to ask whether Jesus considered the substitutionary suffering of the Servant of YHWH "inclusive" or "exclusive" place-taking.[112] Such questions are no doubt important and of significant interest, but they remain the domain of later understanding and reflection and cannot be asked of Jesus himself. Here it is sufficient to note that the Servant's suffering is likely to have been judged by Jesus as the means by which God's redemptive plan for Israel and the world would be realized.

The Necessity of the Passion

The final element of the linguistic carrier to be briefly examined here is the use of the term *dei* in the passion predictions (Matt 16:21; Mark 8:31; Luke 9:22), and the connotations of necessity that it engenders. This term is usually viewed in one of two ways: either it is held to be evidence that Jesus understood his death to be divinely willed,[113] or that because of his political activity, he saw that it was inevitable that he would face persecution and probably death.[114] The *dei* in the latter case is understood to be, if not fate, at least a humanly predictable outcome to a chosen course of action.

However, while I have already argued that Jesus did, in fact, anticipate a premature death, in itself this line of argument does not adequately capture the reason for the *dei* in the passion predictions, nor I contend, does the suggestion of ineluctable divine necessity. The reason I come to this conclusion is based in two points, one theological the other historical. Theologically, divine necessity must always be understood in the context of our discussion in chapter two. That is, since God creates with conditional necessity, contingency is not negated by divine providence and human acts remain free. Furthermore, sinful acts cannot be willed by God because they fall outside the divine providential order and therefore remain entirely the result of the human freedom to withdraw from divine goodness. Thus, the betrayal of Jesus cannot be considered "necessary" in the sense that it was impossible for it to be otherwise, nor can God be said to directly will the death of Jesus. There can be no divine necessity to sinful acts.

112. Bailey, "Concepts of *Stellvertretung*."

113. "There is a compelling divine necessity about this 'must'" (Morris, *The Cross in The New Testament*, 27).

114. Heyer, *Jesus and the Doctrine of the Atonement*, 15.

This consideration directs us then to what was, in fact, necessary—Jesus' willing acceptance of divinely granted human freedom and the inevitable consequences that follow (Matt 26:42; Luke 22:42). In other words, it was necessary to fulfil his mission that Jesus accept the rejection of his kingdom preaching and the consequences of the sinful acts that such rejection entailed. The question is why, within the context of his kingdom expectations, did Jesus consider this necessary?

This is the historical question and given our discussion thus far the answer should already be evident. Firstly, Jesus' appropriation of the Son of man appellation in the passion predictions directs us towards the suffering/victory/vindication motif of Daniel 7 and in that passage it is clear that suffering is a necessary element of God's redemptive plan.[115] Not that God wills Jesus to suffer, but that the rejection which Jesus experienced as the representative Son of man would inevitably have such consequences. This is to be expected all the more when that rejection is understood to result from the conflict with the powers of evil that Jesus had proleptically declared defeated. The anguish that Jesus was remembered to have experienced in the Garden of Gethsemane cannot then, arise from the prospect of imminent death alone, but must be understood to stem from the expectant horror of having to endure the Final Ordeal and the judgment of God that it entailed. Such horror would remain despite the hope that vindication and restoration would follow.

Likewise, the clear influence of Isaiah 40–55 on Jesus' ministry strongly suggests that the representative suffering of Yahweh's servant (however it may be interpreted) would somehow function to realize the reign of God heralded in Isaiah 52:7–12. In such a case, it would be extraordinary if Jesus did not have an expectation of suffering especially since his self-proclaimed mission was to inaugurate the kingdom, a pronouncement that had at its very heart Isaiah 52:7. There is thus more than sufficient evidence from passages that Jesus is known to have reflected upon, to suggest that Jesus would have come to the conclusion that suffering would be a requisite part of God's redemptive plan.

On this basis it would be inappropriate to simply reduce the necessity of the passion to an abstract divine exchange paradigm in which Jesus dies in order to effect salvation. Even putting to one side the misconceptions

---

115. As Hooker notes, if the inclusion of the "Son of man" term here is original (and she argues that it is) then there ought to be some connection between it and the necessity expressed in the word *dei* (Hooker, *The Son of Man in Mark*, 108). McKnight argues similarly for the importance and priority of Daniel 7 in this regard (McKnight, *Jesus and His Death*, 237).

about divine necessity, the Danielic Son of man does not suffer at the hand of God but at the hands of those who reject both God and the inaugurator of the kingdom. *Thus God does not will Jesus to die but rather wills that Jesus remain faithful to his mission and so endure the judgment about to befall the nation.* The difference is crucial and goes a long way to address the arguments of those who would seek to remove the cross from salvation history.

But there is a very important qualification to be noted here, and that is that suffering itself was not necessary in the sense that divine victory was impossible without it. It must always be insisted that God is not necessarily constrained by the acts of the created realm. Thus, God did not cause the reign of evil envisioned by Daniel to oppress the Saints because God was somehow unable to enact the divine plan of redemption until such suffering had occurred. On the contrary, the reign of evil oppressed the Saints because the community in which it reigned categorically failed to will the good. But even though such events are not caused by God, God is nonetheless able to create meaning out of them. This was the conclusion we came to in chapter two where it was argued that God is able to create meaning out of contingent events that transcends the meaning (or lack of meaning) initially constituted. Hence, the suffering that takes place in Daniel 7, Isaiah 53 and, therefore, that which is predicted by Jesus in Mark 8:31 and parallels, has divine meaning created out of it even though such suffering actually occurs as a result of the creaturely failure to will the good. So what is that divine meaning? That, of course, is our fundamental question and we will continue to examine the evidence in the following discussion on the symbolic carrier.

Conclusion

Our analysis of the linguistic carrier is here brought to a close though we have only been able to examine the most important of the Synoptic passages and their influences. We began with the passion predictions and immediately noted that there is no explicit theology of atonement in the very context that one would most expect to find it. Jesus simply predicts that he is to suffer, die and be vindicated without actually specifying any particular purpose for those events. However, we cannot then conclude that Jesus understood his death to be meaningless because the Son of man appellation does provide a clear link to the suffering/vindication motif of Daniel 7, in which the Son of man suffers on behalf of the nation prior to the victory of God. Moreover, the representative element of the Son of man figure strongly suggests that Jesus also saw himself suffering as corporate Israel. In such a case, Jesus suffers on behalf of the nation, enduring the suffering that results from the reign of evil so that the nation may not have to. A crucial point is that Jesus understood that suffering to be part of the Final Ordeal, or tribulation that precedes the coming of the kingdom. Hence, while that suffering is as a result of the present reign of evil, Jesus also understands it to be the judgment of God against the nation. Therefore, atoning significance is found in Jesus' decision to endure that judgment as corporate Israel so that she herself may not have to endure it.

In defense of this we noted three elements: Firstly, Jesus' uncontested use of Isaiah 40–55 to inform his mission validates Jesus' knowledge of the servant tradition and in particular that it would be the suffering of the servant which would realize the heralding of salvation proclaimed in 52:7–12. Again, the suffering of the servant is understood to be the judgment of God against the nation and is followed as in Daniel 7 by victory and vindication. It must be granted that Jesus is not remembered to have directly claimed to be the Servant of YHWH but this acknowledgement does not require the conclusion that Jesus rejected the servant tradition outright.

Secondly, we referred to the martyrdom tradition which demonstrates the clear plausibility for an individual to see his or her suffering as being part of God's judgment against the nation while also having corporate salvific benefits (whether that suffering is understood to be in solidarity with, or on behalf of, the nation).

Thirdly, the "ransom for many" statement of Mark 10:45, regardless of its strength of connection to Isaiah 53 and/or Daniel 7, nonetheless indicates that Jesus did understand his death to have some kind of benefit. Here Jesus is simply remembered as one who would give his life as an act of service in order to redeem many from their current situation.

Finally, we addressed the question of why Jesus saw his death as necessary in terms of his mission to inaugurate the kingdom. Ultimately, Jesus understands his death as necessary because it is through suffering that the victory of God and the judgment of evil is revealed. However, this does not mean that God is the cause of that suffering, or that God directly wills the death of Jesus. On the contrary, what God wills is Jesus' acceptance of his rejection and the suffering that acceptance entailed. Here we have the case of divine meaning being created out of an evil event, in which the cause of the event remains the responsibility of those who withdraw from divine goodness. And that meaning, I have argued, is the meaning that Jesus was creating for his own death, a meaning in which his suffering and death would have redeeming significance for others.

Immediately we can note that this conclusion confronts modern atonement sensibilities which go to great lengths to remove suffering from any possible redemptive significance. But our analysis has not asked what Jesus thought on the basis of recent conceptions of fairness and justice but what the world of meaning was that Jesus created in the context of his mission to inaugurate the kingdom. The question to which we now turn is what does the symbolic carrier bring to this discussion? What meaning or meanings does Jesus constitute for his death through the use of symbols and symbolic action? We will attempt to answer this question through an analysis of the two commonly recognized symbols that pertain to Jesus' death: his cleansing of the Temple and the Last Supper.

Jesus and His Death: The Symbolic Carrier

The Gospels demonstrate that Jesus utilized the symbolic carrier to convey meaning and for once, at least, historical Jesus scholarship presents a consensus. Whether through parables, his works of power or even in his designation of the "twelve," Jesus found in symbols an appropriate way to illustrate the significance of the kingdom.[116] Nowhere is this more true than in the two major symbolic acts that occurred at the beginning and at the end of the last week of Jesus' life: his actions in the Temple and the Last Supper. Recent scholarship acknowledges that the two events are inextricably linked.[117] The strong connection between Jesus' disruption of the Temple operation and the offering of his own body and blood in what appears to be a sacrificial way is taken to be more than coincidental. There seems to be a conscious and intentional act on Jesus' part to connect the dots and thus imbue his death with a meaning that runs through both symbolic acts.

Once this link is recognized the question turns to what that meaning might actually be, and as we might expect, here is where the general consensus ends. But given all that we have argued so far, surely whatever meaning Jesus did choose to embody through these symbolic acts must somehow be connected with his mission to inaugurate the kingdom. And

116. Meyer, *The Aims of Jesus*, 169.

117. Balla, "What did Jesus Think?," 250. The connection probably even extends to the triumphant entry. See McKnight, *Jesus and His Death*, 325–26.

as we have already seen, that mission often entailed constituting a new world of meaning out of that which was corporately intended. Indeed, the provocative nature of both these symbolic acts indicates that this is what was happening here. In each case the corporately constituted world of meaning was being dramatically subverted by Jesus' actions and those confronted by what Jesus did were required to existentially judge for themselves what to make of it.

In the first symbolic act Jesus challenges the Temple's place and function in the coming kingdom of God, an act that is so explosive to the corporately constituted meaning that the chief priests and scribes immediately seek a way to kill him (Mark 11:18). In the second symbolic act the disciples are instructed to eat and drink Jesus' own body and blood, which according to the fourth evangelist immediately turns many disciples away (John 6:52–61). Like any good symbol, both these acts evoke strong feelings in those involved as they are forced to judge the new meaning being symbolically constituted. So then, how should the events be understood in the context of Jesus' mission to inaugurate the kingdom and what impact do these events have on our understanding of Jesus' death? We begin the analysis at the beginning of passion week with Jesus' actions in the Temple.

Jesus and the Temple

It is generally accepted that Jesus' disruptive actions in the Temple were the historical precipitate for his death.[118] Indeed, in Mark's Gospel the Temple incident plays *the* crucial role in bringing Jesus to the attention of the priests and it therefore provides the necessary justification for his later arrest and execution.[119] I argued earlier that Jesus was not blind to the consequences of such a provocative action nor, I would add, does undertaking it regardless of the obvious danger indicate that he had some kind of death-wish. What it suggests instead is that Jesus saw his action as being integral to his proclamation of the kingdom, despite the likely rejection that such an action would elicit. It is most unlikely then, that such a provocative act was born of a sudden impulse or that "consumed with zeal" he lost self-control when confronted with the merchants in the outer court (John 2:17). There is no evidence that Jesus was in the habit of acting randomly and there is no *a fortiori* reason to believe that he did so here. Indeed, Mark tells us that having entered the city Jesus went immediately

---

118. See for example Dunn, *Jesus Remembered*, 638–39.

119. Fredriksen, *Jesus of Nazareth*, 210.

to the Temple where he inspected it thoroughly but because of the late hour he left there, retiring to Bethany for the night (Mark 11:11).[120] It was not until the next day that Jesus actually returned to "cleanse" the Temple and hence Meyer comments that Jesus' actions must have been calculated to some extent.[121]

However, this does not mean that Jesus had a predefined "strategic plan" to follow in which a number of boxes had to be ticked off before his date with destiny. What it means is that his symbolic action had a definite purpose.[122] In other words, Jesus consciously intended whatever it was that he actually did, which should not surprise us given the constitutive function of the symbolic carrier of meaning.

Here I have said "whatever it was," because there continues to be a historical question over the particularities of the disturbance and its probable extent.[123] The tradition at least, is reasonably strong: Jesus upsets the tables of the money-changers and dove sellers and restricts the movement of merchandise through the Temple grounds (Mark 11:15–18; Matt 21:12–13; Luke 19:45–46; John 2:13–16). However, it must be pointed out that this kind of action does not actually *cleanse* the Temple in the liturgical or ritual sense of the term. Jesus does not claim that the Temple is unable to fulfil its cultic function because of national sin, nor does he reject outright the Temple's role in the community.[124] What his quotations of Isaiah 65:7–8 ("a house of prayer for all nations") and Jeremiah 7:11 ("den of

120. Our limited focus means we are not able here to discuss the symbolic meaning of Jesus' entry into Jerusalem with all its royal and messianic overtones.

121. Meyer, *The Aims of Jesus*, 170.

122. So rightly Dunn, *Jesus Remembered*, 637–38.

123. Dunn notes that whatever Jesus actually did, it must have been insignificant enough for the Temple guards and nearby soldiers stationed in the Antonia fortress to ignore (in contrast, see their very quick response to the disturbance in Acts 21:30–35) (ibid., 639). Yet it must also be recognized that Jesus' actions were provocative enough for the chief priests and scribes to immediately seek to have him killed. Some try to circumvent the difference by suggesting Jesus embarked on a Blitzkrieg-style incursion prior to melting away into the crowd before the soldiers could respond. See for example: Chilton, *Rabbi Jesus*, 228–29. But this is difficult to reconcile with the Gospel witness that places Jesus in the temple courts teaching and healing shortly after (Matt 21:14).

124. Maintaining the purity of the Temple was, of course, the business of the priests. Betz, "Jesus and the Purification of the Temple," 459. It should be noted that Jesus' pronouncement of the Temple's destruction (see below) is not a condemnation of the Temple's purpose (to be a place of mediation and reconciliation between God and the covenant people) but an announcement of a new eschatological means to reconciliation created by God out of the continuing sinful actions of the community.

robbers") indicate, is that Jesus was concerned with the corruption of the Temple support systems.[125] Not only did the merchants swindle those who came to offer their sacrifices, but their noisy presence in the outer court diminished the Temple's ability to be a place of worship for all nations.[126]

Jesus' actions must therefore be seen as a critique of its present form of operation, but not necessarily a critique of the sacrificial cultus itself or of those who came to offer their sacrifices. Likewise, Jesus cannot have been critiquing the actual existence of the support services, for they had an important role in facilitating the very function of the Temple. As Fredriksen points out, pilgrims coming from Egypt, Italy or Babylon were hardly likely to carry their own birds and livestock with them for the requisite offerings.[127] And even if they did, there was always a possibility that the Temple priests would deem their offering somehow inappropriate, thereby forcing them to find an alternative animal. Thus, the very nature of sacrificial worship in antiquity required that such support services be available to the community. Jesus' critique must therefore be seen to be against the corruption and extortion of the support services rather than the existence of the support services themselves.[128]

However, to limit the symbolic meaning of Jesus' action to a critique of economic corruption alone underplays the constitutive nature of the symbolic act.[129] Recalling our discussion on constitutive meaning from the last chapter, Jesus' dramatic intervention in the Temple must have had two discernible effects. Firstly, it incorporated an implicit challenge to the

---

125. Betz, "Jesus and the Purification of the Temple," 461–62. See also Wright, *Jesus and the Victory of God*, 419–20; Brondos, "Why was Jesus Crucified?," 492.

126. The extent of the corruption remains unknown (see Wright, *Jesus and the Victory of God*, 420) and the statement here is not meant to imply that all the money-changers and dove sellers were corrupt. But as Gundry notes, there is sufficient evidence to suggest that at least some were (*Mark*, 644–45). This conclusion is supported by the fact that the crowd clearly sympathized with Jesus' action and openly stated their admiration for his teaching (Mark 11:18). Such an attitude suggests there was little concern for those who had their business disrupted. As for whether Jesus' actions were also aimed at ensuring the Temple functioned as a house of prayer for the Gentiles remains a point of contention. However, whatever one concludes on this matter, the point that Jesus critiqued the present operation of the Temple rather than the Temple, or the sacrificial system itself, still stands.

127. Fredriksen, *Jesus of Nazareth*, 209.

128. Betz, "Jesus and the Purity of the Temple," 461 n. 26. The point is made several times throughout the article.

129. I am not here denying the cleansing interpretation but arguing for a meaning that goes beyond it.

community's understanding of the Temple and like the symbolic actions of Isaiah, Ezekiel and Jeremiah, it vividly demonstrated that something was wrong with the status quo.[130] Secondly, Jesus' actions constituted an alternative reality for the Temple and those who were unexpectedly confronted with what occurred were now required to existentially judge what they saw. The result of that judgment depends on the authenticity of the individual but it will always go in one of two ways. Either the newly constituted reality will be accepted or it will be rejected; what the symbolic carrier ensures is that there is no middle ground.[131]

Therefore, the meaning that Jesus constituted for his actions can be seen in the effect that the action engendered. The negative effect is obvious: the chief priests and teachers of the law immediately looked for a way to kill him. The question is why? Such a response is unlikely if Jesus' constituted meaning was merely one against oppressive corruption. Jesus' actions were not significant enough to interrupt the daily operation of the Temple for very long and in fact, we are given no indication in the Gospels that Jesus' actions had any effect on corruption at all. Indeed, it is more than likely that those effected by Jesus' actions simply put their tables the right way up and continued on their business as usual. Hence, to understand the reason for the Temple leadership response we must posit a symbolic understanding that goes beyond the immediate context. This is why Meyer suggests that economic corruption was not the central issue even though its critique is clear.[132] Jesus' action was certainly real and pointed, but its symbolic nature directs us to a larger world of meaning.

Whatever content Jesus may have been constituting for this larger world of meaning, his actions clearly symbolized that something had gone wrong with the existing Temple.[133] This much is not contentious, the crucial question is just what did Jesus think was wrong? Those who hold to a non-eschatological Jesus are forced to postulate a rejection of Temple worship or a rejection of the Temple's purity code as a means to political,

130. Isa 20:1–6 (nakedness); Ezek 4:1–17 (brick); Jer 19:1–15 (smashed pot).

131. This is why suggestions that the Markan narrative of this event is fabricated for rhetorical purposes must be rejected. The constitutive meaning engendered by Jesus' actions would not have had the impact it did *unless* it was rooted in an actual historical event. *Contra*, for example, Seeley, "Jesus' Temple Act."

132. Meyer, *The Aims of Jesus*, 170.

133. Jesus was certainly not alone in this belief. Both the Qumran and Essene communities were, in their own way, critical of the existing Temple and there is mounting evidence that general criticism of the Temple was particularly widespread in the first half of the first-century. Betz, "Jesus and the Purity of the Temple," 460.

social and spiritual oppression.[134] But in the context of Jesus' mission to proclaim the coming of the eschatological kingdom such views are not ultimately persuasive. The Jesus we have seen thus far is concerned to announce the good news of the kingdom, but it is a good news tempered by the fact of imminent judgment. Here we can take advantage of our earlier gains and recall that Jesus understood that judgment was about to befall the nation because it rejected him and his message. This judgment extended not just to the people but also to its national symbols which had been distorted from their original purpose by generations of ideological nationalism. The Temple, as Jesus reminded them, was to be a house of prayer for all nations, yet such was the nationalistic hope of Israel that the Temple itself had become the center of national resistance.[135] Far from being a light to the nations Israel had become myopic, unable to see past its own nationalistic ideals. Marcus Borg raised this point more than twenty years ago when he argued that the Temple had a decisive role in Israel's resistance towards Rome.[136] His corresponding interpretation of Jeremiah 7:11 as a prophetic condemnation of violent resistance may remain debatable, but it nonetheless serves to adequately demonstrate the point:[137] if Jesus saw that the nation had somehow distorted the primary vocation of the Temple then it too would bear the judgment about to befall the nation. As Jesus phrased it, the might of Rome would see to it that not "one stone would be left upon another" (Matt 24:2).

We would expect then to find a strong correlation between Jesus' attitude to the Temple and the coming judgment of God—and so we do. The Gospels' recall that shortly after this incident Jesus predicts that the Temple will, in fact, be destroyed (Mark 13:2), the veracity of which is supported by the later accusation at Jesus' trial (Mark 14:57–60). And when we add the fig-tree judgment (in which Mark pointedly sandwiches the Temple incident), Jesus weeping over Jerusalem, the mocking of Jesus at the cross

134. See the discussion in Fredriksen, *Jesus of Nazareth*, 211–12.

135. Wright, *Jesus*, 420.

136. Borg, *Conflict, Holiness and Politics*, 171–75.

137. Borg contends for the existence of revolutionaries who were using the Temple as a base of operations. Such a view is supported linguistically, since the word for robber (*lestes*) more correctly connotes a brigand who takes by force rather than a "mere" swindler. However, Evans disagrees with Borg completely, arguing that Jesus' actions hardly square with a condemnation of Jewish revolutionaries (Evans, "Jesus' Action in the Temple," 267–68). Wright is more open to the idea, but mollifies Borg's view in suggesting that Jesus' action was against the ideological conception of the Temple as an icon of national resistance, rather than against any particular nationalistic group (Wright, *Jesus and the Victory of God*, 420).

and the charge against Stephen in Acts 6:14, we have a clear picture "not of cleansing or reform, but of destruction."[138] Therefore, in overturning the tables we can appropriately conclude that Jesus was symbolically enacting the destruction of the current Temple.[139] And as Meyer notes; "To evoke, even conditionally, the destruction of "this temple" was to touch not just stone and gold and not only the general well-being but history and hope, national identity, self-understanding, and pride."[140] Little wonder then, that it evoked the negative response from the chief priests that it did.

But the question remains, how does Jesus' prophetic enactment of the Temple's destruction constitute meaning for his own death? Did Jesus intend by his actions to constitute a world of meaning in which it would now be his "body and blood" rather than that of the lamb which would be the effective sacrifice? Was Jesus consciously intending to replace the Temple? The answer is clearly connected with the symbolism of the Last Supper, but before we turn to this most important of symbols, there is a final point to be made. In recounting Jesus' entry into Jerusalem just prior to his symbolic action in the Temple, the Gospel of Luke records that Jesus gave two related reasons for why Jerusalem, and hence the Temple, would be destroyed. The first is because the nation did not accept Jesus' way of peace, and the second is because she did not recognize the time of her grace (Luke 19:41–44). That is, Jesus was remembered to have connected the coming destruction and judgment of the city with his own rejection, a connection that should not surprise us given our earlier argument concerning the Son of man. In this context, Jesus' actions are a demonstration of the eschatological expectation that suffering would precede the victory of God, and the destruction of the Temple is an inevitable element of that suffering.

This means that we cannot interpret Jesus' actions as an indictment on the Temple cultus, for the Temple's role in mediating between God and the covenant community is not criticized. Indeed, Jesus cannot have been

138. Wright, *Jesus and the Victory of God*, 416.

139. I should add here that this meaning is in addition to a critique of the corruption present in the Temple's operation. This should not be understood as a bet-each-way, but the recognition that symbols work on multiple levels. As Evans comments: "Criticism of temple business activities, coupled with a warning (or threat) of destruction, coheres well with the prophetic Scriptures, with Jesus' own prediction of the temple's destruction, and with the charge brought against him at his trial" (Evans, "Jesus' Action in the Temple," 269). See also Sanders, *The Historical Figure of Jesus*, 254–62. Wright, *Jesus and the Victory of God*, 424.

140. Meyer, *The Aims of Jesus*, 183.

intending his disciples to understand his actions as a *prohibition* against participating in the Temple either. For not only do they continue to meet in the Temple courts immediately after Jesus' death and resurrection, the writings of the early Christians give no indication that there existed any kind of anti-Temple Christian Judaism.[141] Therefore, what we need to conclude is that the prophesied destruction of the Temple must be understood within the context of the imminent judgment that Jesus expected to befall the nation.

In this sense the Temple stands in for the nation and Jesus' actions are essentially a portend of the coming judgment. Consequently, when we come to the question of the Last Supper what we should expect to find is not a direct replacement of the Temple itself, but rather a "re-orientation of the Temple order."[142] In fact, according to the accusations at his trial, Jesus claimed that a new Temple would be built, though this time "not with hands" (Mark 14:58). There is an expectation then that the cultic role of the Temple would continue, albeit newly constituted.[143] That Jesus' death is to have a role in constituting this new Temple is suggested by the fourth evangelist ("destroy this Temple, and I will raise it again in three days" (John 2:19b)), but more significant is the way that Jesus intended to endure the impending judgment of God against the nation. If Jesus did intend to symbolically endure the judgment to come, then no matter what may occur historically, Jesus had already made restoration possible. And whatever shape that new Temple would take, its eschatological role would be proleptically present in and through the death of Jesus.[144]

There is then no direct atoning significance to be read from Jesus' actions in the Temple but his actions do point towards a newly restored eschatological Temple, a Temple not built by human hands that finds its inauguration in the death of Jesus of Nazareth.[145] But if the central symbol of Israel's relationship with God was to be constituted afresh, what was it to look like? How was it to function and how, or why, would Jesus' death

141. McKnight, *Jesus and His Death*, 327.

142. Ibid., 326.

143. On the notion of a restored Temple see Meyer, *The Aims of Jesus*, 198; Sanders, *The Historical Figure of Jesus*, 261–62; Wright, *Jesus and the Victory of God*, 425–26.

144. In particular, Meyer, *The Aims of Jesus*, 183–84; O'Collins, *Interpreting Jesus*, 89.

145. Insofar as restoration can be interpreted as salvation (see, for example, Meyer, *The Aims of Jesus*, 200) a saving significance can be argued from the Temple action. However, I prefer to see such significance in relation to Jesus' overall mission as reflected particularly through the Last Supper.

accomplish it? We now turn to the symbolism of the Last Supper in an effort to respond to these questions.

The Last Supper

Along with the shape of the cross, the Last Supper has become the Christian symbol *par excellence*. Every week throughout the world Christians partake of the "body" and "blood" of the Lord in an act that embodies the hope of Christian atonement, forgiveness, peace and reconciliation. There are, of course, differences in Eucharistic practice from one Christian group to the next, but the centrality of the symbol for the Christian life is universally recognized. The Eucharist is, and will always be, something special in the lives of the faithful.

Furthermore, this symbol has great significance for the present discussion because the Last Supper is held to be *the* quintessential carrier of salvific meaning in the life of Jesus. In fact, given the temporal proximity of the meal to Jesus' arrest and crucifixion, if there was to be salvific meaning created for these particular events, then one would expect to find it here. And indeed, the words of the institution in which Jesus is said to have broken the bread and drank from the cup both for the "forgiveness of sins" and on behalf of "many," do provide that expected salvific inference. The challenge is to discern how these inferences should be understood within the context of the meal and the meaning that Jesus intended to create through its symbolic praxis.

It did not take long for the early church to do just that, interpreting the symbolism of the Last Supper in terms of a final sacrifice (Heb 10:1–18), a new Passover and therefore a new exodus (1 Cor 5:7) and an inauguration of a new covenant (Heb 8). Again too, we are confronted with the question of whether Jesus intended the meal to replace the Jewish Temple cult, a consideration that certainly has significant consequences.[146] Of course, as a symbol, the Last Supper is more than capable of incorporating a number of meanings, the question that confronts us is which one(s), if any, did Jesus intend to create? Again, to ask this question is not to imply the irrelevance of later considerations but to reflect on the judgment that Jesus was remembered to have made. So then, where to begin?

146. It has already been argued that Jesus did not intend to replace the Temple cult and we will see this again shortly. *Contra*, in particular, Chilton, *A Feast of Meanings*, 63–74.

Given that the event was remembered in the Synoptics as a Passover meal, we would perhaps do well to start our reflections there.

A Passover Meal?

Immediately we are confronted with the question of the meal itself. Was it actually the Passover celebration? Jeremias classically argued that it was a *seder* meal, but few appear to follow him today.[147] The preponderance of scholarly opinion is more inclined to follow the Johannine chronology than the Synoptics, placing the meal the night before Passover rather than on Passover itself. Of course, this goes against the grain of usual practice in which Markan priority is assumed but one has only to read the relevant sections of Brown's magnum opus to get a feel for the depths of the Johannine evidence.[148] Particularly intriguing is the fact that there is no reference to the Passover lamb at all in the Last Supper accounts. Indeed, if the Passover lamb *was* available to Jesus at the meal then there is enormous significance in the fact that Jesus chose *not* to refer to it.[149] Did Jesus intend to minimize any possible connection between his death and the paschal lamb? Or was he deliberately avoiding any potential connection with the Temple cult as another foreshadowing of its destruction? Or was its absence from the Eucharistic words a direct result of an intention to replace the cult itself?[150] Such questions become far less imposing if the meal itself was not the Passover meal and the absence of the lamb from Jesus' symbolic action is simply explained by the fact that it was not there to be utilized in the first place.

But this conclusion inevitably raises the question of how to understand Mark 14:12, 14, and 16 in which it is clearly stated that Jesus expects to eat the Passover meal that very night. Various attempts at a solution have been made (going as far back as Tatian's *Diatessaron*) but few have commanded much assent.[151] The historical difficulties are simply insur-

147. Jeremias, *The Eucharistic Words of Jesus*, 41–62.

148. And likewise the copious problems that beset the alternative view. Brown, *Death of the Messiah*, 1350–76, esp. 1371–73.

149. For example, had lamb been eaten, would not a saying such as "this lamb is my body" better convey his sacrifice than the mere breaking of bread? McKnight acknowledges that this kind of comment is made from silence but on occasion "silence [can be] golden." For McKnight, it is "nearly incomprehensible" for Jesus to prefer bread over the lamb for his symbolism (*Jesus and His Death*, 270).

150. As Chilton in fact argues (on which see below), (*The Temple of Jesus*, 150–54).

151. See particularly the discussion in Brown, *Death of the Messiah*, 1361–69.

mountable: either Jesus instructed his disciples to prepare for the Passover during the time of the paschal slaughter (Mark) or he was killed at the same time the lambs were immolated (John). The two cannot be historically reconciled. Recognizing this, recent scholarship (again preferring the Johannine chronology) concludes that Mark and hence both Matthew and Luke, have theologized a Passover week meal into the Passover meal itself. Brown surmises that Mark would have been well aware of the historical inconsistency this introduced but probably chose not to be concerned about it because the paschal characterization of the meal was already entrenched in liturgical theology.[152] McKnight and Wright would probably agree since both view this reworking as a strong indication of the importance of the Passover meal to the meaning inherent in Jesus' symbolic actions.[153] This assumes, of course, that the early Christian tradition is indicative of Jesus' own intention, but the context of the Passover week readily suggests that this might be the case. There is little doubt that every meal during that particular week would have been eaten with an awareness of the Passover festivities, and each meal would invoke, even if unintentionally, the events for which the festival was remembered.[154] And if the words and actions of Jesus that night are taken to be authentic, then as we will shortly see, a connection to the exodus tradition is readily discernible.[155] It is, therefore, not at all difficult to perceive Jesus anticipating the Paschal meal by one night, especially if he sensed that his own end was near.[156]

With this in mind, it is of great significance that the Passover festival was designed to celebrate and remember God's redemptive activity. This means that the meaning Jesus created for his death through the words of

152. Ibid., 1370–71. The Pauline tradition of the Eucharist demonstrates that Jesus was understood to be the paschal lamb at a very early stage (1 Cor 5:7). See McKnight, *Jesus and His Death*, 272.

153. McKnight, *Jesus and His Death*, 272; Wright, *Jesus and the Victory of God*, 555–57.

154. McKnight, *Jesus and His Death*, 275. Chilton acknowledges this even though he argues that Jesus had no intention of invoking a Passover context (*The Temple of Jesus*, 150 n. 25).

155. Here I refer to Dunn who argues that despite recognizable liturgical development in each version of the Last Supper tradition there is nonetheless a core memory of what Jesus said and did. The impact of the symbolic actions made a lasting impression and hence carries with it a strong element of authenticity (Dunn, *Jesus Remembered*, 804–5).

156. According to Theissen and Mertz, the whole Last Supper setting implies "a consciousness of imminent death" on the part of Jesus (Theissen and Mertz, *The Historical Jesus*, 430–31).

the institution and the symbolic breaking and sharing of the bread and wine was situated within that wider context. Indeed, it readily allows Jesus to draw upon elements of the great exodus story in the creation of meaning for his own death. Much of this will be familiar and I will only note here some of the more crucial elements.

Firstly, the symbolic usage of bread to refer to Jesus' body is not without importance. In Deuteronomy 16:3 the unleavened bread of the Passover is called the "bread of affliction" because it reminds the people of their suffering in Egypt. Therefore, by connecting his body with the bread of affliction, McKnight argues that Jesus finds in the suffering of Egypt an analogy of his impending death. That is, "he will himself endure suffering not unlike that of the children of Israel. His suffering will lead to an exodus, a redemption not unlike that of the children of Israel."[157] And such a point links the bread to Jesus' death even if the symbolic act of breaking the bread somehow went unnoticed. But the startling, if not shocking element of the meal, is that the bread (and later the cup representing Jesus' blood) is given to the disciples to eat (and drink).[158] The bread of affliction is not broken in abstract but is to be ingested by the believing community so that they might share in the death of Jesus and thereby gain its benefits. This is constitutively new, for the unleavened bread of the Passover is not consumed for its redemptive benefits even if it acquired some form of redemptive significance by virtue of it being an exodus meal. Hence, McKnight contends that having made the identification between his body and the bread, Jesus creates new meaning by offering himself to his followers in order to further offer them the protection of a sacrificial death.[159] If this is accepted, then Dodd's suggestion that the bread took the place of the lamb in this quasi-Passover meal has some merit.[160] The breaking of the bread represents the slaughter of the lamb and evokes the apotropaic (protective) function of the sacrifice.[161] It is, therefore, by Jesus'

157. McKnight, *Jesus and His Death*, 280. In fact, McKnight comments that in the light of Jesus' expectation of the Final Ordeal, it would not be surprising if Jesus understood the Israelite suffering in Egypt as a prototype of that eschatological event.

158. McKnight dismisses any suggestion that the disciples would have understood Jesus' statement literally. Such "unimaginative cannibalistic interpretation[s]" deny the metaphorical power of the symbol (ibid., 283).

159. Ibid., 281.

160. Dodd, *The Founder of Christianity*, 153–54.

161. Sabourin and Lyonnet, *Sin, Redemption and Sacrifice*, 171. Also Young, *The Use of Sacrificial Ideas*, 44; Durham, *Exodus*, 154–55.

death that his disciples will be redeemed from affliction and God will pass over them at the time of judgment. In such a context then, Jesus' death is not about forgiveness or even atonement, it is about protection.[162] Jesus' death protects his disciples from God's judgment, a judgment that Jesus expected to come forthwith.

The cup, which Jesus likens to his own blood continues the apotropaic theme (as the disciples in turn identify themselves with it), but the symbolism also potentially draws upon the covenant ceremony of Exodus 24.[163] Care must, however, be exercised in determining what covenant connotations are actually present in the symbolism of the cup. The primary reason for this concern arises from the demonstrable *lack* of covenant connection with the paschal tradition in Jewish literature. We cannot simply elide the two images together for the significance of the Passover was not construed in covenantal terms.[164] The blood of the paschal lamb, shed for its protective benefits (Exod 12) does not directly parallel the blood of the bulls, shed to inaugurate the covenant (Exod 24). The functions and effects of the blood were not the same.[165] This does not mean, of course, that a covenant connection is untenable, for all four versions of the meal comment that what Jesus offered that night was indeed the cup of the covenant. In fact, for Luke (22:20) and Paul (1 Cor 11:25) it is the cup of the *new* covenant, a qualification intended to recall the actions of Moses in establishing the first covenant while simultaneously insisting that God was doing something eschatologically new. This theme was taken up elsewhere by Paul (Gal 4:24; 2 Cor 3) and figured prominently in Hebrews (8:1–13;

162. The Passover and Paschal lamb not being considered atoning in the Levitical sense. The closest the events of the Passover come to an atoning interpretation is in connection with the Akedah of Isaac. See *Jub* 17:15–18:19; 49:15. Also the discussion in Sabourin and Lyonnet, *Sin, Redemption and Sacrifice*, 265; Wilken, "Melito," 60.

163. Other potential passages are Jer 31:31 and Zech 9:11 and there is some question as to which of the three passages is really paramount in the Last Supper symbolism. McKnight, *Jesus and His Death*, 304–6. However, it is true to say that in much of the literature the Exodus account is taken to be the primary background and we will therefore limit our discussion to it here.

164. Ibid., 306–8. Drawing support from Jeremias, *The Eucharistic Words of Jesus*, 195.

165. "Being covered by blood as *Pesah* differs functionally and effectively from being splashed with blood at the covenant ceremony. In one the person is protected from God's wrath; in the other, a person becomes a covenant member and is warned of extirpation if the covenant terms are ignored. The first is not about forgiveness; the second seals the commitment to YHWH in terms of atonement and purity" (McKnight, *Jesus and His Death*, 307).

9:15). So the question is not whether covenant is an appropriate theme by which to understand Jesus' actions, but whether it was Jesus himself who first constituted the connection.

Contrary to Wright, Dunn and Meyer, McKnight takes the view that Jesus did *not* constitute the connection himself.[166] The covenant imagery was certainly appropriated by the early Christian community and it became foundational for its Eucharistic celebration but McKnight argues that the connection did not originate with Jesus.[167] Determinative in this regard is the fact that it is only here, in the Last Supper tradition, that the explicit concept of covenant emerges. Prior to this point the central theme of Jesus' ministry is the kingdom of God and there is no suggestion in Jesus' teaching that the concept of kingdom is coupled with that of covenant. Indeed, covenant terminology is notably absent from Jesus' preaching,[168] which is why when it suddenly occurs here in the Last Supper accounts it has the appearance of being an "unexpected innovation."[169] It simply does not fit within the wider context of his ministry. In a similar vein, McKnight points out that the Last Supper does not take the form of a covenant ceremony, there is no oath taking (*contra* Exod 24:7), the "blood" is not sprinkled on the disciples nor is a commitment to the new covenant elicited. Thus, he concludes that if Jesus really was "setting forth a new covenant, he does so without specifying it as a covenant."[170] In other words, if Jesus was intending to imbue the Last Supper with a covenantal significance then he went about it in a very subdued way.

One cannot counter this argument with an appeal to the authenticity of the word "covenant" either. Scholarship displays little consensus in this regard; the authenticity of the term is denied just as often as it is affirmed.[171] Therefore, McKnight is not alone when he contends that we can viably understand Jesus to have said "this is my blood," as a simple

---

166. Wright, *Jesus and the Victory of God*, 554–63, esp. 561; Dunn, *Jesus Remembered*, 816; Meyer, *The Aims of Jesus*, 219.

167. McKnight, *Jesus and His Death*, 306–12.

168. Holmén suggests that Jesus was "rather detached from the covenant thinking of his contemporaries" ("Jesus, Judaism and the Covenant," 26). This may explain why Jesus choose to speak in terms of the kingdom rather than in terms of the covenant. Though it should be noted that if Jesus could subvert the nationalistic expectations of the coming kingdom then he could have subverted the covenantal expectations as well. The fact remains, though, that Jesus chose to use kingdom as his primary category.

169. McKnight, *Jesus and His Death*, 310.

170. Ibid.

171. Holmén, "Jesus, Judaism and the Covenant," 5.

parallel to "this is my body."[172] Accordingly, the addition of "covenant" to the phrase would have its origins in the understanding of the early church who found in Jesus' death and resurrection the reality of a new corporate existence.

It must be said that McKnight argues his case well, though it seems to me that the present weight of biblical scholarship contends *for* the authenticity of a covenant connection despite the lack of confidence in the term's exact origin.[173] Predominantly, the question is asked as to whether the early church would have made so much of the covenant typology—especially in its burgeoning liturgy—if it had not first been constituted by Jesus himself. Indeed, given our argument on the importance of constitutive meaning and the impact such meaning has on authenticity this question has significant currency.[174] For as we will see in the following chapter, authenticity to a constituted world of meaning is determined by one's assent to the constituted judgment. Thus, if a covenant hermeneutic was considered to be authentic by the early church then such a judgment had to have been made and assented to. The question is, who made such a judgment? If it was not constituted by Jesus himself then it had to be another figure who had sufficient authority to judge what was authentic for the early Christian community *and, in particular, its liturgical practice.* Since McKnight argues that it can only have been the Pneumatic experience of Pentecost that gave impetus to a covenant interpretation (and as Peter's sermon draws upon Joel rather than the new covenant hermeneutic of Jeremiah or Ezekiel), it must have been an anonymous pre-Pauline Christian who found in Pentecost the reality of a new covenant.[175] The value of this connection would then have been corporately accepted and quickly applied in retrospect to Jesus' actions at the Last Supper and so become foundational in the Eucharistic celebration.

But is this scenario more likely than one in which Jesus himself constituted a covenant meaning? I struggle to see how it can be. The short time frames involved and the significance of the covenant imagery to early Christian practice strongly suggests that only Jesus himself could have had the authority to make such a judgment. Of course, McKnight's observation

172. McKnight, *Jesus and His Death*, 310.

173. Aside from Wright, Dunn and Meyer, one can also note Marshall, *Last Supper and Lord's Supper*, 91–93; Sanders and Davies, *Studying the Synoptic Gospels*, 329. And cautiously, Allison, "Jesus and the Covenant," 65–66.

174. A point McKnight acknowledges though he finds his arguments sufficiently conclusive (*Jesus and His Death*, 306).

175. McKnight, *Jesus and His Death*, 317, 320.

that this is not characteristic of Jesus' teaching and preaching must be acknowledged, but this acknowledgement should not be equated with a denial that Jesus could constitute something new during the Last Supper. Indeed, I think that there is potential for Jesus to have connected the Passover tradition with the notion of covenant because the dispensation of the Mosaic covenant occurs hard on the heels of Israel's redemption from Egypt. The two may not be mutually interpreting but it does not mean that they are unrelated.[176] If, as we have argued, Jesus did understand his death to effect a new exodus, then it is not beyond the realms of possibility for him to have also viewed it as inaugurating a new covenant.[177] The two events go hand in hand: just as redemption from Egypt was followed by the Mosaic covenant, so now redemption through Jesus' protective sacrifice would be followed by the establishment of a new covenant.[178]

Is it possible then, for Jesus to have perceived his death as both a paschal sacrifice and as a covenantal sacrifice? The possibility exists, especially if "blood of the covenant" is taken to be authentic, but this would be, as McKnight points out, constitutively new.[179] However, even if the potential for Jesus' death to be understood as a covenantal sacrifice is rejected, it does not negate the potential for Jesus to expect his death to inaugurate a new covenant. The impetus of what Jesus constitutes here is not how and why his death would achieve this new covenant, but in the reality of its very existence.

A significant point of issue remains, for if in the Last Supper Jesus did intend to inaugurate a new covenant through his death, then he does so without recourse to the central means of Jewish atonement—the Temple.[180]

176. For Wright, to invoke the exodus tradition implies covenant renewal (*Jesus and the Victory of God*, 557, 560).

177. See, for example, Theiss, "The Passover Feast of the New Covenant." Again Wright: "There is no reason to doubt that he intended, in speaking of the final cup of the meal in terms of his own death, to allude to this theme of covenant renewal" (*Jesus and the Victory of God*, 561).

178. Tan, "Community, Kingdom and Cross," 145.

179. It should be pointed out that like a paschal sacrifice, the covenantal sacrifice is not a sin-offering either; the shedding of Jesus' blood would function to inaugurate the new covenant just as Moses' sprinkling of blood upon the people had done to inaugurate the first (Exod 24:8). However, Dunn notes that "we should not play off covenant sacrifice and atoning sacrifice against each other, since there was a tendency to run the two together, evident in the Targums" (*Jesus Remembered*, 816 n. 253). The point being that a covenant could only be formed once the people had been reconciled to God and so an expectation of atonement can be pre-supposed.

180. Wright, *Jesus and the Victory of God*, 557.

That is, Jesus offers his disciples membership of the new covenant on an alternative basis to that of the Temple cult. This is why Wright is correct to insist that the Last Supper and Temple action must mutually interpret each other and are therefore to be taken together in the constitution of meaning.[181] To outline this further we need to go back to Jesus' actions in the Temple which we have already said symbolized its destruction. The Temple cult, of course, was the means of atonement for the community and its prophesied destruction suggests that Jesus perceived its present role as short lived. But did Jesus perceive the Last Supper as its replacement? Bruce Chilton argues that he did; the consuming of bread and wine in a "community created by mutual forgiveness," was a better sacrifice "than the priesthood of the Temple [was] willing to permit."[182] Thus, the bread and wine take the place of the body and blood of the sacrificial animal and are eaten as an acceptable and pure offering to God.[183] In such a case, Theissen and Mertz comment that Jesus would be offering the disciples an alternative to the obsolete "official" cult: "By a new interpretation, the last supper becomes a substitute for the temple cult—a pledge of the eating and drinking in the kingdom of God which is soon to dawn."[184] Indeed, Chilton understands this as the reason for Judas' betrayal. The incendiary rejection of the Temple and the setting up of an alternative atoning cult-act was too much for Judas who perhaps feared exclusion from the nation's constituted accepted means of salvation.[185]

But while such an idea is intriguing and does help explain why Judas left during the meal itself, it fails on at least two accounts. The first is that the New Testament is adamant that the disciples continued to worship in, and associate with, the Temple cult. Why would they continue to do so if they believed that Jesus had denounced the Temple and replaced its effective function with a fellowship meal?[186] But even more telling is the fact that this interpretation has little to do with the aims of Jesus heretofore

---

181. Ibid., 561.

182. Chilton, *A Feast of Meanings*, 71.

183. Chilton, *The Temple of Jesus*, 153.

184. Theissen and Mertz, *The Historical Jesus*, 434.

185. Chilton, *Rabbi Jesus*, 255.

186. An interesting point is made by Jonathan Klawans who remarks that when negative comments about the Temple are discernible within the New Testament, the Eucharist is never mentioned. "If the Last Supper really had been an unambiguously anti-temple act, why not bring it up in such contexts?" (Klawans, "Interpreting the Last Supper," 10).

presented and completely ignores the significance of both the Passover and covenant themes on the interpretation of the elements themselves.[187]

Chilton is, however, right about one thing; the pronouncement of destruction upon the Temple does mean that Jesus expected its role to cease. But Jesus did not view the Mosaic dispensation a failure—after all, it had been a God-ordained order—Jesus was, however, convinced that God was doing something eschatologically new in, and through, him.[188] And there is little doubt that Jesus considered the Last Supper to be symbolic of what God was doing. The eschatological nature of the meal is well recognized and Jesus' apparent eagerness to eat of it indicates a strong desire for the reign of God to come (Luke 22:15). Furthermore, if Luke's addendum of "before I suffer" is taken to be authentic, we have once again an expectation that the coming of the reign of God would be preceded by a period of intense suffering, an expectation that continues into the garden of Gethsemane.

Therefore, at the forefront of Jesus' mind is not the meal itself but the constituted meaning it signifies. Jesus perceives that his suffering and death, represented by the bread and cup, are elements of the new, eschatological work that God is doing. A connection that can be inferred from the more widely attested refusal to drink again of the fruit of the vine until the coming of the kingdom (Matt 26:29; Mark 14:24; Luke 22:18). This was an implicit promise of table fellowship beyond death and demonstrates that Jesus combined his expectation of death with the coming of the kingdom.[189] What we need to conclude then, is that it is not the *meal* that would ultimately displace the Temple in the eschatological kingdom, but *Jesus' own death*.[190] Anthony Bartlett reads Wright well here and it is worth quoting him in full:

> With the destruction of the Temple pronounced, Jesus would offer in its place, a new construction of the central rite of the Jewish people, the Passover, together with its governing story,

187. Expectedly, Chilton views efforts to maintain the paschal connection an "exercise in anachronism." The "appropriate" context for appreciating the Last Supper is cultic purity and Jesus' practice of forgiveness at the table (Chilton, *The Temple of Jesus*, 149–50).

188. As Stuhlmacher notes, the problem for Jesus was not that the Temple cult had failed, the problem was that salvation was now dependent on "accepting God's new eschatological act of election, represented by Jesus" (Stuhlmacher, *Jesus of Nazareth*, 31 n. 41). See also Meyer, *The Aims of Jesus*, 218.

189. Meyer, *The Aims of Jesus*, 218.

190. Wright, *Jesus and the Victory of God*, 558.

the Exodus. *This construction took the old symbols and recast them around his own anticipated death.* But perhaps because the looked-for result was not simply another religious ritual (and a religion with it), but a new human reality, YHWH's Kingdom, Wright is careful to specify that the Eucharist is a quasi-cultic meal. In other words, the eschatological reality it looks toward comes close to overwhelming the cultic aspects, while still allowing them enough purchase to act as metaphors for this radically new event.[191]

Therefore, what Jesus is doing in the Last Supper is drawing upon the stories of the Passover, exodus and covenant and stunningly connecting them to his own body and blood, that is, his own death. This is undoubtedly constitutively new, a creation of meaning for Jesus' death that until this point had not been detailed in the linguistic or incarnate carriers. Previously, Jesus had connected his suffering and death to a representative enduring of the Final Ordeal, and indeed, as the Son of man Jesus would render evil impotent (thus releasing people from spiritual bondage—the promise of which was already seen in his earthly praxis), but now we find it expressed in terms of Israel's greatest release—the exodus. Wright, therefore, concludes that Jesus intended to claim that the new exodus, the return of YHWH as king, would ultimately come about through his own death.[192] It is thus the symbolism of the Last Supper that dramatically connects Jesus' expectation of suffering and death with the eschatological coming of the kingdom.

Finally, reference must be made to the salvific significance given to the cup in the Synoptic accounts. As one might expect, the authenticity of the phrases "forgiveness of sins" and "poured out for many" is hotly debated with many concluding that they are reflective of the tradition's development of understanding rather than *ipsissima verba Jesu*.[193] But even if they are rejected there remains an inherent redemptive symbolism within the Last Supper account that must be recognized. In drawing upon both

191. Bartlett, *Cross Purposes*, 218, emphasis mine.

192. Wright, *Jesus and the Victory of God*, 557.

193. The Matthean "forgiveness of sins" (Matt 26:28) is particularly dismissed as a redaction of his Markan reading though Wright is willing to give the phrase some currency because it ties in well with his forgiveness of sins = return from exile theme (ibid., 561). We should note that Wright does not suggest that the words are Jesus', but he does argue that in them Matthew has captured the symbolic meaning of the meal. McKnight dismisses the words as does Dunn, but Meyer is prepared to give them a hearing: McKnight, *Jesus and His Death*, 305; Dunn, *Jesus Remembered*, 231; Meyer, *The Aims of Jesus*, 219.

the exodus and covenant traditions Jesus symbolically creates redemptive meaning for his suffering and death. He fully expects to share the fruits of the vine with those who follow him in the kingdom to come. Because of this, the comments are not alien to Jesus' constituted meaning and the tradition may very well, as Wright suggests, be reflecting the meaning of the meal, even if the words themselves cannot be directly attributable to Jesus.[194] Thus, for example, the question of whether Isaiah 53 formed a scriptural background to Jesus' actions cannot be simply dismissed on the basis that the only textual allusion is found in redactional texts.[195]

McKnight is more than prepared to acknowledge that Jesus may have connected the Servant text with his own death but he also points out that it is not the only possible background to the meal. Aside from Exodus 24, both Zechariah 9:11 and Jeremiah 31:31–33 are potential contenders, especially if the new covenant motif is to be emphasized.[196] Of course, it is not a matter of either/or. The fact is, all of these texts could have been reflected upon by Jesus in constituting the meaning of the Last Supper and thus remain fruitful avenues for later reflection. However, as always, we must be careful to avoid reading later theological understandings back into Jesus' constituted meaning. What has been outlined here is perhaps the minimum that can be said; Jesus created the symbolism of the Last Supper to reveal that God's eschatological work (occurring in and through him), would redeem his followers for life within the new covenant community and to guarantee them a place at the eschatological banquet to come.

To some this conclusion will be too orthodox to possibly be true, to others it does not go far enough. But the above reflections on the Last Supper arise out of an appreciation for the transformation of meaning that confronted the disciples on that particular evening. Jesus' actions with the bread and wine and the appropriation of the Passover context on a night which was not actually Passover, challenged the disciple's world view and their understanding of redemption within the covenant nation. So while I argued against Chilton's conclusion that Jesus intended the meal to replace the Temple cult, his recognition that Judas was challenged by the meaning Jesus' constituted is right on the mark. What Judas refused to

---

194. Wright, *Jesus and the Victory of God*, 561.

195. For instance, William Farmer does not appeal to these particular phrases when he argues that Jesus connected the Suffering Servant to the new covenant of Jeremiah 31:33 (Farmer, "Reflections on Isaiah 53," 271–72).

196. McKnight, *Jesus and His Death*, 289–90.

do was to accept the meaning that Jesus had newly constituted. The other disciples were also required to judge the new meaning constituted but they accepted it, and thus entered into a new world of authentic existence in which Jesus' death had redemptive significance.

Conclusion

In the Last Supper, Jesus deliberately appropriates the Passover context even though the meal itself most probably took place the night before Passover. This position has two results: Firstly, it explains why Jesus did not make symbolic use of the Passover lamb and secondly, it provides a redemptive context in which the symbolism of the Last Supper functions. Therefore, by identifying his own body with the "bread of affliction," Jesus intended to connect his death with the exodus tradition, possibly even drawing attention to the protective efficacy of such a death. The cup, which Jesus represents as his blood, continues this theme but it also incorporates covenantal significance, a connection implicit within the Paschal meal itself even if the authenticity of the word "covenant" is not granted. This places Jesus' death (and not the meal itself) in direct contrast to the old dispensation, which was now being made redundant by the new and eschatological work of God.

Having pronounced judgment upon the Temple, the central element of the new covenant would be the broken body and shed blood of Jesus himself. Hence, the symbolism of the Last Supper reinforces what we had already discovered through Jesus' expectation that he would endure the Final Ordeal, redeeming the community by taking the judgment of God upon himself. Jesus was convinced that his death would redeem the new community and its redemption would be of the same order as that of the great exodus. This is not to say that Jesus understood his death to therefore be an ineluctable divine necessity "structurally intrinsic to salvation."[197] Such statements are a result of later reflection and developments of theological understanding. Here, in his farewell meal, Jesus creates a symbolic meaning of redemption in which his followers would both be protected from the judgment to come and welcomed into the community of the new covenant.

197. Meyer warns against such a conclusion (*The Aims of Jesus*, 218).

Jesus' Intention for His Death

The amount of material covered in this chapter has been extensive, although it must be said that it is only a drop in the bucket of what could be written about Jesus of Nazareth. However, our task was considerably simplified by the fact of a rather narrow focus and deceptively easy question: what meaning did Jesus create for his suffering and death? Building upon the earlier chapters the investigation was structured along a threefold analysis which examined what meaning could be discerned through the incarnate, linguistic and symbolic carriers. These are, of course, not the only ways to analyze Jesus' expectation and intentions, but as I endeavored to show in the previous chapter, it is an avenue that provides considerable hope for success. So then, having completed the study to the extent that we are able, what can be concluded?

If he had not perceived a premature death already, the death of John the Baptist would have alerted Jesus to the reality that he would probably not live his full three-score and ten. This means that Jesus had more than enough time to reflect upon that possibility and hence create meaning for it, a meaning that went beyond the expectation of a post-mortem vindication. Like John the Baptist, Jesus expected God to come in judgment upon the nation of Israel primarily because of her apostasy. He too called for people to repent and to be aware that the wrath of God was soon to be poured out upon the people via the hand of pagan Rome. But this was not to be a warning without any avenue of hope, for Jesus also proclaimed that the kingdom of God was imminent, and indeed, in and through Jesus it had already made its presence felt. Much of the victory was, of course, proleptic. Jesus still looked ahead to a time when evil would have free reign, the Final Ordeal would occur, precipitating the eschatological battle and the ultimate victory of God. This is not something that Jesus looked forward to in an enthusiastic sense, the sixth petition of the Lord's prayer is evidence enough of that. It was, however, something that Jesus anticipated and at some point in his ministry he came to the conclusion that it would be he himself who would have to endure that tribulation. But ultimate victory over the powers of evil *was* assured and Jesus' praxis foreshadowed that reality.

But how did Jesus' death fit into that reality? Both the passion predictions and Mark 10:45 suggest that the figure of the Son of man held considerable significance for Jesus in this regard. Drawing from Daniel 7, Jesus perceived that he would suffer as the Son of man because his God-given authority had been rejected by the nation, but he also perceived that the suffering which would follow such a rejection could be endured on behalf of the nation itself. The tradition of the Maccabean martyrs provides further evidence in this direction, demonstrating that it was plausibly Jewish for there to be an expectation that suffering could be redemptive for the community. Importantly, Jesus perceived that suffering not in terms of divine willing (in that he saw it as divinely necessary for him to suffer and die in order for God to forgive) but in terms of the eschatological conflict with the powers of evil that presently ruled the nation (world). The Ordeal, is in fact, God's judgment upon the nation (world) for its own apostasy but as the Son of man, Jesus was determined to endure it on behalf of the nation, convinced that God would vindicate him at the proper time. Jesus was also convinced that the vindication he awaited would be extended to those whom he corporately represented.

This redeeming theme is, of course, absent from the passion predictions, but Mark 10:45 does connect the Son of man figure with an expectation that Jesus' life would ransom his followers into the kingdom of God. Exactly how Jesus expected this to occur is not the focus of the passage itself, but if an allusion to Isaiah 53 is allowed it becomes apparent that it is through suffering that God's redemptive plan for Israel—and for the world—would be realized. This conclusion draws us once again to the center of contemporary criticisms of the atonement, but the point here is not to defend any particular atonement theory but to ask what meaning Jesus intended to create for his death. And the meaning conveyed through the linguistic carrier is that Jesus expected to suffer and die as part of the Final Ordeal, an event that would redeem his followers from the judgment of God so that they might be vindicated just as Jesus himself expected to be.

The Temple action and Last Supper provide some further clarity to the meaning that Jesus was constituting for his death. There is little doubt that Jesus' actions in the Temple were critical of the present operation of the Temple cult but we should not, therefore, assume that Jesus was critical of the cult itself. Instead the Temple, which had become the center of the nation's self-reliance, would be destroyed as part of God's judgment upon the nation. But Jesus perceived that judgment not as an end to God's redemptive activity but that God was doing something eschatologically new. It is the symbolism of the Last Supper that confirms Jesus' understanding of this. By utilizing the bread and wine to symbolize his own body and blood, Jesus connects his death to the redeeming activity of God. Drawing upon the Passover context and its implications of covenant renewal, Jesus expresses a conviction that through his death God would redeem his followers just as God had redeemed the Israelites from Egypt. What would result would be a new community, whose authenticity was not based in the old dispensation but was now newly constituted on the basis of Jesus' death. It should also be stressed that it is not the meal itself that affects this redemption but the death of Jesus which, of course, the meal represents. Thus, the symbolic carrier confirms the redemptive meaning that Jesus was creating for his death, a meaning discerned not just from isolated texts but from the impact that Jesus had upon his disciples through both the incarnate and linguistic carriers as well.

So then, where to from here? The next task is to take the results of our efforts and apply them to the theological task of understanding the judgment of Jesus. In other words, how should the theologian successfully reflect on the meaning that Jesus created for his death in developing an atonement motif? Primarily this is a movement from judgment to under-standing, the contention being that a faithful atonement motif will be one that takes due consideration of the constituted judgment of Jesus in the expression of its own understanding. What, exactly, is meant by this will be the focus of the final chapter.

5

From Meaning to Motif

. . . it is difficult to imagine that one soteriological model could express all that one may truly say about the saving significance of Jesus' death.[1]

—Mark D. Baker

IN CHAPTER ONE IT WAS ARGUED THAT AN ATONEMENT MOTIF THAT wished to remain faithful to Christianity would demonstrate a degree of continuity with the meaning that Jesus of Nazareth constituted for his death. That contention still stands, and our analysis of the previous chapter has brought us to the point in which we must now discuss what kind of continuity is, in fact, to be expected. How should we incorporate the meaning that Jesus created for his death into our contemporary presentations? What kind of continuity are we looking for? Are our articulations to be constrained to the categories of Son of man, Final Ordeal, sacrifice or covenant? Or do we have more freedom to create categories of our own making while still remaining faithful to Jesus' constituted intent? These are the primary questions of this chapter and their discussion will conclude the present study.

The Extent of the Meaning Constituted

It should be immediately recognized that the historical evidence presented in the previous chapter did not allow us to arrive at a systematic understanding of the atonement in a similar sense to that, say, of Anselm's *Cur Deus Homo*? Our conclusions were far more circumspect, undoubtedly because the Gospels did not remember a Jesus who mused over the nature of his death in Socratic fashion but a man who was compelled in life

1. Baker, *Proclaiming the Scandal*, 15–16.

and—as he came to comprehend—in death, to inaugurate the kingdom of God. The inescapable conclusion is that Jesus constituted meaning for his approaching death from within a kingdom context and such meaning was not, therefore, an arbitrary imposition upon what was otherwise a meaningless event. In other words, Jesus' death had meaning precisely because he conceived it in terms of his overall mission, which again, is why such an analysis into constituted meaning is so crucial.

However, the obvious consequence of this understanding, and it was certainly evident in the previous chapter, is that the relevant questions on the atonement that concern systematic theology (that is, the fallen nature of humanity and the precise salvific process), had no discernible place in the discussion.[2] We did not, for example, have any occasion to ask whether Jesus believed his death was a propitiatory or expiatory offering. Nor did we have to ask if Jesus thought that by enduring the judgment of the Final Ordeal he would somehow also endure the demands of justice. Nor again, did we have to question whether Jesus believed that by his death he would restore honor to God, or trick the devil into giving up his hold on fallen humanity. None of these questions were asked for the simple reason that the meaning carried through the incarnate, linguistic and symbolic carriers did not raise them.

I would, of course, stress that at no stage did our analysis suggest that a systematic construction is untenable, or that it was impossible for Jesus to have had an understanding that was amenable to such expressions. However, it must be recognized that the Gospels do not articulate Jesus' understanding in this way. What we found instead, was a man who drew upon and reinterpreted both the prophets and the past redemptive acts of YHWH to create a meaning in which his death would have redemptive significance. The Last Supper provides the clearest indication of this expectation, linking the great exodus to the imminent coming of the kingdom, a link made possible by the breaking of his body and the shedding of his blood. Furthermore, this redemptive significance found support in both the linguistic and incarnate carriers, as Jesus' entire life praxis demonstrated the restoration inherent in his kingdom ministry.

And it is the requirement to ascertain this judgment that demanded the rather difficult analysis of the previous chapter. For if we are to take Chalcedon's implications about the humanity of Christ seriously, then it

2. And herein lies one of the great benefits of approaching the cross from an historical perspective. It allows us to examine the constituted meaning of Jesus' death without getting entrenched in the *a priori* assumptions, interests and problems of systematic theology. Lonergan, *Grace and Freedom*, 156.

must be accepted that Jesus conceived his actions from within the context, language and mentality of his own times.[3] And on this score, what our analysis demonstrated was that the meaning that Jesus constituted was a meaning that *above all reflected the reality of the coming of the kingdom*. It is, therefore, historical nonsense to argue that Jesus understood his death in terms of Anselm's satisfaction motif or Grotius' governmental theory or even in terms of Mann's ontological coherence. Such language and concepts were demonstrably not present in the worldview of a first century Jew, even one who was thoroughly convinced that there was a sense of divine destiny about his own work and person. Let me re-iterate: it is not possible to argue that the constituted meaning of the cross is either this or that systematic expression, or that we must somehow defend a particular systematic understanding as belonging to Jesus himself. The fact is, Jesus' constituted meaning remains part of, and connected to, *the story of Israel as a whole and thus should not be interpreted as a systematic discussion on the process of salvation in general*. Again, this is not to say that there is no possibility of a systematic understanding, but that such exposition was not the central element of Jesus' constituted meaning.

Having said all that, I readily acknowledge that the foundations of later systematic expressions are apparent in the Gospels and even more so in the New Testament Epistles as the early church reflected on the nature and function of the cross.[4] But it must be stressed that such motifs are not systematically expressed by Jesus himself but remain a product of understanding of the redemptive judgment that he constituted for his death. What this means is that our salvific expressions cannot afford to be ignorant of the judgment that Jesus made concerning his death and they should, in fact, find their origins therein.

But what are the implications of this point for our discussion going forward? For if Jesus did not express a clear systematic understanding but rather a judgment concerning the soteriological value of his death, how can our further systematic expressions be considered faithful? What, exactly, are our expressions to be faithful to? One answer would be to point to the understandings later developed in the New Testament and to argue for their timeless sufficiency and universal applicability. One could then argue for faithfulness on the basis of a clear connection with Scripture and

3. Hefling, "Christ and Evils," 880–81.

4. We have already seen the potential for Jesus' death to be expressed in terms of a paschal sacrifice, inaugurator of a new covenant, a representative enduring of eschatological judgment and a decisive victory over evil amongst others.

I do not wish to dispute the viability of this point. Indeed, the Scriptural witness has been, and should continue to be, the *sine qua non* of our soteriological discussions and it must be emphasized that any faithful atonement understanding will not contradict or nullify the Word of God.[5]

Yet we must also draw a careful distinction here (to be elaborated on below) between the judgments of truth that the New Testament declares and the Christian faith affirms, and the systematic understanding of that truth. For the theologian who is embedded in a received world of faith the task is not merely to repeat the understandings of the past, but to acknowledge and communicate the revealed truth of the biblical text in the present. Thus, the proliferation of recent atonement motifs, many of which do not explicitly draw upon the symbolism of the New Testament, cannot simply be rejected on the grounds of their differing (that is, non-biblical) categories. Of course, this does not mean that one can approach the text of the New Testament carelessly, for the judgments of truth that are expressed therein are just that, judgments that cannot be denied if one wishes to remain an authentic member of the faith community. However, it does mean that a determination of faithfulness cannot always be ascertained on the basis of a motif's use (or lack of use) of the relevant biblical expression. Importantly, I would strongly insist that this statement is not meant to provoke concerns of relativism, nor is it an underhanded attempt to deny the sufficiency of Scripture. What I am arguing for is simply a recognition that differing articulations have the potential for faithfulness even if a direct appropriation of the New Testament symbols are not made.

But how then are we to judge faithfulness? What is it that makes one's contextualized presentation of the salvation proclaimed in Jesus' death and resurrection authentic? I believe the answer can be found in the distinction between judgment and understanding, a distinction that essentially lies behind what Bernard Lonergan defines as Doctrine and Systematics. And to this we now turn.

Judgment and Understanding

The basis for the above assertion is found in the discussion that took place towards the end of chapter three. There we discussed three worlds: the world of immediacy, the world mediated by meaning and the world constituted by meaning. It was the last of these three that was argued to be

5. As, in fact, we earlier saw Green and Baker affirming: Green and Baker, *Recovering the Scandal*, 217–21.

the most significant for our discussion in chapter four, for it is within the world constituted by meaning that impact occurs and the potential for transformation exists. Thus, in analyzing the impact and transformation that Jesus' constituted meaning had on his followers, we could ascertain via the various carriers of meaning something of the meaning that Jesus constituted.

But there is more to be gained from an investigation into the world constituted by meaning than what we have just described. To begin with, we should recall that in contrast to the world of immediacy the world constituted by meaning requires both understanding and judgment to be effected.[6] This is because it is a world that is created by corporate intention and hence requires a common judgment if it is to take root. Recall too that an individual's authentic existence was predicated on their judgment matching that of the community's judgment. If they judged similarly, then the individual would function as an authentic member of the community. However, if the individual judged differently then he or she could no longer claim authentic existence within *that* community.[7] In such a case, conflict of some sort is inevitable and commonly results in the formation of a separate community, one based on that initial dissenting judgment. And I have argued in the previous chapter that this is precisely what occurred in Jesus' proclamation of the coming of the kingdom. As we saw, Jesus' judgment on what that proclamation meant was based on, yet considerably different from, that constituted by the people of Israel at the time. Importantly, I have stressed that it is also from within that particular context that Jesus judged his death to have redemptive significance. Hence, while it was possible to find points of contact with the Jewish expectation of redemptive suffering it was also recognized that Jesus constituted something entirely new for his death. The Temple action coupled with the Last Supper provided the most significant evidence of this and together demonstrated that the meaning which Jesus constituted, if accepted, would cause a new community to arise. This is not wishful thinking, but the inevitable result of an opposing judgment concerning authentic existence within the constituted community.

And herein lies the foundation of a faithful contemporary atonement motif that engages with the constituted meaning of Jesus of Nazareth. For

---

6. Lonergan, "The Origins of Christian Realism," 241.

7. As was said earlier, one's contrary judgment might actually mean a growth in authenticity, but while authentic to oneself, such a judgment will put one at odds with the community's constitutively defined meaning.

as a result of Jesus' actions (even if one takes issue with my presentation of them), there is a fundamental requirement for those who were confronted by Jesus to existentially judge for themselves the value of Jesus' alternative world of meaning, a world of meaning in which it was now Jesus' death that would ultimately provide the means of divine-human reconciliation and offer membership in the newly constituted community. Hence, it is the continuity of the two judgments—that of Jesus and that of his follow-ers—that determines authentic Christian existence.[8] What this means is that faithfulness to the community arises out of similar judgment rather than the understanding of that judgment. To explain this further it will be necessary to distinguish between belief, understanding and judgment and once again I will make reference to the work of Bernard Lonergan whose discussion on these matters in both *Insight* and *Method in Theology* provides the requisite foundation for my own point.

On Belief, Judgment and Understanding

To examine how the salvific judgment Jesus made might be appropriated in contemporary works on the atonement requires a consideration of the operations of belief, judgment and understanding.[9] Primarily this consid-eration is required because the passage of time demands that the meaning which Jesus constituted be mediated by others. People today are no longer able to directly experience for themselves the challenge which Jesus con-stituted and hence, there is a latent question of belief in the witness of that challenge, and furthermore, what role belief should play in coming to a salvific understanding of the cross. A discussion on the related operations of judgment and understanding is also required because it seems to me that modern atonement perspectives continue to confuse their separate roles when presenting salvific motifs. In Mann and Heim, for example, the motifs described are both judgments as to the salvific value of the

---

8. The two must cohere or what results is not a community based on the consti-tuted meaning of Jesus but on some other dissenting judgment. I am not suggesting either that a common judgment concerning Jesus' death is *all* that constitutes authen-tic existence, but it is a necessary element of such existence.

9. I refer to belief here as opposed to faith because Lonergan distinguishes between the two. Faith for Lonergan is "knowledge born of religious love" and is not derived from the operations of experience, understanding and judging. It is, then, a knowledge that results from being in love with, and deciding on the value of, God. Belief, as we will see, does arise from these cognitive operations, even if they are carried out by an-other. Lonergan, *Method in Theology*, 115; Ogilvie, *Faith Seeking Understanding*, 145.

cross *and* understandings of the salvific process which takes place on the cross. In both cases, the judgment of value arises from the cross' revelatory nature (ontological coherence, scapegoat mechanism) and the understanding of how that judgment effects salvation consequently follows. However, the result of such a presentation is not authenticity within the world of meaning Jesus constituted but an invitation to the world of meaning constituted by the theologian. Of course, the cognitive operations of understanding and judgment are certainly related but this does not mean that they should be confused, and hence, there is a need to examine their distinction here. But before we can adequately discuss their relationship we also need to outline, albeit briefly, what Lonergan terms "immanently generated" knowledge and the means by which it is determined.[10]

Lonergan characterizes knowledge that arises from the operations of experience, understanding and judgment as being immanently generated. The term distinguishes that which we come to know by our own efforts from that which we come to know on the basis of the efforts of others. The three cognitive operations of experience, understanding and judgment are not chosen arbitrarily either, for they are arguably the "triple cord of human knowing."[11] If we were, for example, to ask the question, "what am I doing when I am knowing"? the answer would be a dynamic unfolding of these particular operations.[12] Matthew Ogilvie summarizes Lonergan's position well:

> Just as sense experience alone does not constitute human knowing, Lonergan stresses that neither understanding alone nor judging alone account for human knowing. If understanding lacked the presentations of sensible data, it would have nothing to understand. If understanding lacked judgment, there would be no distinction between fact and fiction. Judgment to the exclusion of understanding is not knowing, but arrogance. Furthermore, judgment isolated from experience simply sets aside fact. For Lonergan, human knowing is neither experience alone, understanding alone, nor judging alone, but a dynamic structure of all three, together constituting human knowing.[13]

10. Lonergan, *Method in Theology*, 43–47. That knowledge arises from a cognitional process in the manner that Lonergan describes will be assumed from this point. Cf. Lonergan, *Insight*.

11. Ogilvie, *Faith Seeking Understanding*, 59.

12. Lonergan, *Insight*, 16–17; Doran, *Theology and the Dialectics of History*, 43.

13. Ogilvie, *Faith Seeking Understanding*, 60.

Knowledge is thus a dynamic process that requires the ongoing unfolding of these three cognitional operations. Just how these operations actually interact is something that Lonergan addresses with considerable detail in Part One of *Insight*. However, it is the specific relationship between judgment and understanding that is worth noting here. In the first place, Lonergan insists that without the prior effort to understand there would be no occasion for judgment. The two do not occur in isolation and if, perchance, one did attempt to judge without the prior act of understanding, then such judgment would essentially be meaningless.[14] Therefore, meaningful judgment occurs as the end result. It is,

> the last act in the series that begins from presentations and advances through understanding and formulation ultimately to reach reflection and affirmation or denial. Thus, the proper content of judgment, the yes or no, is the final partial increment in the process. But this proper content is meaningless apart from the question it answers. With the question it forms an integrated whole.[15]

Again, Lonergan confirms that judgment is not simply a matter of "taking a good look" but arises out of the dynamic unfolding between experience (here presentations) and understanding. But how the judgment of yes or no is arrived at is also significant, for one does not merely understand what one experiences and then decide synchronically one way or the other. It is, as we have already seen in critical realism, a spiraling dialogue between understanding and judgment that allows the ultimate yes/no answer to be given. In other words, it is within this spiraling dialogue (which Lonergan terms *reflective understanding*) that one grasps the "weight" of the evidence at hand and is therefore able to judge appropriately.

"Weighing the evidence" is, of course, a metaphorical euphuism and Lonergan introduces a new term to describe with more precision the fact that an appropriate judgment has been made. The term chosen is *unconditioned*, which he further qualifies as either formal or virtual. A formally unconditioned judgment occurs when there are no conditions whatsoever to be fulfilled. A virtually unconditioned judgment occurs when there are conditions, but these conditions have been met.[16] However, Loner-

14. As he writes in "Cognitional Structure": "To pass judgment on what one does not understand is, not human knowing, but human arrogance" (223).

15. Lonergan, *Insight*, 301.

16. Lonergan writes: "[A] prospective judgment will be virtually unconditioned if (1) it is the conditioned [i.e., there is a question for reflection], (2) its conditions are

gan notes that even if conditions did not exist and one could potentially make a formally unconditioned judgment, the mere act of questioning actually creates conditions, thus denying the judgment formal status.[17] As a consequence, all judgments can only ever reach the status of virtually unconditioned, which is why the act of reflective understanding is always necessary.[18] Indeed, the very function of reflective understanding is to,

> meet the question for reflection by transforming the prospective judgment from the status of a conditioned to the status of a virtually unconditioned; and reflective understanding effects this transformation by grasping the conditions of the conditioned and their fulfilment.[19]

It is, therefore, the virtually unconditioned that we seek because it is only once all the conditions have been met that we can truly answer yes/no to the question for reflection.

Whilst there is no doubt that Lonergan's terminology does take a little getting used to, the point he makes here is well worth the effort to comprehend. The fundamental question of what it is that we are doing when we come to know is answered through the threefold operations of experiencing, understanding and judging. However, true judgment is not simply the result of taking a good look at what we have experienced and understood, but arises from the dynamic unfolding between judgment and understanding, an unfolding that goes on until all the conditions of the judgment have been met. This process Lonergan terms reflective understanding and results in the virtually unconditioned.[20] Now all this is well and good, but what does it mean for a contemporary presentation of the atonement? The answer will be forthcoming shortly but first we must return to the question of belief.

I remarked above that the term "immanently generated" was used to distinguish between knowledge that was discerned directly from our own efforts and that which we come to know by the efforts of others. The implicit assumption is that it is possible to know something that one has not found out for oneself. In other words, not all knowledge is immanently generated

---

known, and (3) the conditions are fulfilled" (ibid., 305).

17. Ibid.

18. Of course, not all judgments are virtually unconditioned, in which case they are more commonly referred to as "guesses."

19. Lonergan, *Insight*, 305.

20. Lonergan acknowledges the influence of J. H. Newman's "illative sense" on his account of reflective understanding (*Understanding and Being*, 351).

and to deny this point would be to blindly insist that one can only know what one has independently experienced, understood and judged.[21] However, knowledge is not confined to what we know in virtue of our personal experience or even our personal grasp of the virtually unconditioned.[22] No one can do all the necessary experiments, nor does anyone unnecessarily repeat that which has already been reliably demonstrated. Indeed, human collaboration inherently requires that we *believe* what others have done and the results they have achieved. If we do not, then advancement in knowledge would become impossible as all our time would be taken up in reproducing the same knowledge over and over again.

In *Insight*, Lonergan gives several examples from the mathematical and scientific fields in which belief in the work of others is repeatedly displayed.[23] In *Method*, some of these examples are given again but in addition he gives a more familiar example from the world of cartography. Drawing our attention to a map of the United States, Lonergan asks whether we know that the locations of each individual city are accurate.[24] If we were to answer "yes" without having actually gone to every city and taken a latitude and longitude reading and then compared it to the location on the map, then our knowledge would be based on belief. Even if we were then to argue that the accuracy of the map is verified every day by countless persons who use the map to fly, sail or drive, only a small proportion of that immanently generated knowledge would be our own. Our knowledge of the map's accuracy is therefore based upon believing the many witnesses who have found the maps acceptable. Thus, the conclusion to be drawn here is twofold. Firstly, belief itself is not opposed to human rationality nor is it somehow to be limited to the religious sphere; and secondly, belief results in a judgment of fact based upon the knowledge of another.[25]

This second point highlights a crucial feature of belief. The judgment that results is not immanently generated (that is, it does not result from reflective understanding) but is *an assent based on the trust of one's sources*. Importantly, that trust is not uncritical, for the source is evaluated (attentively, intelligently, reasonably and responsibly) on their ability to

21. Lonergan, *Method in Theology*, 41–47.

22. Lonergan, *Insight*, 726.

23. Ibid., 726–28.

24. It must be remembered that Lonergan was writing before the era of cartographic satellites and the reproduction of the example here should not be taken as a comment on the accuracy of current surveying practices but for its heuristic value.

25. See Ogilvie, *Faith Seeking Understanding*, 183.

arrive at a virtually unconditioned judgment on the basis of their own immanently generated knowledge.[26] Such knowledge can be confirmed by others and the value of believing the initial judgment can be realized and subsequently communicated. Belief, then, must be acknowledged as a judgment, but it is not an affirmation of the truth of one's own understanding but an assent to the virtually unconditioned that is communicated by another. Belief therefore conveys judgment and not understanding which is why religious belief cannot be expected to provide an understanding of the mysteries of faith.[27] Rather, belief allows one to assent to the fact of those mysteries, an assent that then fosters understanding.

Both Augustine and Anselm argued for this very point when they contended for the axiom *crede ut intelligas* (believe that you may understand). And it is this point that we must come to grips with if we are to successfully appropriate the constituted meaning of Jesus. The reason for this is twofold. In the first place, I have contended that Jesus constituted meaning for his death and that meaning was not a systematic expression of the process of salvation but a judgment based on reflective understanding of his own life and ministry. In other words, Jesus' knowledge that his death would have redemptive significance was immanently generated. Accordingly, this knowledge challenged the current world view of his followers and they were required to existentially judge for themselves the value of this alternative world of meaning. Now this judgment had the potential to be made by virtue of reflective understanding, since the world of meaning that Jesus constituted was experienced by the disciples and therefore could be understood and judged in the immediate sense. Yet as Dunn emphasized, the disciples began to believe Jesus from the very start, which suggests that their knowledge of this world primarily arose from their trust in Jesus as a source of virtually unconditioned judgment. In other words, in their own reflective act of understanding what the disciples grasped was not immanently generated knowledge of the constituted world of meaning, but the value of deciding to believe the person and judgment of Jesus. Hence, the disciples did not have to immediately understand how Jesus' death would be redemptive to know that it was so. Their knowledge was based on the judgment of Jesus rather than in their own cognitive operations.

---

26. This is the third stage of a total of five stages that Lonergan identifies operating in belief but such discussion is not required here. See Lonergan, *Insight*, 728–32; Lonergan, *Method in Theology*, 44–46.

27. Ogilvie, *Faith Seeking Understanding*, 153.

It was, of course, only post-Easter that the disciples were able to process the consequences of such an assent, but this in itself points to the second reason for the importance of belief in our argument. That is, what establishes authentic existence in the world of meaning that Jesus constituted is not the understanding of that world but the assent to its virtually unconditioned judgment. The Gospels certainly present the disciples as authentic followers of Jesus but this was not because they understood what Jesus was doing—they clearly did not. No, they were authentic members because they believed in him and in the value of his judgment. This is of vital significance for contemporary articulations of the atonement because it locates faithfulness *not in the form of its expression but in the judgment it makes*. In other words, what makes our atonement discussion faithful to the constituted meaning of Jesus is not whether our understanding demonstrably matches that of Jesus, but whether the judgment we make concerning the death of Jesus faithfully reflects that which he himself made. As was suggested earlier, this point can be further clarified by an appeal to Lonergan's distinction between the functional specialties of Doctrines and Systematics.

On Doctrines and Systematics

In Lonergan's transcendental method the functional specialty *Doctrines* directly precedes that of *Systematics* and both are found in the more personal phase of theological reflection that begins with *Foundations*.[28] Without engaging in unnecessary detail, according to Lonergan the key to Foundations is intellectual, moral and religious conversion.[29] Such an emphasis is given because at this point in the theological method it is no longer a matter of investigating, comparing and analyzing the data, but of its personal and corporate appropriation. As Lonergan notes, the undertaking of Research, Interpretation, Historical inquiry and Dialectics (the four prior functional specialties) does not require a particular commitment to what one is investigating.[30] However, the task of theology does not cease with Dialectics, but must go on to include the doctrines of faith accepted

28. I use the capital designation throughout this discussion to make reference to Lonergan's functional specialties. Where the words are found without capitalization they hold their usual non-technical meaning.

29. "Normally it is intellectual conversion as the fruit of both religious and moral conversion; it is moral conversion as the fruit of religious conversion; and it is religious conversion as the fruit of God's gift of grace" (Lonergan, *Method in Theology*, 267–68).

30. Ibid., 268.

at conversion, and from there the understanding of such doctrines and their subsequent communication in both pastoral and missional aspects. Hence, conversion lies at the heart of both Doctrines and Systematics, and as we will see, the task of Doctrines is to codify the realities of conversion into more formal terms prior to their subsequent systematic expression. With that said, our focus here is not simply to discuss two particular stages in theological method but to highlight the value of distinguishing between Doctrines and Systematics because of the insight both specialties offer to the development of soteriological motifs.

As Lonergan defines it, doctrines express judgments of fact and judgments of value.[31] They are concerned, then, with the affirmations and negations of theologically relevant questions of reflection and as such correlate well with the judgment that arises from a confrontation with constituted meaning. This means that doctrines are not an expression of understanding. Rather they are statements of what constitutes authentic existence within the community that chooses to call itself, in this case, Christian. And because they are constitutive of authenticity, such statements have a certain level of permanence. This is all the more so for Christian doctrines since "they are not just data but expressions of truths and, indeed, of truths that, were they not revealed by God, could not be known by man."[32] Hence, the functional specialty Doctrines is concerned to state the religious community's confession of what can be known of God and God's activity in creation. As such, the assent to doctrine remains within the realm of faith but it is an assent that is based on lived experience within the community as much as cognitive acceptance.[33]

However, Lonergan notes that while doctrines are asserted and assented to, the measure of understanding that accompanies the assent of faith is highly variable.[34] He gives the example of Irenaeus who acknowledged that one believer could be more articulate and knowledgeable than another, but that does not mean the former was more a believer than the latter.[35] The two are equally believers, it is merely their level of understanding that differs. With this in mind, it cannot then be the *understanding* of the doctrine that determines authentic existence but the *acceptance* of the doctrine. And this allows for considerable difference in understanding to

31. Ibid., 132.

32. Ibid., 325.

33. And lived experience includes a personal relationship with Christ, however mediated such a relationship might be by the community.

34. Lonergan, *Method in Theology*, 349–50.

35. Ibid., 350, citing Irenaeus, *Adv. Haer.*, I, 10. 3.

exist between authentic members of the community without negating the validity of their individual membership.[36]

But if an understanding of a doctrine can differ, and indeed, change over time, then so too must its articulation.[37] And it is precisely the expression of the meaning of doctrines that is the business of the functional specialty *Systematics*. In short, Systematics promotes an understanding of the realities affirmed in Doctrines. Both aim at understanding truth, but they do so in different manners. Lonergan again:

> Doctrines aim at a clear and distinct affirmation of religious realities: its principal concern is the truth of such an affirmation; its concern to understand is limited to the clarity and distinctness of its affirmation. On the other hand, systematics aims at an understanding of the religious realities affirmed by doctrines. It wants its understanding to be true, for it is not a pursuit of misunderstanding. At the same time, it is fully aware that its understanding is bound to be imperfect, merely analogous, commonly no more than probable.[38]

Hence, the aim of Systematics is not to increase certitude but to promote understanding. In other words, Systematics is not about establishing the facts but is an effort to provide "some inkling as to how it could possibly be that the facts are what they are."[39] And it should be recognized that such understanding is never going to be definitive, not just because the context for grasping such meaning varies, but because it would be folly—if not blasphemous—to expect an exhaustive understanding of the divine transcendent mystery.

The relationship between Doctrines and Systematics is far more complicated than that just described but such complexities do not negate the fundamental distinction between the two specialties.[40] The point to be made here is that as an exercise in *fides quaerens intellectum*, systematic theology does not determine the content of faith but is an attempt to

---

36. Meynell, *The Theology of Bernard Lonergan*, 20.

37. "Human understanding develops over time and, as it develops, human concepts, theories, affirmations, courses of action change. Such change is cumulative" (Lonergan, *Method in Theology*, 325).

38. Ibid., 349.

39. Ibid., 336.

40. As Robert Doran notes, what Lonergan says in his chapter on Systematics is not to be contradicted, but it does not say all that can be said (Doran, "Bernard Lonergan and the Functions of Systematic Theology," 570).

express such faith in a systematic fashion.[41] And since that synthesis is centered in the mysteries of faith, its "understanding must remain permanently imperfect, hypothetical, analogical, and open to development."[42] Hence, it should be accepted that an understanding of a particular doctrine is open to changes of expression *insofar* as the doctrine itself remains faithfully asserted. This means, of course, that the systematic task must be approached attentively, intelligently, reasonably and responsibly or the understanding it communicates will not bear appropriately on the mysteries of faith. But if done fittingly, differences in expression will be seen to be benign (due, for example, to differences in culture) rather than as an offence arising from a lack of intellectual, moral, or religious conversion. As Meynell writes, in themselves, "[B]enign differences testify to the vitality of faith, since one's grasp of it, if deep and genuine, will be expressed in the terms and conceptions proper to one's own culture."[43] This also signifies that fruitful and faithful meanings will never emerge from an understanding that does not cohere with the asserted doctrine. Here, as elsewhere, the truth of *crede ut intelligas* remains.

So what, then, does this line of reasoning mean for the present discussion? Essentially it is this: the presentation of how the death of Jesus reconciles humanity to both God and one another should not be taken as proof of the doctrine that Jesus' death does, in fact, save. Atonement motifs are not viable forms of theological rationalism. What they are, are attempts to understand the divine offer of redemption in, and through, the death and resurrection of Jesus of Nazareth. If this is accepted, then the various motifs themselves should not be classified as individual and competing doctrines but rather as instances of exactly what should be occurring under the functional specialty of Systematics. Here again we should note that there never has been a defined dogma concerning the *pro nobis* nature of redemption. What, for example, Nicea and Chalcedon did for the incarnation and ontological constitution of Christ has no direct parallel in the history of Christian soteriological discourse. Indeed, perhaps there cannot be such a clarity of definition, especially if one considers that the meaning of the cross is best expressed dramatically because of its symbolic and aesthetic nature. As Robert Doran notes:

> The mystery of redemption is one whose articulation, precisely as a mystery, remains perhaps forever the symbolic expressions

41. Ormerod, "What is the Task of Systematic Theology?"

42. Doran, "Functions of Systematic Theology," 577.

43. Meynell, *The Theology of Bernard Lonergan*, 24.

of a "position," the *esthetic* and *dramatic* presentation of a truth that, affirmed as truth, is constitutive of the community of believers.[44]

This means that an attempt to grasp the meaning of salvation in Christ from within the theologian's own context is not to present a new doctrine, nor is it to present an alternative means to authentic Christian existence. It is, instead, to explain the salvific significance of the cross in a manner relevant to the current community, whether that community consider themselves authentically Christian or not.[45] The "dramatic" element of that articulation that Doran highlights here is something to which we will return below, but to draw the present point to a close it must be insisted that there is room for contextually coherent expressions of the meaning of the cross as long as they remain faithful to the salvific judgment that Jesus himself constituted. What now remains is to make some relevant observations about the development of contemporary expressions, a journey in the given context from constituted meaning to theological motif.

From Constituted Meaning to Theological Motif

As I have contended all along, the journey towards a contemporary coherent atonement motif must begin with the constituted meaning of Jesus of Nazareth. However, the meaning to be appropriated is not a systematic construction as we saw, but the judgment Jesus made concerning the soteriological value of his death. In other words, we must judge as "true" or "authentic" the salvific meaning divinely created out of the contingent cross event. This is, and must be, the non-negotiable element of an authentically Christian interpretation of the cross. Modern theologians do not have a *tabula rasa* with which to work, but a slate that is already etched in detail with the dramatic artistry of the redeeming God. We are not at liberty to fill the etches in and start again, nor can we arbitrarily break the slate and chisel a new one. The meaning manifest by Jesus through the incarnate, linguistic and symbolic carriers is an historical reality and has a bearing on our understanding, not just in the world of meaning constituted then, but in the world that we constitute now.

44. Doran, "Functions of Systematic Theology," 580, emphasis original.

45. Insofar as the community is authentically Christian, context sensitive presentations of the salvific meaning of the cross will aid in their ongoing Christian journey. If the community is not yet Christian, then such presentations are missional in focus.

Encountering the Cross: Meaning and Dramatic Art

This is especially evident when we consider the dramatic artistry inherent in the incarnate carrier. Earlier it was argued that the incarnate carrier incorporates all the other carriers of meaning because it essentially characterizes the meaning of a person. I made special and categorical use of it in the previous chapter because it provided a ready means of explicating Jesus' actions from within a historical context, but it should not be forgotten that as a totalizing expression of meaning, the incarnate carrier also includes an artistic component. Hence, it is appropriate to consider for a moment what it might mean to approach the life of Jesus as a dramatic work of art.

This is certainly not a new theological conception. One only has to look to Hans Urs von Balthasar's multi-volume *Theo-Drama* to discover a thoroughgoing dramatic analysis of God's activity in creation.[46] Raymund Schwager too, makes good use of the category of drama to construct a five-act presentation of God's redemptive activity in Jesus of Nazareth.[47] And more recently, Robert Jenson has outlined the viability of understanding the life of Jesus as a dramatically coherent story, a story that involves both divine and human narratives.[48] I believe such analysis is fruitful, and if time and space permitted, would provide some important contributions to the present discussion. However, it is not necessary to do so at this point, because our focus on the transition from meaning to motif is not directly dependent upon dramatic categories but on the way meaning is discerned through dramatic art. And to this end we have already made the pertinent comments in chapter three and these can be readily drawn upon here.

Recalling then, our earlier discussion, there are two particular conclusions that can be drawn. The first is that since art itself inherits meaning from the artist we can note that the life and death of Jesus must be understood as meaningful. And the second, is based on the fact that art must be experienced for its meaning to be discerned.[49] In other words, when it comes to understanding the meaning of Jesus' death, we must enter into the world of the artist and experience it first-hand. We can be told what the cross might mean, we can read what someone else experienced in their own encounter with it, but unless we experience the cross for ourselves, we

---

46. Balthasar, *Theo-Drama*.

47. Schwager, *Jesus in the Drama of Salvation*.

48. Jenson, "Christ as Culture 3." All three articles in the series are instructive.

49. What Lonergan calls *elemental* meaning (*Method in Theology*, 63).

will not understand its redemptive power.[50] Of course, as I have argued, the cross is an historical event, which means that our contemporary encounter with it is not physical but is symbolically mediated through preaching and liturgy.[51] And this is the recognizable domain of atonement motifs, which expound not its historical detail but its religious significance.

Some might argue, though, that this is tantamount to the two-cross theory, in which the historical actuality of the cross is subjugated to its symbolic appropriation. Have we not then, inadvertently let in through the back door an understanding that we rejected at the beginning? To borrow from the Apostle Paul, *by no means*. In approaching the death of Jesus from an artistic perspective, the meaning of the cross is found to be present in *two* ways. It must always be remembered that it is primarily present in the manner in which it is imbued by the artist (Jesus), which means that the meaning evoked through the dramatic encounter with the art itself remains secondary. The postmodern rejection of this understanding has itself been challenged in chapter three, and the argument there for the potential of objective historical knowledge is equally applicable here. It relies, of course, on authentic subjectivity, in that one approaches the symbolic meaning of the cross attentively, intelligently, reasonably and responsibly. But to the extent to which this is successfully done, the meaning constituted by the artist will bear upon the meaning encountered in the art itself.

Thus, an encounter with dramatic artistry can never be an arbitrary experience because the life and death of Jesus of Nazareth has a meaning that exists independently of the interpreter. Indeed, this is what the incarnate carrier guarantees for it demonstrates not only that Jesus imbued his life and death with meaning but that such meaning can be encountered. And this means that such an encounter cannot be free from its historical context even though it evokes a dynamic operation between the participant and the art. For in a manner similar to the disciple's own encounter with Jesus' constituted meaning, the participant has the potential to arrive at the meaning of the art in two ways. Reflective understanding does take place because one experiences the art and is, therefore, able to understand and judge the art on that basis. Yet one cannot ignore the meaning of the art that is also communicated through belief in the artist's judgment. And this is the crucial point, for the meaning one discovers in their own

---

50. Again Augustine's *crede ut intelligas* is apparent.

51. Hence the reason why the Eucharist has the significance it does in Christian worship.

encounter with the cross cannot then *contradict or nullify the meaning of the artist and still claim to be faithful to the artist's intent.*

Certainly, it is always possible for one to find other meanings in the encounter that go beyond that which the artist intended (artistic expression has a way of evoking unintended meaning).[52] But one cannot claim faithfulness to the artist if that unintended meaning contradicts the meaning originally constituted. In this sense the meaning constituted in the dramatic art is a *terminus a quo*, which is another reason why we cannot conclude that there are two distinct crosses. We can, of course, articulate that unintended meaning in terms suitable to our contemporary culture and community but we must nevertheless ensure that our articulations remain faithful to the constituted judgment. For if we were to negate the original judgment then we would also redefine authenticity and this is not the role of a developing motif that claims continuity with the Christian tradition. Three important points for a contemporary atonement presentation follow from this conclusion.

There Is Theological Significance in Jesus' Intentional Judgment

The first is banal but must be stressed: we cannot be ignorant of the judgment that Jesus intended to create for his death or any faithfulness to that judgment will be arrived at accidentally rather than intentionally. Hence, an investigation into the constituted meaning of the historical Jesus is not only of historical interest but contains substantial theological significance.

Jesus' Intention Unlocks the Meaning of the Cross Event

Secondly, Jesus, as the self-revelation of God, is the interpretive key to the dramatic act of redemption that God creates out of the contingent cross event. It is in Jesus that the divine artist's intent is to be found, a point which insists that the meaning that Jesus constitutes for his death must provide the requisite contour for our own encounter with the cross. Again, if a Chalcedonian Christology is to be upheld then the judgment that Jesus made concerning his death must be understood to be delivered by God incarnate. Thus, there is divine meaning created for the suffering

52. As Lonergan notes, art is not autobiography. In the encounter with the art the participant interacts with the elemental meaning and grasps what is significant but such understanding is not constrained to the stroke and brush of the artist (*Method in Theology*, 63–64).

and death of Jesus of Nazareth, and that meaning was "neither necessary or incidental. It was intentional."[53]

But here lies the major sticking point for much of the contemporary discussion today. Not because there is a belief that God is incapable of creating meaning out of contingent events, but because it is taken to be an anathema that God would do so for events that are particularly evil.[54] I recounted the reasons for this understanding in chapter one and my arguments against such a conclusion in chapter two. Again I would reiterate that God is able to create meaning out of evil events without either justifying the evil of that event or requiring the theological understanding that such events are divinely necessary. Evil acts can have no divine cause because it is impossible for them to be providentially willed by God. Instead, evil acts and events occur because created humanity fails to will the good that God desires. But, such evil acts *having occurred*, God is free to create meaning out of them, and in our case, imbue such an acknowledged evil event with redemptive significance. Importantly, we should not conclude then, that redemptive significance can be found because the event was evil, nor that further events of evil will possess *mutatis mutandis* similar meaning. The significance of the cross is not found in the evilness of the event, but in the God who creates meaning out of it and such meaning must be divinely revealed and not assumed.[55] Because of this, contemporary atonement motifs that attempt to negate the potential for divine meaning to be created out of the cross event must be rejected.

As an example, consider the recent work *Proverbs of Ashes* from the pens of Feminist theologians Rita Nakashima Brock and Rebecca Ann Parker.[56] Their work is not a presentation of an atonement motif *per se*, but a narrative exploration into their own experiential search for salvation. It is pathos-heavy, drawing as it does on their own traumatic experiences and it consistently attempts to underline the failure of traditional Christian soteriological expressions to mediate transcendent presence. The problem

---

53. Hefling, "Christ and Evils," 881.

54. In passing it is worth commenting that if evil is not a privation but a thing in itself that God must separate Godself from (the only conclusion one can draw from this perspective), then how can God act to redeem an evil situation? The inevitable answer is that God cannot so act. This was actually the reason why Augustine left the Manichees, their dualist conception of God made God powerless in the face of evil (Augustine, *Confessions*, 7.5).

55. It is, in fact, a genuine operation of *creatio ex nihilo* since God actively creates meaning out of the meaningless.

56. Brock and Parker, *Proverbs of Ashes*.

for Brock and Parker is that violence and suffering (the cornerstone of traditional motifs) do nothing to mediate salvation but completely annihilate love and obliterate "the spaces in which spirit breathes."[57] To contend otherwise is said to perpetuate suffering and to continue to abuse the oppressed. The only way to resist and redress this horror is to act for justice and be soteriologically "present" to one another. Parker writes:

> I began to understand that violence is resisted by those who reverence the sacred presence of human beings and themselves embody such presence in the world. Individuals and communities protect life by taking actions that keep faith with their knowledge of something other than the lessons of oppression, or abuse, or violence. The practice of loving involves more than obeying an ideal, applying a principle, or imitating a model. Loving acts emerge from the grace we have come to know in the presence of one another. It is by being faithful to the power of presence that we learn to love.[58]

For Parker then, the way to healthy and whole relationships is through the healing presence of love that counters the destruction that violence brings. And this is how both authors choose to understand the work of Jesus of Nazareth. Divine salvation is not offered on the basis of Jesus' death ("no one was saved by the execution of Jesus"), but rather in and through the presence of love as it is mediated through Jesus' life.[59] And that love is found not just in the example of Jesus, but in any situation in which the presence of God is felt.[60] Thus, it is concluded that salvation is personally apprehended as the presence of God becomes real in each of our lives.

As a reflection of a subjective encounter with the dramatic artistry of Jesus of Nazareth the model presented by Brock and Parker is at the same time an achievement and a failure. That is to say, their discussion is, in a very loose sense, an understanding of the life and death of Jesus of Nazareth. Yet it is also most clearly not an understanding that finds value in the judgment that Jesus constituted.[61] Indeed, it becomes apparent very

57. Ibid., 10. And thus, cannot be salvific in any sense.

58. Ibid., 110.

59. Ibid., 211.

60. Ibid., 252.

61. Elsewhere Brock argues that this is precisely the point, for to posit that Jesus is the center of Christianity is to give priority to individual existence rather than to the "larger sanctity of community." This acts to reinforce the violence of power but also prevents the potential for divine presence to be mediated in community (Brock, *Journeys by Heart*, 68). I would suggest that what Brock is actually seeking here is a

early on in their discussion that the judgment that Jesus made concerning his death would have no bearing on their discussion in any way. To be sure, the story of Jesus is taken to be an expression of divine presence but that is as far as his contribution goes. Hence, their motif struggles with the question of authenticity, because even if the previous chapter's conclusions are rejected, it is nonetheless the case that authentic existence is based on the successful appropriation of the meaning that Jesus did, in fact, constitute. The "motif" presented here has no need for, or connection to, the meaning imbued by the artist. It is completely self-contained within the understanding of the participant. This is, perhaps, to be expected given the authors' rejection of the potential for divine meaning to be created out of the cross event, but that rejection also implies that the only meaning expressed will be that of the participant's own encounter. However, this is to deny any value to the artist's intention and functions to submit the constituted meaning of the dramatic art to the perils of inauthentic subjectivity.

Now, by no means should this criticism be taken as a rejection of the author's experiences or that God is unable to mediate salvation through divine presence. Indeed, I believe it is actually possible to explicate salvation in terms of presence from within the meaning that Jesus constituted (is not the expectation that YHWH would return itself representative of divine presence?). But what I do seek to illustrate here is that in rejecting the potential for divine meaning for the cross event, Brock and Parker inevitably deny their "motif" authenticity within the constituted meaning of Jesus. And thus, their discussion will provide little benefit to those who seek to remain authentic members of the community so defined.[62]

Faithfulness Is Required in Appropriating Jesus' Judgment

The third point I wish to make is that it is not required, nor is it even appropriate, for contemporary motifs to "mold" the intention of Jesus to fit their own particular presentations. What I mean by this is seen in the three examples I gave in chapter one, in which Mann, Heim and Milbank interpreted Jesus in a way that supported their particular presentations. For Mann, Jesus intended to demonstrate the divine offer of, and the

---

redefined community.

62. Something that Brock and Parker would probably accept given that Parker has previously acknowledged that her understanding can only be considered Christian if what it means to be "Christian" is heavily redefined (Brown and Parker, "For God So Loved the World?," 27–28). Hence, what both authors are actually calling for, is that a differing judgment be accepted and thus they seek to define a new community.

potential for, ontological coherence—the possibility of narrative whole-ness. For Heim, Jesus intended to reveal the scapegoat mechanism and through that revelation debunk the mechanism's power and thus create the possibility for a community to be based on love rather than mimetic violence. For Milbank, Jesus intended to become *homo sacer* in order that he might be able to forgive on behalf of every unique victim and thus make it possible for humanity to viably forgive one another.

In each of these presentations the Jesus presented is far removed from the Jesus we discovered in the previous chapter. One could then assume that their particular models of atonement should be abandoned because the Jesus they write about and appropriate is not the Jesus who constituted meaning for his death. The answer, I believe, is yes *and* no. Yes, because the Jesus they write about is not historically viable, but no because these motifs are not necessarily nullifying the judgment that Jesus made. We will consider these three examples in more detail below, but the point to be drawn here is that it is not necessary for us to project back onto Jesus' consciousness our own understanding of the salvific judgment that was constituted. We do not have to make the understanding of Jesus fit our atonement motifs, what we have to ensure is that our atonement motifs faithfully appropriate the judgment that Jesus made.

With these three points in mind, and by way of example, we will now consider what impact the above discussion might have on the presenta-tions we considered in chapter one.

Alan Mann: Atonement for a "Sinless" Society

Mann's conception of Jesus' death as the visible representation of onto-logical coherence has significant potential, although in its present form it suffers somewhat from its own narrative incoherence. The crux of my disagreement with Mann lies, as is to be expected, in his abandonment of the historical Jesus and, in the present context, what that means for the au-thenticity of Mann's own community. For in ignoring the judgment made by Jesus of Nazareth, Mann is inevitably forced to create a new judgment for his community of implied readers to subsequently judge for them-selves. What this means is that the community which forms on the basis of Mann's presentation is not an authentic member of the community which Jesus constituted, but a member of the community that Mann constitutes. Now I doubt that this is what Mann intended to achieve, but I would argue that it is, in fact, what has occurred.

Interestingly, the judgment that Mann creates for Jesus' death is not all that far removed from our analysis of the previous chapter. Both have argued that Jesus' death has redemptive significance and both point to the transcendent nature of the salvific act. However, Mann's presentation would have significantly more impact if his analysis of ontological coherence was demonstrated from within the constituted meaning of Jesus rather than being applied as somewhat of a *tertium quid* to the Gospel narrative. And I would suggest that this is actually more than possible since, as Wright has convincingly demonstrated, the meaning that Jesus created for his own death resides within (but is not limited to) the story of Israel herself. Thus, the meaning that Jesus creates for his death is part of that story and therefore can be argued to have narrative coherence. Of course, as we saw, the meaning that Jesus constitutes goes well beyond that of Israel's narrative but this is precisely where Mann could have found the example of ontological coherence that he contends his community desperately seeks. For in challenging the status quo with his own constituted meaning Jesus pronounced what Mann would call his "ideal-self." The challenge for Jesus was to live that call, to live as if the reality of the kingdom was already at hand. This the Gospels declare he did, and thus Jesus stayed within the meaning he constituted and hence his "real-self" cohered with his "ideal-self." Again, this is seen pre-eminently in the cross because it is there that Jesus ultimately had to endure the judgment of the kingdom, and moreover, the fact that he endured it intentionally powerfully displays the ontological coherence that Mann contends is necessary in the postmodern search for salvation.

Framed in such a way, Mann's presentation carries more weight for it does not ignore the divine meaning created for the cross event. Nor does it attempt to force Jesus' self-understanding into that which has little historical merit. Indeed, it demonstrates the potential for Mann to draw upon the ontological coherence that Jesus' life and death displays from *within* a first-century context. A systematic exposition of this nature could then be argued to be faithful to the constituted meaning of Jesus and at the same time be expressed in a way that brought that redemptive judgment home to the postmodern community. Considerably more would need to be argued before such a thesis would convince, especially in regard to the possible relationship between ontological coherence and the Scriptural witness, but that is not the intent of the present discussion. Yet already the little that has been suggested demonstrates the potential for a systematic understanding of Jesus' death to include ontological coherence.

S. Mark Heim: Saved from Sacrifice

In Heim's model, the Gospels reveal the scapegoat mechanism and thereby overcome it, since to reveal the mechanism is to make it impotent. And Heim contends that Jesus himself had the same goal, intentionally siding with every victim in order to break the sacrificial cycle. The problem, as was argued, was that Heim completely ignores the kingdom motif in Jesus' ministry. His conception of Jesus standing in solidarity with all victims has scriptural merit but his elevation of that relationship beyond the kingdom message cannot be supported historically. Therefore, in a similar way to Mann, Heim fails to adequately incorporate the constituted judgment of Jesus within his own presentation. What we have instead, is a judgment concerning the cross that is projected onto the life and praxis of Jesus, rather than forming a systematic understanding from the judgment that *is* historically constituted. But is this observation the death knell for the Girardian anthropological insight? Not at all. In fact, the Girardian perspective holds considerable potential for directing our attention to the non-violent constitution of community that results from the salvific activity of the cross. On this, I limit myself to the following pertinent comments.

In the first place there is no need to insist that Jesus intended to reveal, or was even aware of, the scapegoat mechanism. Indeed, from within the context of the coming of the kingdom there is very little historical evidence that such a feature of community construction and maintenance was obviously in mind. Jesus was not remembered to have spoken directly about or against the scapegoat mechanism, nor is Heim's re-reading of passages such as Matthew 23 ultimately convincing. I would contend that Wright's account of these passages is far more telling; to my mind he convincingly demonstrates their contextual applicability to the overall story that Jesus narrated about imminent judgment. Hence, to suggest that what Jesus was really talking about is actually the scapegoat mechanism, is to force onto Jesus' self-understanding an expectation that has very little historical credence. Not only does this undermine Heim's presentation, it also functions to negate the very real potential that Jesus' own judgment has for such a Girardian informed understanding.

And that potential can be seen in the way that Jesus defines authenticity for the new community. In the discussion on the Last Supper it was noted that in the symbolic use of the bread and the wine, Jesus directs his disciple's attention to his own death. Furthermore, Jesus' actions indicated that he expected his death to take the place of the Temple cult; it would now function to mediate the presence of God to the new covenant community. Further still, the Last Supper also demonstrates that Jesus considered it necessary that his *followers participate in his death*. Not in the sense of going to the cross in solidarity with him, of course, but symbolically, through the partaking of the bread and wine. Jesus' exhortation to the disciples that they "eat and drink" is strongly suggestive that authenticity within the newly constituted covenant community depended upon such participation.[63]

Now as an example, it might well be argued that from a Girardian perspective, the meal itself actually functions to subvert the scapegoat mechanism. How so? Because it fundamentally rejects the ongoing sacrificial violence deemed necessary to maintain the community by emphasizing the once-for-all nature of Jesus' own death *and* the participation in that death of the covenant community. Indeed, this is something that Heim actually points to in the title of his work since we are, in fact, "saved from sacrifice" in that having died with Christ, the scapegoat mechanism loses its restorative power. This is because authenticity within the community that Jesus constitutes is not dependent upon maintaining the status quo of our own community but in the abandonment of ourselves "in Christ" to the community of God. It is in a community such as this that permanent harmony becomes possible, because peace is no longer found in the limited efficacy of the scapegoat but in the corporate participation in Christ's death. We have, as the apostle Paul said, been baptized into Christ's death (Rom 6:3–8) and in corporate death there is no longer any need for further scapegoating.

Importantly, the Girardian insight requires the acknowledgement that outside the newly covenanted community the scapegoat mechanism still operates. Indeed, Heim's contention that redemptive sacrifice was precisely what the Jewish leaders were seeking is a significant insight and one worth reflecting upon. But it is not necessary to judge Jesus' actions and intentions for his death as an effort to directly expose the scapegoat mechanism. Instead, I believe there is ample room to apply a Girardian understanding to the salvific, kingdom-focused, judgment that Jesus made and in so doing, discover significant material for a contemporary systematic expression.

Undoubtedly, these points warrant further development but for now it is enough to demonstrate that a systematic understanding of the

---

63. Readily evidenced by the importance placed on the Eucharist by the early Church.

meaning of the cross does not require an abandoning of the historically constituted meaning in order to be effective.

John Milbank: Being Reconciled

Milbank's presentation is more difficult to assess, mainly because of the intense obfuscation that permeates his work but also because he does not articulate an atonement motif *per se*. As I outlined earlier, *Being Reconciled* is primarily concerned with the category of *gift*, of which atonement is but a component part. Nevertheless, there are some important comments that can be made within the context of the present discussion.

In the first place, Milbank is very concerned to draw our attention to the experience of abandonment suffered by the historical Jesus. This need arises from a conception that if Jesus is to truly stand in solidarity with every victim then he needs to be the definitive victim, cast out, abandoned and ultimately one considered *homo sacer*. Furthermore, it is important to note that in Milbank's argument, it is only in dying as a *homo sacer* that Jesus' offer of human forgiveness becomes possible for us to accept. Hence, there is great stress placed on the necessity of Jesus' abandonment if forgiveness is to be received at all. This presents an obvious conflict with our own analysis since Milbank also insists that such abandonment requires the cross event to be historically meaningless. And thus, Jesus cannot have constituted meaning for his death but must have passively accepted its meaninglessness in order to suffer as the definitive victim. In such a case, meaning is only discerned post-resurrection as the reality of what occurred begins to be divinely revealed to the disciples. Yet does this not introduce tension between the human and divine judgments of the cross, in that Jesus must judge the cross meaningless whilst God nevertheless imbues it with soteriological value? This is a tension difficult to reconcile, especially given Milbank's extensive emphasis on the value of the incarnation to his argument. In any case, our analysis of the previous chapter contends rather strongly that Jesus did, in fact, constitute salvific meaning for his death and thus there is no reason for insisting that the constituted meaning of Jesus must be different to that created by God.

That is, of course, as long as one accepts that it is possible for Jesus to remain in solidarity with every victim whilst constituting meaning for his own suffering. And it would be foolishness to suggest that we are in any position to try and answer this question beyond pointing to our contention in chapter two in which it was said that meaning can be created for evil events without justifying them (which means, in this context, without negating the horror of the victim). It would no doubt require more discussion, but perhaps it could be demonstrated that Jesus' historical acceptance of his own rejection—coupled with the above potential to create meaning for evil events without justifying them—would adequately ensure Jesus' status as a universal victim. I would expect Milbank to disagree, inasmuch as he contends that (a) Jesus could not have been *homo sacer* if he held on to dignity in death, and thus, could not enter into solidarity with every victim especially those who suffer meaninglessly; and (b) he continues to overlook the significance of, and meaning inherent in, the Last Supper texts. But these are questions for another time. The point to be made here is that in its current form, Milbank's presentation must be rejected for to deny that Jesus constituted meaning for the cross event is to negate the value of his salvific judgment and locate its meaning entirely in the encounter of the participant. The end result is inevitably a failure to grasp what truly defines authenticity for the Christian community.

Conclusion

The above three examples are by no means complete and each deserves further discussion, yet enough has been said to demonstrate the value of appropriating the constituted meaning of Jesus for contemporary motifs. Without encountering the meaning constituted by the artist, authentic understanding is impossible. One may, of course, constitute one's own meaning independent of the artist's intention but one cannot do so and still claim continuity with the intent of the artist. For Brock and Parker such an outcome is the necessary price to pay for their conception of the restorative mediation of divine presence. For Mann, Heim and Milbank their departure from the constituted meaning of Jesus is rather more unintended. Indeed, in each of the above examples I have tried to demonstrate that it is possible to maintain continuity with the constituted judgment of Jesus whilst still articulating that judgment in terms understandable to the author's respective communities.

Again, I would stress that authenticity to the soteriological judgment of the cross is not found in appropriating exactly the same understanding that Jesus of Nazareth expressed. In the first place we simply do not have sufficient evidence to discern exactly what that understanding may have been, and in the second, the New Testament itself demonstrates that expressions of the cross' salvific power are not limited to a single understanding. However, this is not a license to abandon the historically constituted meaning of the cross in our contemporary presentations. To do so would be to reject the divine meaning created out of the cross event in favor of constructions of our own making. On the contrary, authenticity is dependent upon encountering the imbued meaning of the artist. It remains the task of the theologian to express that imbued meaning in a way understandable to his or her community.

Meaning and Motif

What I have attempted to do in this chapter is to demonstrate the viability of incorporating the historical judgment of Jesus in contemporary atonement discussions. The key is to recognize the difference between judgment and understanding, and to comprehend the relationship of belief to both operations. Moreover, it must be stressed that it is fundamentally coherence in judgment that defines authenticity and not the level or expression of one's understanding of that judgment. Hence, it is possible to articulate the saving message of the cross—that is, the judgment that Jesus constituted for his death—without necessarily having to understand that judgment in terms of, for example, Son of man, Paschal lamb, covenant and the like. Without a doubt these terms and concepts remain invaluable, and are certainly worthy of detailed consideration and investigation. But they do not necessarily constrain our articulations of the atonement for they are not in themselves what determines authenticity.

What *is* necessary is that we uphold the judgment that Jesus made concerning his death, for it is the judgment of God-incarnate, the eternal Word who intentionally incorporates suffering and death into the divine soteriological narrative. This is the proclamation of the New Testament and must be believed if we are to have any understanding of what occurs on the cross at all. At this point we must re-iterate the importance of *fides quaerens intellectum* because it is, fundamentally, the theological task: to identify and accept the revealed truth of the gospel and moreover, to explore and communicate its meaning. This has unashamedly been the present objective in regard to the cross of Jesus of Nazareth, who is called Christ. The saving power of the cross is the cornerstone of the Christian message and the contemporary challenges facing its articulation are no reason to abandon or retreat from its discussion. But they are reason enough to carefully consider how the atonement should be articulated today and what it is that constitutes authenticity within Christian soteriological discussion.

Afterword

What I have attempted to demonstrate herein is the ongoing potential for theology to articulate the meaning of Jesus' death in a way that remains both faithful to the Christian tradition and yet sensitive to the needs of any given community. Hence, the task has not been to assert any one particular motif or understanding of the cross as *the* expression of faithful Christianity. Such an assertion (be it for any particular motif) needs to be rejected, not because individual motifs lack understanding or coherence but because the communication of the saving message of the cross must be received personally, if it is to be received at all. And as community and culture change—and change they will—the onus is on the theologian to express the saving significance of the cross in a way in which the community can continue to receive such a message. For while Christianity is right to proclaim the death of Jesus of Nazareth as universally significant for salvation, it must be recognized that such significance is not limited to a first, third or fifteenth-century context. It needs to be constantly articulated, and re-articulated, in a manner which is contextually coherent.

Now, it is clear that some motifs will find higher receptivity than others and will remain valuable and meaningful over several generations. Christian history has already demonstrated the truth of this. And where a motif remains meaningful within a given community there is no need to arbitrarily abandon its articulation. Yet to categorically assert that any one particular motif transcends culture and the corresponding challenges that confront the changing world is to relegate that motif to eventual anachronism and ultimate irrelevance. As was argued, systematic understandings cannot claim permanence, for they remain the aesthetic presentations of a transcendent mystery. What I have contended *is* permanent in the Christian proclamation of the cross event is the redemptive judgment that was divinely created out of the horror of Jesus' death. And it is here, I believe, that authenticity in atonement articulation is to be found.

Therefore, differences in articulations cannot be judged on the way in which the redemptive significance of the cross is expressed, but on whether they demonstrate sufficient coherence with that redemptive judgment. In other words, it is the meaning that Jesus of Nazareth constitutes for his death which needs to be appropriated in our contemporary articulations. This is to make two assertions: that (a) the cross is an actual historical event and (b) God is able to create meaning out of the event despite its inherent evil and contingency. These two assertions have two corresponding corollaries. The first locates the divine soteriological narrative in the historical realm, an emphasis which should not be interpreted as a negation of the transcendent nature of salvation. It does, however, require an acknowledgement that God's redemptive activity is not a *deus ex machina* that somehow operates irrespective of the created realm. It is to affirm to the contrary that God acts in, and is revealed through, the historically constituted meaning of Jesus of Nazareth. This is why I have argued for the appropriateness of historical investigation to the theological task, despite such an argument exposing theology to the joys and challenges that lie therein. The second enables an understanding in which meaning can be created out of the suffering and death of Jesus of Nazareth without justifying the act(s) of evil that caused and effected that suffering and death.

Now it is true that a reliance on classical theism in order to defend this position does place the discussion firmly in the Western tradition, and thus criticism could be brought to bear on the way this localization limits the argument's applicability. Yet no theology is ever worked out in a vacuum, and the present challenges to the notion of redemptive suffering in Western academic literature (the context in which we are engaged) demand an appropriate response. Of course, evil as a privation *is* meaningless and there is nothing inherently redemptive in suffering itself. This much should be strongly asserted. Yet to correspondingly deny that redemptive meaning can be created out of the event *ex nihilo* without implicating God in its violence and horror is to misunderstand the nature of divine action. God does not—cannot—will the death of Jesus of Nazareth, for the unintelligibility of evil cannot be related to the intelligibility of God's providential action. What God can only will is that Jesus accept the consequences of the sins of others, not because redemption requires some kind of macabre necessity to sinful acts, but because God has created a world in which the creature has the ability to withdraw from divine goodness. However, having discerned his own rejection, and being obedient to the will of God to the end, Jesus was able to constitute meaning for that rejection, meaning that has not just historical but theological significance. If God was, indeed, in Christ reconciling the world to Godself, then historical investigation into the death of Jesus is not only relevant but crucial to the atonement discussion.

Yet theology and historical Jesus studies tend to make uncomfortable bedfellows. The problem is not one of applicability but rather historiography. A commitment to faith tends to be viewed as antithetical to historical investigation while a "faith-less" perspective has little bearing on a theological perspective. However, I have contended that a critical realist view of historical investigation overcomes such concerns because (a) it denies the possibility of an unbiased interaction with history; (b) it contends that objectivity is not a matter of "taking a good look"; and (c) it sufficiently takes into account the spiraling dialogue that occurs between the historical object and the historian. With such an approach, theologians can engage in matters of historical interest without projecting themselves or their prior considerations onto the object. The task is certainly not an easy one and requires, as was said, a commitment to authentic subjectivity. But difficulty does not necessitate abandonment and theologians can viably investigate history without having to deny their faith perspective.

It should also be stressed that the contention that Jesus constituted meaning for his death is not asserted from some theological *a priori*, but arises as a natural conclusion from the movement from the world of immediacy into the world constituted by meaning. This larger world of meaning that Jesus' constituted evoked not just a challenge to the corporately intended status quo, but dramatically invited transformation for those who judged value in that alternative reality. What conveyed that challenge were the various carriers of meaning, all of which combined to reveal the world of meaning that Jesus constituted. And our investigation into the incarnate, linguistic and symbolic carriers revealed a world in which it was concluded that Jesus judged his death to have redemptive value. This value is apparent in Jesus' decision to endure the judgment of the Final Ordeal on behalf of the nation. This is not something that Jesus looked forward to in an enthusiastic sense, but it was an event that he anticipated given the opposition his ministry encountered. And, according to Daniel 7, such rejection would usher in the Final Ordeal and result in the ultimate victory of God. Therefore, in Jesus' death, evil would be judged and the kingdom of God would be made manifest. However, it was not until the Last Supper that the importance of Jesus' death for the constitution of the new community became manifest. Coupled with the Temple action, the breaking of bread and the drinking of the cup symbolized the arrival of a new exodus and pointed towards the existence of a new eschatological covenant. That his followers would be redeemed by this action is made clear in the expectation that they would drink of the fruit of the vine again in the kingdom of God.

Crucially, this conclusion leads to a judgment of redemptive value rather than one of systematic understanding. This is why I argued in the final chapter that there is, in fact, no systematic expression to be gained from the analysis. What we have instead is a judgment that Jesus made concerning the redemptive value of his death. Some conclusions can, of course, be drawn about this judgment as we have just said. But they are not conclusions that define the theological expression of atonement. If they were, then we would have to limit all discussion of the meaning of the cross to a Paschal eschatological context. The New Testament does not do this and nor do such requirements need to be arbitrarily enforced on contemporary articulations. What is important is the judgment that is constituted, and significantly *that judgment is sufficient to contend for authenticity in contemporary articulations.*

In other words, we do not have to conform our presentations to an understanding that is only hinted at in the Gospels. What we have is a responsibility to assent to the judgment that Jesus made, which is why the discussion on belief is so important. Belief itself is a judgment, but it is a judgment of value not an expression of understanding, one that is made on the basis of trust in one's source rather than on one's own immanently generated knowledge. And as I have argued, it is this coherence with the judgment of Jesus that constitutes authenticity in contemporary atonement discussion.

Bibliography

Alison, James. *The Joy of Being Wrong: Original Sin through Easter Eyes*. New York: Crossroad, 1998.

Allison, Dale C. *Constructing Jesus: Memory, Imagination, and History*. London: SPCK, 2010.

———. "Jesus and the Covenant: A Response to E. P. Sanders." *Journal for the Study of the New Testament* 29 (1987) 57–78.

Althaus, Paul. *The Theology of Martin Luther*. Translated by Robert C. Schultz. 2nd ed. Philadelphia: Fortress, 1966.

Anselm, Saint, Archbishop of Canterbury. *Why God Became Man: Cur Deus Homo?* Translated by Jasper Hopkins and Herbert Richardson. Toronto: E. Mellen, 1985.

Aquinas, Thomas. *The De malo of Thomas Aquinas*. Translated by Richard Regan. New York: Oxford University Press, 2001.

———. *In Aristotelis Libros Peri hermeneias*. Casali: Ioseph Angrisani, 1955.

———. *Quæstiones disputatæ de potentia Dei*. Westminster: Newman, 1952.

———. *Scriptum Super Sententiis*. Amersham: Avebury, 1980.

———. *Treatise on Separate Substances*. Translated by F. J. Lescoe. West Hartford: Saint Joseph College, 1959.

———. *Truth*. 3 vols. Translated by Robert W. Schmidt. Chicago: Henry Regnery, 1952–1954.

Arendt, Hannah. *Eichmann in Jerusalem: A Report on the Banality of Evil*. London: Penguin, 1992.

Aristotle. *Nicomachean Ethics*. Translated by H. D. Apostle. Dordrecht: D. Reidel, 1976.

———. *Physics*. Translated by Robin Waterfield. Oxford: Oxford University Press, 1996.

Augustine, Saint. *The Confessions of Saint Augustine*. Translated by John K. Ryan. New York: Image, 1960.

Bailey, Daniel P. "Concepts of *Stellvertretung* in the Interpretation of Isaiah 53." In *Jesus and the Suffering Servant: Isaiah 53 and Christian Origins*, edited by William H. Bellenger Jr. and William R. Farmer, 223–50. Harrisburg, PA: Trinity, 1998.

Baker, Mark D., ed. *Proclaiming the Scandal of the Cross: Contemporary Images of the Atonement*. Grand Rapids: Baker Academic, 2006.

Balla, Peter. "What Did Jesus Think about His Approaching Death?" In *Jesus, Mark and Q: The Teaching of Jesus and its Earliest Records*, edited by Michael Labahn and Andreas Schmidt, 239–59. Sheffield: Sheffield Academic Press, 2001.

Balthasar, Hans Urs von. *Theo-Drama: Theological Dramatic Theory*. 4 vols. San Francisco: Ignatius, 1988–1998.

Barrett, C. K. "The Background of Mark 10:45." In *New Testament Essays: Studies in Memory of T. W. Manson*, edited by A. J. B. Higgins, 1–18. Manchester: Manchester University Press, 1959.

Bibliography

Bartlett, Anthony W. *Cross Purposes: The Violent Grammar of Christian Atonement.* Harrisburg, PA: Trinity, 2001.

Bauckham, Richard. *Jesus and the Eyewitnesses: The Gospels as Eyewitness Testimony.* Grand Rapids: Eerdmans, 2006.

Beasley-Murray, G. R. *Jesus and the Kingdom of God.* Grand Rapids: Eerdmans, 1986.

Bernard, of Clairvaux. *Contra quaedam capitula errorum Abelardi epistola CXC seu tractatus ad Innocentium pontificem.* PL 182.1069.

Betz, Hans Dieter. "Jesus and the Purification of the Temple (Mark 11:15–18): A Comparative Religion Approach." *Journal of Biblical Literature* 116/3 (1997) 455–72.

Betz, Otto. "Jesus' Gospel of the Kingdom." In *The Gospel and the Gospels,* edited by Peter Stuhlmacher, 53–74. Grand Rapids: Eerdmans, 1991.

Boersma, Hans. *Violence, Hospitality and the Cross: Reappropriating the Atonement Traditions.* Grand Rapids: Baker Academic, 2004.

Borg, Marcus. *Conflict, Holiness and Politics in the Teachings of Jesus.* Vol. 5 of *Studies in the Bible and Early Christianity.* New York: Mellen, 1984.

Bostock, David. *Aristotle's Ethics.* Oxford: Oxford University Press, 2000.

Bracken, Joseph A. *The Divine Matrix: Creativity as Link between East and West.* Maryknoll, NY: Orbis, 1995.

———. "Response to Elizabeth Johnson's "Does God Play Dice?"" *Theological Studies* 57 (1996) 720–30.

Braine, David. *The Reality of Time and the Existence of God.* Oxford: Clarendon, 1988.

Brock, Rita Nakashima. *Journeys by Heart: A Christology of Erotic Power.* New York: Crossroad, 1992.

Brock, Rita Nakashima, and Rebecca Ann Parker. *Proverbs of Ashes: Violence, Redemptive Suffering, and the Search for What Saves Us.* Boston: Beacon, 2001.

Brondos, David. "Why was Jesus Crucified? Theology, History and the Story of Redemption." *Scottish Journal of Theology* 54 (2001) 484–503.

Brown, Joanna Carlson, and Rebecca Ann Parker. "For God So Loved the World?" In *Christianity, Patriarchy and Abuse: A Feminist Critique,* edited by Joanna Carlson Brown and Carole R. Bohn, 1–30. Cleveland: Pilgrim, 1989.

Brown, Raymond E. *The Death of the Messiah: From Gethsemane to the Grave.* Vol. 1. New York: Doubleday, 1994.

———. "The Pater Noster as an Eschatological Prayer." In *New Testament Essays,* 275–320. New York: Image, 1968.

Brümmer, Vincent. *Atonement, Christology and the Trinity: Making Sense of Christian Doctrine.* Hampshire: Ashgate, 2005.

Bryan, Steven M. *Jesus and Israel's Traditions of Judgement and Restoration.* Society for New Testament Studies 117. Cambridge: Cambridge University Press, 2002.

Bultmann, Rudolf. *Jesus and the Word.* New York: Scribner's, 1985.

———. "The Primitive Christian Kerygma and the Historical Jesus." In *The Historical Jesus and the Kerygmatic Christ: Essays on the New Quest of the Historical Jesus,* edited by C. E. Braaten and R. A. Harrisville, 15–42. New York: Abingdon, 1964.

———. *Theology of the New Testament.* Translated by Kendrick Grobel. 2 vols. New York: Scribner's, 1951–1955.

Burkett, Delbert. *The Son of Man Debate: A History and Evaluation.* Cambridge: Cambridge University Press, 1999.

Burrell, David B. *Aquinas: God and Action.* Notre Dame: University of Notre Dame Press, 1979.

———. *Freedom and Creation in Three Traditions.* Notre Dame: University of Notre Dame Press, 1993.

Calvin, John. *Institutes of the Christian Religion.* Translated by Ford Lewis Battles. 2 vols. Philadelphia: Westminster, 1960.

Casey, M. "General, Generic and Indefinite: The Use of the Term 'Son of Man' in Aramaic Sources and in the Teaching of Jesus." *Journal for the Study of the New Testament* 29 (1987) 21–56.

Chadwick, H. *Lessing's Theological Writings.* London: Black, 1956.

Childs, Brevard S. *Isaiah.* Louisville: Westminster John Knox, 2001.

Chilton, Bruce. *A Feast of Meanings: Eucharistic Theologies from Jesus through Johannine Circles.* Leiden: Brill, 1994.

———. *Rabbi Jesus: An Intimate Biography.* New York: Doubleday, 2000.

———. *The Temple of Jesus: His Sacrificial Program within a Cultural History of Sacrifice.* University Park: Pennsylvania State University Press, 1992.

Clark, Gordon H. *Religion, Reason, and Revelation.* Philadelphia: Presbyterian & Reformed, 1961.

Clarke, Randolph. *Libertarian Accounts of Free Will.* Oxford: Oxford University Press, 2003.

Collingwood, R. G. *The Idea of History.* Oxford: Oxford University Press, 1946.

Collins, John J. "The Son of Man in First-Century Judaism." *New Testament Studies* 38/3 (1992) 448–66.

Crossan, J. D. *The Cross That Spoke: The Origins of the Passion Narratives.* San Francisco: Harper & Row, 1988.

———. *The Historical Jesus: The Life of a Mediterranean Jewish Peasant.* New York: Harper Collins, 1992.

Cyre, Susan. "Fallout Escalates Over 'Goddess' Sophia Worship." *Christianity Today* 38 (1994) 71.

Davies, W. D., and Dale C. Allison. *Matthew.* International Critical Commentary. London: T. & T. Clark, 1988–1991.

Derrida, Jacques. *Dissemination.* Translated by Barbara Johnson. Chicago: University of Chicago Press, 1981.

Descartes, René. *Meditations on First Philosophy.* Translated by John Cottingham. Rev. ed. New York: Cambridge University Press, 1996.

Dodd, C. H. *The Founder of Christianity.* London: Collins, 1971.

Doran, Robert M. "Bernard Lonergan and the Functions of Systematic Theology." *Theological Studies* 59/4 (1998) 569–607.

———. *Theology and the Dialectics of History.* Toronto: University of Toronto Press, 1990.

Dowd, Sharyn, and Elizabeth Struthers Malbon. "The Significance of Jesus' Death in Mark: Narrative Context and Authorial Audience." *Journal of Biblical Literature* 125/2 (2006) 271–97.

Dunn, James D. G. *Jesus Remembered.* Vol. 1 of *Christianity in the Making.* Grand Rapids: Eerdmans, 2003.

———. *A New Perspective on Jesus: What the Quest for the Historical Jesus Missed.* Grand Rapids: Baker Academic, 2005.

———. *The Theology of Paul the Apostle.* London: T. & T. Clark, 1998.

Bibliography

Durham, John I. *Exodus*. Word Biblical Commentary. Waco: Word, 1987.

Evans, C. A. "Context, Family and Formation." In *The Cambridge Companion to Jesus*, edited by Markus Bockmuehl, 11–24. Cambridge: Cambridge University Press, 2001.

————. "Jesus' Action in the Temple: Cleansing or Portent of Destruction?" *The Catholic Biblical Quarterly* 51/2 (1989) 237–70.

————. "Jesus and the Continuing Exile of Israel." In *Jesus and the Restoration of Israel: A Critical Assessment of N. T. Wright's* Jesus and the Victory of God, edited by Carey C. Newman, 77–100. Downers Grove, IL: InterVarsity, 1999.

Farmer, William R. "Reflections on Isaiah 53 and Christian Origins." In *Jesus and the Suffering Servant: Isaiah 53 and Christian Origins*, edited by William H. Bellenger Jr. and William R. Farmer, 260–80. Harrisburg, PA: Trinity, 1998.

Fredriksen, Paula. *Jesus of Nazareth, King of the Jews: A Jewish Life and the Emergence of Christianity*. London: Macmillan, 1999.

Frei, H. W. "Theological Reflections on the Accounts of Jesus' Death and Resurrection." In *Hans Frei: Theology and Narrative: Selected Essays*, edited by George Hunsinger and William Placher, 45–93. Oxford: Oxford University Press, 1993.

Funk, R. W., and R. W. Hoover. *The Five Gospels: The Search for the Authentic Words of Jesus*. Sonoma, CA: Polebridge, 1993.

Garrett, Graeme. *God Matters: Conversations in Theology*. Collegeville, MN: Liturgical, 1999.

George, Timothy. *Theology of the Reformers*. Nashville: Broadman, 1988.

Girard, René. *The Scapegoat*. Translated by Yvonne Freccero. Baltimore: John Hopkins University Press, 1986.

————. *Things Hidden Since the Foundation of the World*. Translated by Stephen Bann and Michael Metteer. Stanford: Stanford University Press, 1987.

————. *To Double Business Bound: Essays on Literature, Mimesis and Anthropology*. Baltimore: John Hopkins University Press, 1988.

————. *Violence and the Sacred*. Translated by Patrick Gregory. Baltimore: John Hopkins University Press, 1977.

Gorringe, Timothy. *God's Just Vengeance: Crime, Violence and the Rhetoric of Salvation*. Cambridge Studies in Ideology and Religion 9. Cambridge: Cambridge University Press, 1996.

Green, Joel B., and Mark D. Baker. *Recovering the Scandal of the Cross: Atonement in New Testament and Contemporary Contexts*. Downers Grove, IL: InterVarsity, 2000.

Greene, Colin J. D. *Christology in Cultural Perspective: Marking Out the Horizons*. Carlisle, UK: Paternoster, 2003.

Grudem, Wayne. *Systematic Theology: An Introduction to Biblical Doctrine*. Grand Rapids: Zondervan, 1994.

Gruenler, Royce Gordon. "Atonement in the Synoptic Gospels and Acts." In *The Glory of the Atonement: Biblical, Historical and Practical Perspectives*, edited by Charles E. Hill and Frank A. James III, 90–105. Downers Grove, IL: InterVarsity, 2004.

Gundry, Robert H. *Mark: A Commentary on His Apology for the Cross*. Grand Rapids: Eerdmans, 1993.

Gunton, Colin E. *The Actuality of Atonement: A Study of Metaphor, Rationality and the Christian Tradition*. Edinburgh: T. & T. Clark, 1988.

———. *Becoming and Being: The Doctrine of God in Charles Hartshorne and Karl Barth*. Oxford: Oxford University Press, 1978.

———. *Yesterday and Today: A Study of Continuities in Christology*. London: Darton, Longman & Todd, 1983.

Haight, Roger. *Jesus: Symbol of God*. Maryknoll, NY: Orbis, 1999.

Hall, Douglas John. *The Cross in Our Context: Jesus and the Suffering World*. Minneapolis: Fortress, 2003.

Hartshorne, Charles. *Creative Synthesis and Philosophic Method*. London: SCM, 1970.

———. *The Divine Relativity: A Social Conception of God*. New Haven: Yale University Press, 1948.

Hartshorne, Charles, and William. L. Reese, eds. *Philosophers Speak of God*. Chicago: University of Chicago Press, 1953.

Hefling, Charles. "Another Perhaps Permanently Valid Achievement: Lonergan on Christ's (Self-) Knowledge." *Lonergan Workshop* 20 (2008) 127–64.

———. "Christ and Evils: Assessing an Aspect of Marilyn McCord Adams's Theodicy." *Anglican Theological Review* 83/4 (2001) 869–83.

Heim, S. Mark. *Saved From Sacrifice: A Theology of the Cross*. Grand Rapids: Eerdmans, 2006.

Heyer, C. J. den. *Jesus and the Doctrine of the Atonement*. Harrisburg, PA: Trinity, 1998.

Hick, John. "God as Necessary Being." *The Journal of Philosophy* 57/22–23 (1960) 725–34.

Holmén, Tom. "Jesus, Judaism and the Covenant." *Journal for the Study of the Historical Jesus* 2/1 (2004) 3–27.

Hooker, Morna D. *Jesus and the Servant*. London: SPCK, 1959.

———. "On Using the Wrong Tool." *Theology* 75 (1972) 570–81.

———. *The Son of Man in Mark: A Study of the Background of the Term "Son of Man" and Its Use in St. Mark's Gospel*. London: SPCK, 1967.

Horsley, R. A. "The Death of Jesus." In *Studying the Historical Jesus: Evaluations of Current Research*, edited by Bruce Chilton and C. A. Evans, 395–422. Leiden: Brill, 1994.

———. *Jesus and the Spiral of Violence: Popular Jewish resistance in Roman Palestine*. San Francisco: Harper & Row, 1987.

Hoye, William J. *Actualitas Omnium Actuum: Man's Beatific Vision of God as Apprehended by Thomas Aquinas*. Edited by Georgi Schischkoff. Monographien zur Philosophischen Forschung 116. Meisenheim am Glan: Anton Hain, 1975.

Hume, David. *Dialogues Concerning Natural Religion*. Edited and with introduction by Stanley Tweyman. London: Routledge, 1991.

Hunsinger, George. "The Politics of the Nonviolent God: Reflections on René Girard and Karl Barth." *Scottish Journal of Theology* 51/1 (1998) 61–85.

Jenkins, Keith. *On "What is History?": From Carr and Elton to Rorty and White*. London: Routledge, 1995.

Jenson, Robert. "Christ as Culture 3: Christ as Drama." *International Journal of Systematic Theology* 6/2 (2004) 194–201.

Jeremias, Joachim. *The Eucharistic Words of Jesus*. London: SCM, 1966.

———. *New Testament Theology*. Translated by John Bowden. New York: Scribner's, 1971.

———. *The Prayers of Jesus*. London: SCM, 1967.

Bibliography

Johnson, Elizabeth A. "Does God Play Dice? Divine Providence and Chance." *Theological Studies* 57 (1996) 3–18.

Jonge, Marinus, de. *God's Final Envoy: Early Christology and Jesus' Own View of His Mission.* Grand Rapids: Eerdmans, 1998.

———. "Jesus' Death for Others and the Death of the Maccabean Martyrs." In *Text and Testimony*, edited by T. Baarda et al., 142–51. Kampen: Kok, 1988.

Jüngel, Eberhard. *God as the Mystery of the World: On the Foundation of the Theology of the Crucified One in the Dispute between Theism and Atheism.* Translated by Darrell L. Guder. Grand Rapids: Eerdmans, 1983.

Kähler, Martin. *The So-Called Historical Jesus and the Historic, Biblical Christ.* Philadelphia: Fortress, 1964.

Käsemann, Ernst. "Das Problem Des Historischen Jesus." In *Exegetische Versuche und Besinnungen*, 187–214. Göttingen: Vandenhoeck and Ruprecht, 1960.

———. "The Problem of the Historical Jesus." In *Essays on New Testament Themes*, 15–47. Translated by W. J. Montague. London: SCM, 1964.

Keck, Leander E. *Who Is Jesus? History in Perfect Tense.* Studies on Personalities of the New Testament. Columbia: University of South Carolina Press, 2000.

Kelly, Anthony J. "Dimensions of Meaning: Theology and Exegesis." In *Transcending Boundaries: Contemporary Readings of the New Testament*, edited by Rekha M. Chennattu and Mary L. Coloe, 41–55. Rome: LAS, 2005.

Kenny, Anthony. *Aquinas on Being.* Oxford: Clarendon, 2002.

———. *Aquinas on Mind.* Edited by John Marenbon. Topics in Medieval Philosophy. London: Routledge, 1993.

———. *The Five Ways: St. Thomas Aquinas' Proofs of God's Existence.* London: Routledge & Keegan Paul, 1969.

Kierkegaard, Søren. *The Concept of Anxiety: A Simple Psychologically Orienting Deliberation on the Dogmatic Issue of Hereditary Sin.* Translated by Reidar Thomte. Princeton: Princeton University Press, 1978.

Klawans, Jonathan. "Interpreting the Last Supper: Sacrifice, Spiritualisation, and Anti-Sacrifice." *New Testament Studies* 48 (2002) 1–17.

Leibniz, G. W. "The Monadology." In *Philosophical Texts*, 267–81. Oxford: Oxford University Press, 1998.

———. "Principles of Nature and Grace, Based on Reason." In *Philosophical Texts*, 258–66. Oxford: Oxford University Press, 1998.

Lonergan, Bernard. "Christ as Subject: A Reply." In *Collection: Papers by Bernard Lonergan, S. J.*, edited by Frederick E. Crowe, 154–84. New York: Herder and Herder, 1967.

———. "Cognitional Structure." In *Collection: Papers by Bernard Lonergan, S. J.*, edited by Frederick E. Crowe, 205–21. New York: Herder and Herder, 1967.

———. *De Verbo Incarnato.* 3rd ed. Rome: Gregorian University Press *ad usum auditorum*, 1964.

———. "Dimensions of Meaning." In *Collection: Papers by Bernard Lonergan, S. J.*, edited by Frederick E. Crowe, 232–45. New York: Herder and Herder, 1967.

———. "Existenz and Aggiornamento." In *Collection: Papers by Bernard Lonergan, S. J.*, edited by Frederick E. Crowe, 222–31. New York: Herder and Herder, 1967.

———. "The Future of Christianity." In *A Second Collection*, edited by William F. J. Ryan and Bernard J. Tyrrell, 149–64. Philadelphia: Westminster, 1974.

―――. *Grace and Freedom: Operative Grace in the Thought of St. Thomas Aquinas.* Vol. 1 of *Collected Works of Bernard Lonergan.* London: Darton, Longman and Todd, 2000.

―――. *Insight: A Study of Human Understanding.* Vol. 3 of *Collected Works of Bernard Lonergan.* 5th ed. Toronto: University of Toronto Press, 1992.

―――. "An Interview with Fr. Bernard Lonergan, S. J." In *A Second Collection,* edited by William F. J. Ryan and Bernard J. Tyrrell, 209–30. Philadelphia: Westminster, 1974.

―――. *Method in Theology.* London: Darton, Longman and Todd, 1972.

―――. "The Natural Desire to See God." In *Collection: Papers by Bernard Lonergan, S. J.,* edited by Frederick E. Crowe, 81–91. New York: Herder and Herder, 1967.

―――. "On God and Secondary Causes." In *Collection: Papers by Bernard Lonergan, S. J.,* edited by Frederick E. Crowe, 58–63. New York: Herder and Herder, 1967.

―――. *The Ontological and Psychological Constitution of Christ.* Translated by Micael G. Shields. Vol. 7 of *Collected Works of Bernard Lonergan.* Toronto: University of Toronto, 2002.

―――. "The Origins of Christian Realism." In *A Second Collection,* edited by William F. J. Ryan and Bernard J. Tyrrell, 239–262. Philadelphia: Westminster, 1974.

―――. *Philosophy of God, and Theology.* Philadelphia: Westminster, 1973.

―――. "Theology in Its New Context." In *A Second Collection,* edited by William F. J. Ryan and Bernard J. Tyrrell, 55–68. Philadelphia: Westminister, 1974.

―――. *Understanding and Being: The Halifax Lectures on Insight.* Edited by Elizabeth A. Morelli and Mark D. Morelli. Toronto: Toronto University Press, 1990.

Luther, Martin. *The Bondage of the Will.* Translated by James I. Packer and O. R. Johnston. Old Tappan: Fleming H. Revell, 1957.

Mann, Alan. *Atonement for a "Sinless" Society: Engaging with an Emerging Culture.* Edited by Pete Ward. Faith in an Emerging Culture. Milton Keynes, UK: Paternoster, 2005.

Marshall, I. Howard. *Last Supper and Lord's Supper.* Exeter: Paternoster, 1980.

Matustik, Martin Joseph. *Mediation of Deconstruction: Bernard Lonergan's Method in Philosophy: The Argument from Human Operational Development.* Lanham, MD: University Press of America, 1998.

McCabe, Herbert. *God Matters.* London: Chapman, 1987.

McDonald, H. D. *New Testament Concept of Atonement: The Gospel of the Calvary Event.* Cambridge: Lutterworth, 1994.

McDowell, John C. "Much Ado about Nothing: Karl Barth's Being Unable to Do Nothing about Nothingness." *International Journal of Systematic Theology* 4/3 (2002) 319–35.

McGinn, Bernard. "The Development of the Thought of Thomas Aquinas on the Reconciliation of Divine Providence and Contingent Action." *The Thomist* 39 (1975) 741–52.

McGrath, Alister. *Luther's Theology of the Cross.* Oxford: Blackwell, 1985.

―――. *Nature.* Vol. 1 of *A Scientific Theology.* Edinburgh: T. & T. Clark, 2001.

McInerny, Ralph. *Aquinas on Human Action: A Theory of Practice.* Washington, DC: The Catholic University of America Press, 1992.

McKnight, Scot. *Jesus and His Death: Historiography, the Historical Jesus, and Atonement Theory.* Waco: Baylor University Press, 2005.

Meier, J. P. *A Marginal Jew: Rethinking the Historical Jesus.* 3 vols. New York: Doubleday, 1991–2001.

Merback, Mitchell. "Reverberations of Guilt and Violence, Resonances of Peace: A Comment on Caroline Walker Bynum's Lecture." *Bulletin of the German Historical Institute* 30 (2002) 37–50.

Mertens, Herman-Emiel. *Not the Cross, but the Crucified: An Essay in Soteriology.* Louvain Theological and Pastoral Monographs 11. Grand Rapids: Eerdmans, 1992.

Meyer, B. F. *The Aims of Jesus.* London: SCM, 1979.

———. *Critical Realism and the New Testament.* Princeton Theological Monographs. Allison Park, PA: Pickwick, 1989.

———. *Reality and Illusion in New Testament Scholarship: A Primer in Critical Realist Hermeneutics.* Collegeville, MN: Liturgical, 1994.

Meynell, Hugo A. *The Theology of Bernard Lonergan.* American Academy of Religion Studies in Religion 42. Atlanta: Scholars, 1986.

Milbank, John. *Being Reconciled: Ontology and Pardon.* Radical Orthodoxy. London: Routledge, 2003.

———. *Theology and Social Theory: Beyond Secular Reason.* Oxford: Blackwell, 1990.

Milton, John. *Paradise Lost.* Harlow: Longman, 1971.

Moltmann, Jürgen. "The Cross as Military Symbol for Sacrifice." In *Cross Examinations: Readings on the Meaning of the Cross Today*, edited by Marit Trelstad, 259–63. Minneapolis: Augsburg Fortress, 2006.

Mongeau, Gilles. "The Human and Divine Knowledge of the Incarnate Word." *Josephinum Journal of Theology* 12 (2005) 30–42.

Morgan, Robert. "The Historical Jesus and the Theology of the New Testament." In *The Glory of Christ in the New Testament: Studies in Christology in Memory of George Bradford Caird*, edited by L. D. Hurst and N. T. Wright, 187–206. Oxford: Clarendon, 1987.

Morris, Leon. *The Cross in The New Testament.* Exeter: Paternoster, 1965.

Newman, John Henry. *An Essay in Aid of a Grammar of Assent.* Notre Dame: University of Notre Dame Press, 1979.

O'Collins, Gerald. *Interpreting Jesus.* Introducing Catholic Theology 2. London: Geoffrey Chapman, 1983.

Ogilvie, Matthew C. *Faith Seeking Understanding: The Functional Specialty, "Systematics," in Bernard Lonergan's* Method in Theology. Marquette: Marquette University Press, 2003.

Ormerod, Neil. "Chance and Necessity, Providence and God." *Irish Theological Quarterly* 70/3 (2005) 263–78.

———. *Method, Meaning and Revelation: The Meaning and Function of Revelation in Bernard Lonergan's* Method in Theology. Lanham, MD: University Press of America, 2000.

———. "What is the Task of Systematic Theology?" *Australian EJournal of Theology* 8 (2006) n.p.

Pannenberg, Wolfhart. "Dogmatic Theses on the Doctrine of Revelation." In *Revelation as History*, edited by Wolfhart Pannenberg, 123–158. London: Macmillan, 1968.

———. "Eternity, Time and Space." *Zygon* 40/1 (2005) 97–106.

———. *Jesus—God and Man.* Translated by Lewis L. Wilkins and Duane A. Priebe. London: SCM, 1968.

———. *Systematic Theology*. 3 vols. Translated by Geoffrey W. Bromiley. Grand Rapids: Eerdmans, 1988–98.

Parmenides. *Fragments: A Text and Translation*. Translated by D. A. Gallop. Toronto: Toronto University Press, 1984.

Peterman, E. L. "Redemption (Theology Of)." In *New Catholic Encyclopedia*, edited by Berard L. Marthaler, 11:973–89. Detroit: Thomson Gale, 2003.

Peters, Ted. *God—The World's Future: Systematic Theology for a Postmodern Era*. Minneapolis: Fortress, 1992.

Pinnock, Clark H. "Between Classical and Process Theism." In *Process Theology*, edited by Ronald Nash, 316–27. Grand Rapids: Baker, 1987.

———. *Most Moved Mover: A Theology of God's Openness*. Grand Rapids: Baker Academic, 2001.

———. "Open Theism: An Answer to My Critics." *Dialog: A Journal of Theology* 44/3 (2005) 237–45.

Pitre, Brant. *Jesus, the Tribulation, and the End of Exile: Restoration Eschatology and the Origin of the Atonement*. Grand Rapids: Baker Academic, 2006.

Plato. *Sophist*. Translated, with introduction and notes by Nicholas P. White. Indianapolis: Hackett, 1993.

———. *Timaeus*. Translated, with introduction by Donald J. Zeyl. Indianapolis: Hackett, 2000.

Rad, Gerhard von. *Old Testament Theology*. Translated by D. M. G. Stalker. Edinburgh: Oliver and Boyd, 1962.

Ray, Darby Kathleen. *Deceiving the Devil: Atonement, Abuse, and Ransom*. Cleveland: Pilgrim, 1998.

Ricoeur, Paul. "The Hermeneutics of Testimony." In *Essays on Biblical Interpretation*, edited by L. S. Mudge, 119–54. London: SPCK, 1981.

———. *Memory, History, Forgetting*. Translated by K. Blamey and David Pellauer. Chicago: University of Chicago Press, 2004.

Riley-Smith, Jonathan. *The First Crusade and the Idea of Crusading*. Philadelphia: University of Pennsylvania Press, 1986.

Robinson, J. A. T. "The Last Tabu?" In *Twelve More New Testament Studies*, 155–70. London: SCM, 1984.

Rocca, Gregory P. "Aquinas on God-Talk: Hovering over the Abyss." *Theological Studies* 54/4 (1993) 641–61.

Rosenberg, Randall S. "Christ's Human Knowledge: A Conversation with Lonergan and Balthasar." *Theological Studies* 71 (2010) 817–45.

Rowland, Tracey. "Divine Gifts to the Secular Desert." *Reviews in Religion and Theology* (2004) 182–87.

Sabourin, L., and S. Lyonnet. *Sin, Redemption and Sacrifice: A Biblical and Patristic Study*. Rome: Biblical Institute, 1970.

Sanders, E. P. *The Historical Figure of Jesus*. London: Penguin, 1993.

———. *Jesus and Judaism*. London: SCM, 1985.

Sanders, E. P., and M. Davies. *Studying the Synoptic Gospels*. London: SCM, 1989.

Schleiermacher, F. D. E. *On Religion: Speeches to Its Cultured Despisers*. Translated by John Oman. Louisville: Westminster, 1994.

Schwager, Raymund. *Der wunderbare Tausch: Zur Geschichte und Deutung der Erlösungslehre*. Munchen: Kösel, 1986.

Bibliography

———. *Jesus in the Drama of Salvation: Toward a Biblical Doctrine of Redemption.* New York: Crossroad, 1999.

Schweitzer, Albert. *The Quest of the Historical Jesus: A Critical Study of Its Progress from Reimarus to Wrede.* Translated by W. Montgomery. London: Adam & Charles Black, 1948.

Searle, John R. *The Construction of Social Reality.* New York: Free Press, 1995.

Seeley, D. "Jesus' Temple Act." *The Catholic Biblical Quarterly* 55/2 (1993) 263–81.

Snodgrass, Klyne R. "Reading and Overreading the Parables in *Jesus and the Victory of God.*" In *Jesus and the Restoration of Israel: A Critical Assessment of N. T. Wright's Jesus and the Victory of God,* edited by Carey C. Newman, 61–76. Downers Grove, IL: InterVarsity, 1999.

Soelle, Dorothee. *Suffering.* Translated by Everett R. Kalin. Philadelphia: Fortress, 1975.

Southern, R. W. *Saint Anselm: A Portrait in a Landscape.* Cambridge: Cambridge University Press, 1990.

Spinoza, Benedictus de. *Ethics.* Translated by Andrew Boyle. London: Dent, 1989.

Stuhlmacher, Peter. *Jesus of Nazareth—Christ of Faith.* Translated by Siegfried S. Schatzmann. Peabody, MA: Hendrickson, 1988.

Stump, Eleonore. *Aquinas.* Arguments of the Philosophers. London: Routledge, 2003.

Swinburne, Richard. *The Christian God.* Oxford: Clarendon, 1994.

Tan, Kim Huat. "Community, Kingdom and Cross: Jesus' View of Covenant." In *The God of Covenant: Biblical, Theological and Contemporary Perspectives,* edited by Jamie A. Grant and Alistair I. Wilson, 122–55. Leicester: Apollos, 2005.

Theiss, Norman. "The Passover Feast of the New Covenant." *Interpretation* 48/1 (1994) 17–36.

Theissen, G., and A. Mertz. *The Historical Jesus: A Comprehensive Guide.* London: SCM, 1998.

Theissen, G., and D. Winter. *The Quest for the Plausible Jesus: The Question of Criteria.* Translated by M. E. Boring. Louisville: Westminster John Knox, 2002.

Thucydides. *History of the Peloponnesian War.* Translated by Rex Warner. London: Penguin, 1988.

Torrance, Thomas F. *Divine and Contingent Order.* Oxford: Oxford University Press, 1981.

Tracy, David. *The Achievement of Bernard Lonergan.* New York: Herder and Herder, 1970.

Trelstad, Marit, ed. *Cross Examinations: Readings on the Meaning of the Cross Today.* Minneapolis: Augsburg Fortress, 2006.

Turner, Denys. "'Sin Is Behovely' in Julian of Norwich's *Revelations of Divine Love.*" *Modern Theology* 20/3 (2004) 407–22.

Tyrrell, George. *Christianity at the Crossroads.* London: Allen and Unwin, 1963.

Vanhoozer, Kevin J. "The Hermeneutics of I-Witness Testimony: John 21:20–24 and the Death of the Author." In *First Theology: God, Scripture and Hermeneutics,* 257–74. Downers Grove, IL: InterVarsity, 2002.

Vermes, Geza. *Jesus in His Jewish Context.* Minneapolis: Augsburg Fortress, 2003.

Watts, Rikki. "Jesus' Death, Isaiah 53 and Mark 10:45: A Crux Revisited." In *Jesus and the Suffering Servant: Isaiah 53 and Christian Origins,* edited by William H. Bellenger Jr. and William R. Farmer, 125–51. Harrisburg, PA: Trinity, 1998.

Wawrykow, Joseph P. *The Westminster Handbook to Thomas Aquinas.* Louisville: John Knox, 2005.

Weaver, J. Denney. *The Nonviolent Atonement*. Grand Rapids: Eerdmans, 2001.

———. "Violence in Christian Theology." *Cross Currents* 51/2 (2001) 1–21.

Wiesel, E. *All Rivers Run to the Sea: Memoirs*. Vol. 1, *1928–1969*. New York: HarperCollins, 1996.

Wilken, Robert L. "Melito, The Jewish Community at Sardis, and the Sacrifice of Isaac." *Theological Studies* 37/1 (1976) 53–69.

Williams, Delores S. "Black Women's Surrogacy Experience and the Christian Notion of Redemption." In *Cross Examinations: Readings on the Meaning of the Cross Today*, edited by Marit Trelstad, 19–32. Minneapolis: Augsburg Fortress, 2006.

Williams, Sam K. *Jesus' Death as Saving Event: The Background and Origin of a Concept*. Missoula, MT: Scholars, 1975.

Wippel, John F. *The Metaphysical Thought of Thomas Aquinas: From Finite Being to Uncreated Being*. Washington, DC: Catholic University of America Press, 2000.

Wolterstorff, N. P. "Does God Suffer?" *Modern Reformation* 8/5 (1999) 45–47.

Wright, N. T. *Evil and the Justice of God*. London: SPCK, 2006.

———. "Jesus." In *Early Christian Thought in Its Jewish Context*, edited by John Barclay and John Sweet, 43–58. Cambridge: Cambridge University Press, 1996.

———. *Jesus and the Victory of God*. Christian Origins and the Question of God 2. Minneapolis: Fortress, 1996.

———. "Jesus, Israel, and the Cross." In *SBL 1985 Seminar Papers*, edited by K. H. Richards, 75–95. Chico, CA: Scholars, 1985.

———. *The New Testament and the People of God*. Christian Origins and the Question of God 1. Minneapolis: Fortress, 1992.

———. "The Servant and Jesus." In *Jesus and the Suffering Servant: Isaiah 53 and Christian Origins*, edited by William H. Bellenger Jr. and William R. Farmer, 281–97. Harrisburg, PA: Trinity, 1998.

Young, Frances M. *The Use of Sacrificial Ideas in Greek Christian Writers from the New Testament to John Chrysostom*. Patristic Monograph Series 5. Philadelphia: Philadelphia Patristic Foundation, 1979.

Subject Index

Anselm, Bishop of Canterbury, x, 2–4,
  27, 98, 210, 212, 220
Aquinas, Thomas, x–xi, 31, 36, 38–50,
  52–53, 56, 58–74, 79, 84,
  87–89, 92n205
artistic carrier, 143, 144, 152
atonement,
  criticism of, 4, 6, 25, 94, 208
  and divine meaning, 29–30, 95
  in contemporary discussions, 10–24,
    29–30, 32–33, 101, 186, 213,
    229, 232–37
  and Jesus' intent, 6, 9–10, 24–25,
    97–100, 150, 209–10, 215, 221,
    243–44
  models of, 2–3, 181, 208, 210, 224,
    227
  violence in, 26–27
Augustine, Bishop of Hippo, 27, 38, 77,
  220, 227n50, 229n54
authentic/authenticity,
  Christianity, xi, 5, 225, 237–38
  criteria of, 124, 131n106, 166
  existential judgment of. *See*
    judgment, existential.
  human fulfilment, 12, 101
  words/life of Jesus, 131n105,
    161n38, 167–68, 169n70, 196,
    199–201, 203–4, 206
  subjectivity, 114, 116–17, 125–27,
    227
  testimony, 120

carriers of meaning. *See* meaning,
  carriers of.
Chalcedon, Chalcedonian, 9, 87, 91,
  94, 211, 224, 228
Christ of faith, xiii, 108, 119

conditional necessity, 58–59, 62–64,
  74–75, 82, 84, 182
constitutive,
  doctrines as C for authenticity,
    222, 225
  Jesus' life as C for faith, 103–4,
    107–8
  of Jesus tradition, 130, 197, 200–
    201, 204
  meaning. *See* meaning,
    constitutive.
contextualisation, 14, 98, 100
contingency, contingent,
  in creation, 41, 44, 54–55, 63, 82
  and divine meaning, 25, 29, 31, 36,
    95, 229, 242
  and God's knowledge, 58–64, 85
  and providence, 39, 53, 58, 64
  and the cross event, 35–36, 65,
    83–84, 225, 228
  vs necessity, 34, 37–42, 46, 54–56,
    59–63, 182
covenant, covenantal,
  atonement, redemption *through*, 2,
    133, 205–6, 210, 212n4, 238,
    244
  community, nation, xi, 156–57,
    165, 175, 188n124, 192, 235
  and Last Supper, 194, 198–203, 208
  promise, 158–59
creatio ex nihilo, 35, 44, 51, 55, 61,
  82, 85
critical realism, realist, ix, xi, 31–32
  106, 114–15, 117, 119, 125–27,
  135n125, 151, 217, 243
cross,
  divine necessity, 148, 182, 184, 206
  interpretations of, xiii, 7, 98–99,
    148

functions of meaning, x, 137–38

Girard, Girardian, 11, 14–15, 17, 19,
20n62, 22, 170, 234–35

historical Jesus. *See* Jesus of history.
historical Jesus scholarship. *See* Jesus *in*
scholarship (historical Jesus).
historiography, 31–32, 105–6, 108,
125–26, 151, 243
homo sacer, 22–23, 232, 236–37

immanently generated, 216, 218–20,
244
impact,
as generative of faith, 129–33, 149,
151
transformation of meaning, 32,
128, 133–134, 138, 140–41,
148–49, 214
incarnate carrier, 141, 146–47, 154,
164, 166, 204, 211, 226–27
instrumental cause, 50, 52–53, 88–89
intersubjective carrier, 142–44

Jesus
and atonement theology, 10, 13,
20, 24, 100
of history, xiii, 6, 10, 14, 82, 94,
102–10, 119, 127–28, 129–30,
150, 228
incarnation, 6, 9, 19–21, 23–24, 30,
73n144, 84, 88, 91–92, 98, 101,
103, 142, 165, 224, 236
intention for death. *See* death of
Jesus, Jesus' intention for.
knowledge of divine will, 90, 92,
208
meaning of death. *See* death of
Jesus, meaning of.
psychological constitution, 88,
90–91
self-understanding, x, 7, 98, 100,
104, 128, 132–34, 141, 151,
171, 174, 179–81, 192, 233–34
in scholarship (historical Jesus), 9,
19–20, 23, 32, 102, 110, 117,
133n114, 150–51, 153n10, 161,

166, 168, 171, 181, 186, 196,
199–200
Jesus Seminar, 167
John the Baptist, 131, 153–54, 156,
159–60, 207
judgment,
divine, 156–57, 236
eschatological, 155–56, 177, 212
existential J of authenticity, x, 104,
118–19, 137–41, 190, 200, 206,
209, 213–16, 221–23, 225, 228,
231–32, 234–35, 238
Salvific, 32, 215, 225, 232, 237
and understanding, 32, 213, 215,
217–18, 238
virtually unconditioned, 217–21
kerygma, 8, 100, 102–4, 148
kingdom of God,
brings judgment, 155–57, 161–64,
170
as eschatological hope, 158–59
as future, 154, 177, 203
and Jesus' mission, ix, 19, 23–24,
154, 181, 183–87, 191, 199,
211–12
has come, 159–60, 207, 233
victory of, 177

Last Supper, xi, 11, 13–14, 23, 98, 100,
152n7,152n8, 186, 192–208,
211, 214, 234–35, 237, 243
linguistic carrier, 146, 165–66, 182,
184, 208–9
Lord's Prayer, 161, 163, 207
Luther, Martin, 27, 75–76

Maccabean tradition, 156n23, 174–75,
208
martyrs, martyrdom 22–23, 132, 167,
173–76, 185, 208
meaning,
carriers of, xi, 32, 141–48, 214,
226, 243
constitutive, 32, 112n47, 128, 134,
136–39, 141, 147, 188–89,
190n131, 214n7
created *ex nihilo*, 85, 86n184,
229n55, 242

Author Index

Ancient Document Index

69062864R00159

Made in the USA
Middletown, DE
04 April 2018